The

Broadview

Book

of

Common

Errors

in

English

The

Broadview

Book

of

Common

Errors

in

English

A Guide
to Righting Wrongs

4TH EDITION

Don
LePan

broadview

Canadian Cataloguing in Publication Data

LePan, Don, 1954-
  The Broadview book of common errors in English

4th ed.

Includes index.

ISBN 1-55111-318-X

1. English language — Errors of usage. 2 English language — Errors of usage — Problems, exercises, etc. 3. English language — Grammar. I. Title. II. Title: Common Errors in English

PE1460.B76 1999   428.2   C99-931922-1

Broadview Press Ltd. is an independent, international publishing house, incorporated in 1985.

North America:

PO Box 1243, Peterborough, Ontario, Canada K9J 7H5

3576 California Road, Orchard Park, NY, USA 14127

within North America: (705) 743-8990 (phone); (705) 743-8353 (fax)

UK and Europe:

Turpin Distribution Services Ltd., Blackhorse Rd., Letchworth, Hertfordshire, SG6 1HN   United Kingdom

(1462) 672555 (phone); (1462) 480947 (fax)

Australia:

St. Clair Press, PO Box 287, Rozelle NSW 2039 (02)818 1942

elsewhere:

Please order through local wholesalers or direct from North America.

www.broadviewpress.com

Broadview Press Ltd. gratefully acknowledges the financial support of the Book Publishing Industry Development Program, Ministry of Canadian Heritage, Government of Canada.

PRINTED IN CANADA

Contents

Form

Preface

Let me focus this time on a core issue that I have only skirted in the prefaces to early editions: in what sense are errors in grammar and usage wrong? *Are* they in fact wrong in any meaningful sense? Should "wrong" in this context be read as always having quotation marks around it?

Too often this sort of question becomes so infused with assumed political content that it is not taken seriously. On the one hand the conservative is likely to regard the question of whether "you" is a formation inherently superior to the vulgar "y'all" or "youse" as unworthy of debate. Of course the form established as correct is superior; of course the colloquialism is debased. On the other side are those who regard it as an article of faith that there are no universal or objectively verifiable truths, and that consequently there can be no rational justification for preferring "you" to "youse" or "y'all".

Is "Would you like anything else?" correct and "Would youse like anything else?" incorrect in the same way that "12 x 3 = 36" is correct and "12 x 3 = 35" incorrect? Or in the same way that "The capital of Burkina Faso is Ouagadougou" is correct and "The capital of Burkina Faso is Harare" is wrong? Surely not, as we must recognise as soon as we recognise how odd it would be to say that "Would youse like anything else?" is false. "12 x 3 = 35" and "The capital of Burkina Faso is Harare" are false; they do not correctly make connections between symbolic systems of numbers or of language and a structure of reality that (albeit with certain qualifications) all of us assume to exist. But "youse" does connect with a structure of reality. In fact, as the cognitive scientist Steven Pinker points out, it makes such a connection with a greater degree of precision than does currently correct usage:

> The mavens lament the loss of conjugal distinction in "he don't" and "we was". But this has been the trend in standard English for centuries. No one minds that we have abandoned the

> second-person singular form of verbs, as in "thou sayest." And
> by this criterion it is the non-standard dialects that are superior,
> because they provide their speakers with second-person plural
> pronouns such as "y'all" and "youse" (20).

Returning for a moment to Burkina Faso may help us to sense the
way in which "youse" and "y'all" may fairly if in a limited sense be
thought of as wrong. The sentence "The capital of Upper Volta is
Ouagadougou" is wrong in something like the same sense that
"Would youse like anything else?" is wrong. Both use the symbolic
system of language to correspond to an understood reality. But in
both cases the signs used are not those used under currently
accepted conventions; though a few may still cling to the old usage,
almost everyone has now adopted the 1984 change of name (from
Upper Volta to Burkina Faso) for the area surrounding the
headwaters of the Volta River. "Upper Volta" certainly still
corresponds to reality; it is not false. But nor is it right.

But why stick to the conventional? Is it possible to justify standard
English from first principles as the best form to use? On pedagogical
grounds it seems to me that the acquiring of a knowledge of English
grammar and syntax is an enormously helpful way of strengthening
habits of abstract thought. But that speaks to the value of a
by-product, not to the thing itself. It may be that there are only two
essential justifications for standard English: ease of communication,
and elegance of expression. The first of these is to a large extent
obvious, but it is worth stressing that the ease of communication
which standard forms or conventions of usage make possible extends
not only from individual to individual but also from one culture to
another, and over very long periods of time. It has been often noted
but bears repeating that the ordinarily literate person in our own
time is able to respond to the language of Shakespeare in a way that
the ordinarily literate person in Shakespeare's day was quite unable
to respond to *Beowulf*, simply because the conventional codification
of grammar and usage that print made possible has drastically
slowed down the rate of linguistic change. (This may be becoming
less true; Cullen Murphy has interestingly suggested that the
development of electric and then of electronic methods of
reproducing sound has given the sloppy and unruly nature of the

spoken word a much greater influence on the shaping of the language and on the speed of change than it had in the sixteenth through nineteenth centuries [22].)

The second legitimate argument in favour of standard English is by far the weaker, and I will readily concede that elegance of expression is often achievable outside the confines of standard English. But complex syntactical and grammatical pathways will inevitably tend to have been worn smoother in a greater variety of ways in long-established conventions of formal expression. Colloquial or non-standard usages may have an inimitable freshness to them or in other syntactical ways may appeal strongly in ways with which standard English cannot compete. But they are unlikely to consistently lend themselves to long and elegantly balanced combinations of clauses and phrases in the way that the mainstream of our culture has been training standard English to do for centuries.

* * *

If this book is prescriptive, then, it should be understood that it is prescriptive only in a context that recognises correct English as a matter of convention, not as one in which one form is understood to be necessarily or absolutely better than another. Sentences such as "use 'aggravate' to mean 'make worse,' not to mean 'annoy' or 'irritate'" should always be taken as a convenient short form for "in formal written English, if you wish to conform to the most commonly accepted conventions of usage, use...." And, to return to the example with which I began, "y'all" and "youse" are alternative, arguably superior forms, that we may legitimately reject only on the grounds of convention.

On other specific issues, though, the case for standard usage is sometimes considerably stronger. The confusion of "uninterested" and "disinterested," for example, will if "disinterested" is driven from the field represent a measurable loss of the communicative capacity of the English language. If we lose "disinterested" it will become more difficult and more cumbersome to express a variety of meanings. Yet there can be no question that many who are unperturbed by "disinterested" having largely been swamped by "uninterested" — indeed, many who do not even recognise the distinction — cringe at the supposed abomination of "youse" or "y'all." Indeed, I must confess to having been among the cringers until I read and was entirely persuaded by Pinker's argument. What such cases drive home to us is the degree to which the assumptions we make about standard English may be linked to irrational sentiments such as social snobbery or gender-based prejudice. (How many there still are that ludicrously claim "fisher" and "chair" to be 'more awkward' than the longer and cumbersome forms "fisherman," "chairman.") There are good reasons for not abandoning standard English — but good reasons as well to keep questioning our own assumptions about it.

* * *

One of the ways in which this book differs from many other guides to grammar and usage is the degree to which it is open to change in language, and the degree to which it attempts to resist the assumption that where the English language is concerned, change implies debasement. Thus in the chapter on part of speech conversions in this edition such previous entries such as "liaise" and "mandate" have been dropped. I am not at all sure that the back formation of a verb from the noun "liaison" is a pretty thing. But nor am I sure that my own bias against it reflects anything more than habit; certainly I find it difficult in many cases to find more economical replacements. I cannot convince myself that the prejudice against such words is any better grounded than was the bias a generation or two ago against using "contact" as a verb. Similarly, I used to believe that "meet with," which appeared quite suddenly in the 1980s, was merely a wordy expansion of "meet"; why add the proposition? But as I now realise, "meet with" as it is normally used has a subtly different meaning; it functions not as a longer stand-in for "meet" but as a short form for "have a meeting with." "Finalize" still grates slightly on my ear too. But sometimes "finish" just does not capture the sense, and "finalize" is more concise than "make final" or "put into final form." A comparison of current usage with attitudes of the mid twentieth century may be instructive as to whether or not there are any good grounds today for objecting to "finalize":

> *Finalize* is not standard: it is special, and it is a peculiarly fuzzy
> and silly word. Does it mean "terminate," or does it mean "put
> into final form"? One can't be sure, really, what it means, and
> one gets the impression that the person using it doesn't know,
> either, and doesn't want to know. (Strunk and White 75-76)

That may have been true in 1957, when the first edition of *The
Elements of Style* appeared, or even in 1972, when the second edition
was published. But no one today uses "finalize" to mean "terminate;"
that denotation has dropped away, and the word's meaning has
stabilized as "put into final form."

If Strunk and White are now out of date on the particulars, this
remains a good example of the wisdom of their advice to writers that
one danger of "adopting coinages too quickly is that they will bedevil
one by insinuating themselves where they do not belong" (75-76).
What was a fuzzy and confusing coinage in the 1950s has found a
clearly-defined place in the language of the 1990s. And even
conservative arbiters such as Strunk and White recognise that
language must change, and that this is not in itself a bad thing. In the
end guides such as this one should continually strive for a balance
between the value of continuity in language and in usage, and the
value of language as a living thing; without change there can be no life.

* * *

In one area in particular this guide is not only unresistant to change
but embraces change: the move towards bias-free language. In this
one area a different sort of "correctness" than the correctness I have
thus far been speaking of is involved. Call it political correctness if
you will, but however it is referred to it concerns things that are right
and wrong in a sense that goes far beyond questions of what is
conventional or convenient. The point involved here is that language
can have an important part to play in helping us to do the right thing.
To treat men and women on an equal footing; to avoid
discrimination on the basis of religion, or race, or class — language
can be used to help accomplish all of these goals.

An increased emphasis on the ways in which language can help or
hinder social change of this sort is an important change from early
editions. The discussion of bias-free language forms one of the

longer chapters in the book, and provides a much more thoroughgoing treatment of these issues than did early editions — or than do most other concise guides to usage. And it is largely this aspect of the book that the new subtitle addresses. The perhaps-too-obvious pun is intended at one level to reflect the lack of solemnity with which issues of correctness are approached in this book; this is a guide to writing wrongs, and to how to put them right. But at another level the subtitle is intended to face head-on the paradox of correctness; even those who do not see correctness in the English language as possessing any intrinsic importance treat other sorts of right and wrong as vitally important. Language can indeed be used to help in righting wrongs, and I hope this book may help.

* * *

It may well be that the greatest single improvement for recent editions of this book is in the binding. Many readers had requested that something be done to make the book physically easier to use, but a number had also disparaged the clunky cardboard dividers/ ring-binding format that has been so much in vogue for student writing guides. A lay-flat binding is, I hope, the perfect compromise.

Recent entries to the book include newly-common confusions of sound-alikes such as "reluctant" and "reticent"; the misuse of "refute" to mean "deny"; and the misuse of quotation marks as an indicator of emphasis. As one would expect, there are dozens of new examples. As before, these have been taken largely from published sources, including many from justly-respected writers. The spirit throughout is to regard errors in writing as problems of a sort that we all have to work on, not as signifiers of inferiority.

Several changes have been intended to make the book more readily usable for university students. The section on referencing has been expanded, with separate chapters now devoted to MLA, APA and Chicago styles. Chapters have been re-organized so as to incorporate into the structure of the book a progression from individual words to larger questions of style, with a full chapter now devoted to general issues regarding writing process and structure. Also given a full chapter for the first time in this edition is the topic of writing with computers.

I had rather assumed in preparing early editions that if university instructors were to assign this book (as many have done), they would do so in conjunction with another book on writing style and writing process—something such as Janet Giltrow's marvellous introduction to *Academic Writing*, for example. (Or, indeed, that they might turn to *The Broadview Guide to Writing*, which combines material from this book with a great deal of useful advice by Doug Babington of Queen's University on the process of essay writing). An increasing number of university professors and writing instructors, however, seem to prefer to expose their students to relatively little writing about writing in the abstract, and to look for books about writing that will function more as reference guides to the nuts and bolts of the thing than as full-scale textbooks. Some say that discussions of writing process and of essay structure have more impact with their students if done in class or in individual meetings. Some simply say that their students respond better to books in a concise format. Some argue that even books renowned for the wisdom of their advice about writing process and style (*The Elements of Style* perhaps foremost among them) in fact often focus far more on style at the word-by-word and sentence-by-sentence level than on the large issues of essay construction. They argue too that the habits of thought which need training and practice in order to structure clauses, sentences, and paragraphs coherently also operate in the structuring of the essay, the report, even the dissertation. And some simply suggest that the one truly effective way to learn how to construct longer pieces of writing most effectively is by doing it, paying attention to the comments made about it, and doing it again. Whatever the rights or wrongs of these views, it seems clear that concise guides such as this one are now widely regarded as strong candidates for use as university-level reference texts, and I have thus tried to accommodate the concerns of instructors at the university level.

That said, however, this also remains very much a book designed to be of interest and of use to writers and lovers of language outside the academic community. To such readers the change from early editions that may be of most interest is the addition of a mini-dictionary of variants in the largest traditional areas of English usage: Australia, Canada, England, and the United States. Quite aside from its inherent interest and usefulness I hope this little section of the book may help to underscore the sense in which particular usages are correct or incorrect. To refer to the body of water behind a dam as being itself "a dam" is certainly wrong to a North American, but not to an Australian, or for that matter to a Zimbabwean. Such examples should act as a reminder that a guide such as this one is inevitably a book as much about difference as it is about right and wrong.

Don LePan
Calgary, 1999

Works Cited

Murphy, Cullen. "The Lay of the Language: The Decline of Semantic Distinction, and What it Suggests About Linguistic Evolution." *Atlantic Monthly* May 1995: 20-22.

Pinker, Steven. "Grammar Puss: The Fallacies of the Language Mavens." *New Republic* 31 Jan. 1994: 19-24.

Strunk, William Jr., and E.B. White, *The Elements of Style*. 2nd ed. New York: Mamillan, 1972.

Acknowledgements

To the list of those thanked in the Acknowledgements to early editions I should add the names of a number of people who have offered helpful advice in recent years: R.W. Cooley of the University of Saskatchewan, Tom Hurka and Ann Levey of the University of Calgary; Reid Gilbert of Capilano College; Barbara Conolly, Mical Moser, Julia Gaunce, and Heidi Standell, all of Broadview; Eileen Eckert and Terry Teskey (both free-lance editors based in Calgary); and Andrew Bailey, who has been a wonderful copy editor.

Preface to the Second Edition

Re-reading five years later the Preface to the first edition of this book, with its focus on the 'correctness versus creativity' debate in education, I am struck both by how much has changed and by how much has remained the same.

Certainly the debate in educational circles — and in society as a whole — over the value of teaching formal grammar and of emphasizing correct English usage has not gone away; if anything it has grown and intensified. Too many educators still see correctness and creativity as antithetical to each other. And perhaps as well too many on the political left see the push for correct English as only one manifestation of a much broader effort by those on the right to impose a conservative agenda on education, and on society generally.

To be fair, their fears are not always entirely groundless. It is an unfortunate fact that *some* of those striving to re-trench 'the basics' in the schools would also like to see the end of multiculturalism, the abolition of the progressive income tax, and elimination of all moves towards gender equality. For that reason it is crucial to emphasise that many of us who would like to see higher levels of reading and writing skill in society are on the political left; that many of us would be appalled were the issue of higher standards of English to be hijacked by purveyors of a reactionary political agenda. That must not — and need not — be allowed to happen.

A useful litmus test of the motivations of those striving for better English is the attitude taken towards certain issues of perennial controversy: issues such as *that* and *which*, part of speech conversions, split infinitives, and gender neutral language. To always take a hard line on issues such as these is to be reactionary rather than conservative; it is to take a stand against the flexibility that is one of the greatest strengths of the English language; and it is to fight against the natural process of change and of growth that must occur in the history of any language. It is one thing to struggle against the confusion of *it's* with *its* or of *unexceptional* with *unexeptionable*; that is a struggle to preserve meaning and subtlety in our language. But it is quite another to struggle to preserve in the late twentieth century all of the rules codified by eighteenth and nineteenth century grammarians; that is to set dogma above common sense. Usage keeps changing, and as in any other part of life, change need not imply debasement.

I should perhaps add a note concerning the cover of the new edition, which is intended to express something of the philosophy behind the book as a whole. The reader may already have been surprised to find quotations from Milton and from the Bible in amongst the 'errors'. Though the distinction between *imply* and *infer* has not been universally observed in any era, it was certainly established well before *Paradise Lost*; it is hard not to feel that in this instance the great poet simply got it wrong. And certainly the reader will find throughout this book examples of common errors committed by well-known writers. The point of including them is in no way to suggest that these writers are somehow less accomplished for having made a few mistakes. Rather it is to suggest that *we* need not feel badly when we catch ourselves making mistakes; even the best writers do it.

But what of Psalm 121? Are we to 'correct' the King James phrasing, "I will lift up mine eyes unto the hills"? Certainly there is a redundancy here, and yet what a world separates "lift up mine eyes to the hills" from "lift up my book from the table". This is surely one of those times when we must be sensitive to circumstances that admit of exceptions; here the gain in rhythm completely outweighs any loss in 'correctness'.

Also included are two examples of the 'every' problem. On the one hand an anonymous writer claims that "every Prime Minister must do what he believes is right" (and thereby suggests that only males make Prime Ministers). On the other hand no less an authority than Samuel Johnson ignores the supposed singularity of *everyone* in writing that in some cultures "everyone sacrifices a cow or more, according to their different degrees of wealth or devotion." Which is right — the sentence that conforms to the eighteenth century rule on subject-verb agreement, or the sentence that sacrifices the rule to convenience and gender-neutral language? (We may well doubt, of course, if the latter was the decisive concern for Samuel Johnson.) To my mind it is the discussion of such issues that most enlivens the study of English grammar and usage. For the most part this book is simply a guide to what everyone acknowledges to be correct. But in a number of areas there *is* no consensus — and it is probably healthy that there should not be.

The other quotations on the cover *are* errors without qualification, and some of them are really quite amusing; "British Left Waffles on Falklands" is my own favourite, but I hope you will enjoy them all. For I can see no harm in laughing at our mistakes — provided that we never assume as we do so that we are ourselves somehow immune. (I have purposely included a *mitigate/militate* error on the cover, since this is one that I always have to pause over if I am to get it right, and don't always do so even then.) If we are prepared to laugh at our own mistakes as heartily as we laugh at those of others we can only be the better for it.

To those thanked in the Acknowledgements to the first edition I should add the names of George Kirkpatrick, who was a great help in the preparation of the first edition, and of Ingrid Berzins, who in editing this edition has saved me from the embarrassment of seeing a number of errors, both common and uncommon, find their way into print.

Don LePan
Peterborough, October 1992

Preface to the First Edition

Languages are always notoriously difficult subjects to study. Is it in fact possible to <u>study</u> in order to improve your English, or does improvement only come through a process of osmosis the more one reads and writes? The body of public opinion has swung wildly back and forth on this issue over the past thirty years. In the 1950s and 60s the prevailing view among educators was that students were being constricted by an excessive emphasis on correctness over creativity. Writing in 1952, Donald J. Lloyd expressed what would soon be conventional wisdom, in an article entitled, "Our National Mania for Correctness":

> In school and out, in print and out, we can leave usage to its natural nurse, the unforced imitation of the practices which are actually current among educated people. We can use our English courses in school and college, not to give drill on questionable choices among common alternatives, demanding that one be taken as right and the others as wrong, but to give practice in reading and writing. We can learn to write for the idea, and go for the idea without regard for anything else. Then our young people will come to maturity confidently using their pencils to find out what they think and get it down on paper; then our scholars will come to write simply, clearly and brilliantly what they brilliantly know.

Given the experience of the seventies and eighties, it is difficult to suppress a smile at such grand illusions. Language does change, and there will always be disagreement as to various points of usage. But most of us have come to appreciate in the course of the past generation that the level of communication in our society will not be raised by leaving students to sort out English usage in their own. Learning that certain forms of English usage are considered to be superior to others, far from damming the flow of creativity, can help to create the channels through which creativity can be best expressed.

Common Errors in English

Our belief, then, is that the study of English usage is both possible and desirable; this book is designed to help you discover and correct the mistakes in your writing. If you are working as part of a class, ask your instructor to help you identify the mistakes that you make most often. Study the relevant sections in the book with particular care, and then do the corresponding exercises at the back of the book. These are keyed to the numbered entries in the body of the text, so that each exercise can be checked and corrected by the student. This feature also enables the book to be used by those who are trying to improve their English outside of any course of formal instruction.

The question of formal grammar is always a slightly touchy one among teachers at all levels. Some more traditional instructors like to teach set classes in formal grammar, while many others prefer to teach grammatical points as they arise out of literary passages or out of the students' work. Still others - especially in certain of our more prestigious universities - do not believe they should be teaching writing skills at all; they feel such skills should have been learned by students in primary and secondary school. It is hoped that this book will be of use to members of all camps. The key points of grammar are clearly laid out in an appendix at the end of the book, where they can be used as a reference to grammatical points as they arise. The mistakes themselves are for the most part organized around certain grammatical patterns, but the teacher can easily teach them (and the student learn them) while making little or no reference to the grammatical terms themselves. Similarly, the teacher who wishes to avoid grammar entirely can simply assign the book for the student to work through independently, and concentrate on literature in class.

Some educators maintain that students should not be exposed to errors, but only to correct English. If this were possible it would be wonderful, but in the real world students will inevitably be exposed to innumerable errors in any case. If the students are not taught to recognise and correct them, many of these errors will become embedded in their patterns of speech and writing. Most authorities nowadays therefore recommend extensive work with the specific errors most commonly made by any given group of students. To avoid teaching the students how to make errors, however, teachers should always be careful when using this approach to emphasise the *correct* way much more strongly than the error.

Among those who have made helpful suggestions as to the errors that should be included and the approach that should be taken in this book are the following: Professor Maurice Legris of the University of Alberta, Professor Tom Hurka of the University of Calgary, Professor Tom Marshall of Queen's University, Professors Robert Lovejoy and M.I. Cameron of Carleton University, Professor Robert Chambers of Trent University, Marjorie Holmes of Algonquin College, Molly Blyth of Sir Sanford Fleming College, and Terry Teskey of Calgary. Their assistance is gratefully acknowledged, though responsibility for any errors in the book remains our own.

Don LePan
George Kirkpatrick
Peterborough, November 1987

this time to Naomi,

and to Dominic

Words

VERBS AND VERB TENSE DIFFICULTIES

The Infinitive

Although not properly speaking a verb tense, the infinitive is the starting point for building a knowledge of verb tenses; the infinitive is the most basic form of the verb. Some examples of infinitives are *to go, to be, to do, to begin, to come, to investigate.* The infinitive form remains the same, of course, whether the action referred to happens in the past, the present, or the future.

1. **Split infinitives:** The most commonly made mistake involving infinitives is undoubtedly the slang substitution of *and* for *to*, especially in the expression *try and do it* for *try to do it* (see under Usage for a fuller treatment). The great issue in this area among grammarians, however, is the split infinitive — the infinitive which has another word or words inserted between *to* and the verb:

wrong The time has come to once again go to the polls. Economic conditions are likely to greatly influence the outcome, and the Prime Minister has promised to forcefully speak out in defence of the government's fiscal record.

With re-united infinitives, the same passage looks like this:

right The time has come to go once again to the polls. Economic conditions are likely to influence greatly the outcome, and the Prime Minister has promised to speak out forcefully in defence of the government's fiscal record.

On what grounds can the second passage be considered better? It comes down to a matter of sound and rhythm. To most ears *to go once again* and *to speak out forcefully* are preferable to the split alternatives, but *to influence greatly* seems more awkward than *to greatly influence*. Happily, most authorities are now agreed that it is not a grievous sin to

Common Errors in English # 1.

split an infinitive; Philip Howard, editor of *The Times of London*, calls the split infinitive "the great Shibboleth of English syntax," and even the traditionalist H.W. Fowler allows that while "the split infinitive is an ugly thing, we must warn the novice against the curious superstition that splitting or not splitting makes the difference between a good and a bad writer."

This is not to say that the splitting of infinitives should be encouraged. In many cases a split infinitive is a sign of wordiness; in cases such as the following it is better to drop the adverb entirely:

poor	The Chairman said it was important to really investigate the matter thoroughly.
better	The Chairman said it was important to investigate the matter thoroughly.

Like all verb forms, most infinitives have both an <u>active</u> and a <u>passive</u> voice. The active, which is more common, is used when the subject of the verb is doing the action, whereas the passive is used when the subject of the verb is receiving the action, or being acted <u>on</u>. *To do, to hit, to write* are examples of infinitives in the active voice, while *to be done, to be hit, to be written* are examples of infinitives in the passive voice.

The Simple Present Tense

	singular	plural
1st person	I say	we say
2nd person	you say	you say
3rd person	he, she, it says	they say

2. **Subject-verb agreement**: The simple present tense seems entirely straightforward, and usually it is. Most of us have no difficulty with the first person or the second person. But almost all of us occasionally have problems in writing the third person correctly. All too often the letter *s* at the end of the third person singular is left out. The simple rule to remember is that whenever you use a verb in the third person singular of the simple present tense, it <u>*must*</u> end in *s*.

wrong	He go to Vancouver at least once a month.

right   He goes to Vancouver at least once a month.

wrong   The litmus paper change colour when the solution is poured into the beaker.

right   The litmus paper changes colour when the solution is poured into the beaker.

(*Paper*, which is the subject, is an *it* and therefore third person singular.)

It is not particularly difficult to ensure that the subject agrees with the verb in the above examples, but even professional writers often have trouble with more complex sentences. Here are two common causes of subject-verb agreement errors:

(a) The subject and verb are separated by a long phrase or clause.

wrong   The state of Afghanistan's roads reflect the chaotic situation. (*The Toronto Star*)

right   The state of Afghanistan's roads reflects the chaotic situation.

Here the writer has made the mental error of thinking of *roads* as the subject of the verb reflect, whereas in fact the subject is the singular noun *state*. "The state reflect..." would immediately strike most people as wrong, but the intervening words have in this case caused grammatical confusion.

wrong   As the statement by Belgium's Prime Minister about his country's deficit and unemployment problems indicate, many nations are in the same shape, or worse. (*The Globe and Mail*, Sept. 22, 1993)

right   As the statement by Belgium's Prime Minister about his country's deficit and unemployment problems indicates, many nations are in the same shape, or worse.

(The subject is the singular noun *statement*, so the verb must be *indicates* rather than *indicate*.)

wrong   Courses offered range from the history of the Greek and Roman world to the 20th century, and covers Britain, Europe, North America, Africa and the far East.

(History Dept. Prospectus, Birkbeck College, University of London, 1997)

right   Courses offered range from the history of the Greek and Roman world to the 20th century, and cover Britain, Europe, North America, Africa and the far East.

Sometimes a long sentence can in itself throw off a writer's sense of subject-verb agreement, even if subject and verb are close together. In the following example the close proximity of the subject *simplifications* to the verb has not prevented error:

wrong	The decline in the quality of American leadership is mirrored in the crude simplifications which characterises the average American's view of the world.
	(*The Guardian*, April 19, 1987)
right	The decline in the quality of American leadership is mirrored in the crude simplifications which characterise the average American's view of the world.

(b) The error of using *there is* **instead of** *there are* **when the subject is plural has become more and more frequent in writing as well as speech. When these two expressions are used, remember that the subject comes <u>after</u> the verb; use** *is* **or** *are* **depending on whether the subject is singular or plural.**

wrong	There's more Stars with our Stripes.
	(Advertisement for the Sentinel Equity Fund, June 1987)
right	There are more Stars with our Stripes.

3. **Habitual action:** The simple present tense is often used to express what is called *habitual* action — the way an action ordinarily, or habitually occurs. The simple present tense is used to name such action *even if* the main verb of the sentence is in the past or future tense.

wrong	The professor told us that Jupiter was the largest planet.
right	The professor told us that Jupiter is the largest planet.
	(Jupiter has not stopped being the largest since he spoke.)

The Present Progressive (or Continuous) Tense

	singular	**plural**
1st person	I am saying	we are saying
2nd person	you are saying	you are saying
3rd person	he, she, it is saying	they are saying

4. **Verbs not normally used in the continuous tenses:** In English the continuous tenses are not normally used with many verbs which have to do with feelings, emotions, or senses. Some of these verbs are *to see, to hear, to understand, to believe, to hope, to know, to think* (meaning *believe*), *to trust, to comprehend, to mean, to doubt, to suppose, to wish, to want, to love, to desire, to prefer, to dislike, to hate.*

wrong	He is not understanding what I meant.
right	He does not understand what I meant.

Common Errors in English # 3.

The Simple Past Tense

	singular	**plural**
1st person	I finished	we finished
2nd person	you finished	you finished
3rd person	he, she, it finished	they finished

5.   The occasional problems that crop up with the simple past tense usually involve irregular verbs. The use of *may, might* is a good example:

wrong   Bands such as U2 and Simple Minds gained a foothold in North America through campus radio; without it they may not have broken through.

right   Bands such as U2 and Simple Minds gained a foothold in North America through campus radio; without it they might not have broken through.

6.   Two other verbs that often cause problems with the simple past tense are *lie* and *lay*. The difficulty many people have in keeping these straight is often ascribed to other factors, but is in part also attributable simply to the forms of the tenses; the past tense of *lie* is the same as the present tense of *lay*. Also, the past participle of *lie* is *lain*, not *laid*.

informal   Many in our party have just laid down and rolled over; they cannot get over the fact that we have lost control of the House of Representatives.
(Representative Kweisi Mfume, November 1994)

right   Many in our party have just lain down and rolled over; they cannot get over the fact that we have lost control of the House of Representatives.

Given the inherent confusion of the tense forms, the difficulty of getting one's tongue round 'lain down' rather than 'laid down,' and the fact that almost anyone will know what meaning is intended with these words, many authorities now feel that the distinctions are not worth troubling over except in formal written English.

Common Errors in English # 5.

The Past Progressive (or Continuous) Tense

	singular	**plural**
1st person	I was leaving	we were leaving
2nd person	you were leaving	you were leaving
3rd person	he, she, it was leaving	they were leaving

The problems that sometimes occur with the past continuous tense are the same as those that occur with the present continuous (see above, number 4). Remember to avoid these tenses when using verbs having to do with feelings, emotions, or senses (e.g. *see, hear, understand, believe, hope, know, think, trust, comprehend*) and when using the verb *to have* to mean *own, possess,* or *suffer from.*

| *wrong* | At that time he was believing that everything on earth was created within one week. |
| *right* | At that time he believed that everything on earth was created within one week. |

The Simple Future Tense

	singular	plural
1st person	I will arrive	we will arrive
2nd person	you will arrive	you will arrive
3rd person	he, she, it will arrive	they will arrive

The only significant difficulty in using the simple future tense occurs over the issue of when to use *shall*, which has for the most part given way to *will* in ordinary usage. But it will never disappear; most of us who would never dream of wading through the pages and pages many authorities offer on when to use *will* and when to use *shall* nevertheless sense instinctively moments when *shall* lends the resonance of added conviction to a verb.

| *milder* | We will not fail. |
| *more determined* | We shall not fail. |

.The Future Progressive (or Continuous) Tense

	singular	**plural**
1st person	I will be finding	we will be finding
2nd person	you will be finding	you will be finding
3rd person	he, she, it will be finding	they will be finding

Common Errors in English # 6.

The Perfect Tenses

As used to refer to the perfect tenses, the word *perfect* means *completed*; as you might expect, then, the perfect tenses are often (though not always) used to express actions that have been completed. They are formed by combining some form of the verb *to have* with a past participle (e.g., *opened, finished, believed, done*).

The Present Perfect Tense

	singular	plural
1st person	I have worked	we have worked
2nd person	you have worked	you have worked
3rd person	he, she, it has worked	they have worked

7. One way in which this tense is used is to speak of past actions which may continue into the present, or be repeated in the present or future. In the sentence, "Margaret Atwood has written a number of books," for example, the form of the verb shows that she will probably write more; she has neither died nor given up writing.

A simple enough practice in normal usage, but, in the long sentences often attempted as part of academic writing, it is easy to become confused:

wrong   Since it called the First World Food Congress in 1963, the Food and Agriculture Organization has said clearly that the world, with the science and technology then known, had enough knowledge to ensure man's freedom from hunger. Successive world congresses and conferences have repeated this contention.
(from a paper given by a distinguished professor at a 1985 academic conference)

Here the writer has evidently chosen the present perfect, thinking that he is referring to a situation which has continued on into the present. But when he refers to the *science and technology then known* and to *successive world congresses and conferences* he has cut off the 1963 conference from any grammatical connection with the present. This is again the sort of mistake that most writers can only catch during the revision process.

Common Errors in English # 7.

right   When it called the First World Food Congress in 1963, the Food and Agriculture Organization said clearly that the world, with the science and technology then known, had enough knowledge to ensure man's freedom from hunger. Successive world congresses and conferences have repeated this contention.

The Past Perfect Tense

	singular	plural
1st person	I had believed	we had believed
2nd person	you had believed	you had believed
3rd person	he, she, had believed	they had believed

Since the verb remains unchanged in all these forms, the past perfect is one of the easiest tenses to remember. What is difficult is learning how and when to use it. In English, however, there are quite definite rules about when the past perfect tense should be used. Its chief use is to show that one action in the past was completed before another action in the past began. Here are some examples:

I told my parents what <u>had happened</u>.

> (The happening occurred before the telling.)

By the time the group of tourists left Zimbabwe, they <u>had formed</u> a very favourable impression of the country.

> (The forming occurred before the leaving.)

When he had gone I thought very seriously about what he <u>had said</u>.

> (Both the going and the saying occurred before the thinking.)

The usefulness of the past perfect tense can be clearly seen in passages in which the writer wishes to flashback, or move backwards in time. If you compare the following passages, you will see that the use of the past perfect tense in the second passage removes any confusion about the order in which the events happened. In the example below, when only the simple past tense is used, it sounds as if the dead snake is able to crawl.

wrong   The tail was still moving, but the snake itself was quite dead. It crawled out from under a rock and slowly

Common Errors in English # 7.

	moved towards me as I was lowering the canoe at the end of the portage.
right	The tail was still moving, but the snake itself it was quite dead. It had crawled out from under a rock and had moved slowly towards me as I had been lowering the canoe at the end of the portage.

(In the second passage it is clear that the snake approached this person <u>before</u> it died, and not afterwards.)

Perhaps the most common occasions in which we use the past perfect tense are when we are using indirect speech:

> She said that she <u>had knocked</u> on my door in the morning, but that there had been no answer.

(The knocking happened before the saying.)

> The Committee Chairman repeatedly asked Col. North when the President had known of the diversion of funds to the Contras.

(The knowing happened before the asking.)

In a few cases it is possible to correctly speak of two actions which happened one after the other in the past by using the simple past tense for both actions. The use of the word *after*, for example, often makes it clear that the first action was completed before the other began.

---

8. Writers often neglect to use the past perfect to name the earlier action when they are speaking of two (or more) actions that happened at different times in the past.

wrong	He asked me if I talked to his secretary before coming to him.
right	He asked me if I had talked to his secretary before coming to him.

wrong	By the time the Allies decided to resist Hitler, the Nazis built up a huge military machine.
right	By the time the Allies decided to resist Hitler, the Nazis had built up a huge military machine.

wrong	Johnson's girlfriend, Marsha Dianne Blaylock, said she knew Williams since October 1984, when she and Johnson began their relationship.

(news report, *Chattanooga Times*, Aug. 9, 1985)

right	Johnson's girlfriend, Marsha Dianne Blaylock, said she had known Williams since October 1984, when she and Johnson began their relationship.

(Note that like the present perfect, the past perfect is very frequently required with *since* or *for*.)

The past perfect is also used to indicate that a past action occurred over a prolonged period:

> In the early 1960s Sonny Bono was a disheveled pop singer and songwriter with hippie tendencies; by the time of his death in 1998 he had become a conservative Republican member of the House of Representatives.

wrong
> In 1970, 10 per cent of Chile's families did not have sufficient income to satisfy the minimum food requirements recommended by international organizations; in 1983 the figure grew to 32 per cent.
> (*New York Review of Books*, May, 1988)

right
> In 1970, 10 per cent of Chile's families did not have sufficient income to satisfy the minimum food requirements recommended by international organizations; by 1983 the figure had grown to 32 per cent.

right
> ...in 1983 the figure was 32 per cent.

(The original suggests that the figure had remained at 10 per cent in every year from 1970 to 1983, and then jumped in the course of one year to 32 per cent.)

The Future Perfect Tense

	singular	**plural**
1st person	I will have gone	we will have gone
2nd person	you will have gone	you will have gone
3rd person	he, she, it will have gone	they will have gone

The Conditional

	singular	**plural**
1st person	I would go	we would go
2nd person	you would go	you would go
3rd person	he, she, it would go	they would go

The conditional tense is used when we are speaking of actions which would happen *if* certain conditions were fulfilled. Here are some examples:

> If I <u>wanted</u> to go to Australia, I <u>would have</u> to fly.

> If I <u>drank</u> a lot of gin, I <u>would be</u> very sick.

Common Errors in English # 8.

I would lend Joe the money he wants if I trusted him.

Notice that each of these sentences is made up of a main clause, in which the conditional tense *would have*, *would be*, etc., is used, and a subordinate clause beginning with *if*, with a verb in the simple past tense (*wanted, drank, trusted,* etc.). In all cases the action named in the *if* clause is considered by the speaker to be unlikely to happen, or quite impossible. The speaker does not really want to go to Australia: she is just speculating about what she would have to do if she did. Similarly the second speaker does not expect to drink a lot of gin: if he did, he would be sick, but he does not plan to. In the same way, the speaker of the third sentence does not trust Joe: he is speaking about what the situation would be if he did trust Joe. Situations like these which are not happening and which we do not expect to happen are called *hypothetical situations*: we speculate on what would happen *if...* but we do not expect the *if...* to come true.

If we think the *if...* is likely to come true, then we use the future tense instead of the conditional in the main clause, and the present tense in the subordinate *if* clause, as in these examples:

If I drink a lot of gin, I will be very sick.

(Here the speaker thinks that it is very possible or likely that he will drink a lot of gin.)

If I want to go to Australia, I will have to fly.

(Here the speaker thinks that she may really want to go.)

Notice the difference between the following two sentences:

If a socialist government is elected, the American administration will not be pleased.

(Here the writer thinks that it is quite possible or likely that the socialists will be elected.)

If a socialist government were elected, the American administration would not be pleased.

(Here the writer is assuming that the socialists probably will not be elected.)

---

9. **The subjunctive**: Notice in the above example that *were* is used instead of *was*. This is what is known as the subjunctive mood, used in certain cases to denote actions that are wished for or imagined. Years ago there were many more types of sentence in which the subjunctive was used than there are now, but it has by no means disappeared.

Common Errors in English # 9.

If we can't even get this much done, God help us. [not *God helps us*]

If I were you, I'd do what she says. [not *if I was you*]

Suffice it to say that the subject is a controversial one. [not *suffices it...*]

Be that as it may, the central assertion of Smith's book is irrefutable. [not *is that...*]

The doctor advises that he stop smoking immediately. [not *that he stops*]

wrong	If a bank was willing to lend new businesses very large amounts without proper guarantees, it would go bankrupt very quickly.
right	If a bank were willing to lend new businesses very large amounts without proper guarantees, it would go bankrupt very quickly.

10. Some writers mistakenly use the conditional tense or the present tense (instead of the past tense) in the *if* clause when they are using the conditional tense in the main clause.

wrong	If I want to buy a car, I would look carefully at all the models available.
right	If I <u>wanted</u> to buy a car, I would look carefully at all the models available.
	(The speaker does not want to buy a car.)
or	If I <u>want</u> to buy a car, I will look carefully at all the models available.
	(The speaker may really want to buy a car.)
wrong	If television networks would produce fewer series about violent crime, parents would allow their children to watch even more television than they do now.
right	If television networks produced fewer series about violent crime, parents would allow their children to watch even more television than they do now.

Remember that the <u>past</u> tense (or with the verb *to be*, the subjunctive) is used in the *if* clause whenever the conditional tense is being used in the main clause.

The Past Conditional Tense

	singular	plural
1st person	I would have gone	we would have gone
2nd person	you would have gone	you would have gone
3rd person	he, she, it would have gone	they would have gone

Common Errors in English # 10.

This tense is used in conditional sentences in which we are speaking of actions which never happened. It is used in the main clause, with the past perfect tense being used in the *if* clause.

> If I had studied harder, I would have passed.
>
> (meaning that in fact I did not study very hard, and did not pass)
>
> If Kitchener had arrived at Khartoum a day earlier, he would have saved Gordon and the rest of the British garrison force.
>
> (meaning that Kitchener did not come early enough, and was not able to prevent the 1885 massacre at Khartoum)

11. Some people mistakenly use the past conditional tense in both clauses of sentences such as these; remember that the past conditional should be used only in the main clause; use the past perfect in the *if* clause.

wrong	If the Titanic would have carried more lifeboats, hundreds of lives would have been saved.
right	If the Titanic had carried more lifeboats, hundreds of lives would have been saved.
wrong	If the 'Yes' campaign in Quebec would have won 200,000 more votes, the course of Canadian politics in the mid-1990s would have been very different.
right	If the 'Yes' campaign in Quebec had won 200,000 more votes, the course of Canadian politics in the mid-1990s would have been very different.

Active and Passive Voice

12. As many authorities have pointed out, in most cases writers can make their sentences less wordy and more effective by using the active voice rather than the passive.

wrong	The election was lost by the premier. (Passive —7 words)
right	The premier lost the election. (Active — 5 words)
wrong	Union power was seen by them to have constrained the possibilities for full investment, and for achieving full employment.
	(from the first draft of a manuscript by a professor)
right	The shareholders thought that union power had constrained the possibilities for full investment, and for achieving full employment.

Common Errors in English # 11.

The vice, one should note, is not the passive voice *per se*, but the wordiness it sometimes gives rise to.

Other Tenses

The present perfect continuous tense — I have been running, you have been working, etc.

The past perfect continuous tense — I had been looking, you had been following, etc.

The future perfect continuous tense — I will have been sleeping, they will have been studying, etc.

The conditional continuous tense — I would be bringing, she would be starting, etc.

The past conditional continuous tense — I would have been working, he would have been driving, etc.

DANGLING CONSTRUCTIONS

Dangling Participles and Infinitives

A present participle is an *-ing* word (*going, thinking* etc.). When combined with a form of the verb *to be*, participles form part of a complete verb. They can also be used in a number of ways on their own, however:

> The President felt that visiting China would be unwise at that time.
>
> (Here *visiting China* acts as a noun phrase.)

> Having taken into account the various reports, the Committee decided to delay the project for a year.
>
> (Here *having taken into account the various reports* acts as an adjectival phrase modifying the noun *Committee*.)

13. **Dangling present participles or participial phrases**: The danger of dangling occurs with sentences such as the second example above. If the writer does not take care that the participial phrase refers to the subject of the main clause, some absurd sentences can result:

wrong	Waiting for a bus, a brick fell on my head.
	(Bricks do not normally wait for buses.)
right	While I was waiting for a bus, a brick fell on my head.
wrong	Leaving the room, the lights must be turned off.
	(Lights do not normally leave the room.)
right	When you leave the room you must turn off the lights.

In sentences such as these the amusing error is relatively easy to notice; it can be much more difficult with longer and more complex sentences. Experienced writers are especially alert to this pitfall if they begin a sentence with a participle or participial phrase that describes a mental operation; they are wary of beginning by *considering, believing, taking into account, remembering, turning for a moment* or *regarding*.

wrong	Believing that he had done no wrong, the fact of being accused of dishonesty infuriated Col. North.
right	Believing that he had done no wrong, Col. North was infuriated at being accused of dishonesty.
or	Col. North was infuriated at being accused of dishonesty; he believed he had done no wrong.

Common Errors in English # 13.

wrong	Considering all the above-mentioned studies, **the** evidence shows conclusively that smoking can **cause** cancer.
right	Considering all the above-mentioned studies, **we** conclude that smoking causes cancer.
better	These studies show conclusively that smoking can cause cancer.
wrong	Turning for a moment to the thorny question of Joyce's style, the stream of consciousness technique realistically depicts the workings of the human mind.
right	Turning for a moment to the thorny question of Joyce's style, we may observe that his stream of consciousness technique realistically depicts the workings of the human mind.
better	Joyce's style does not make *Ulysses* easy to read, but his stream of consciousness technique realistically depicts the workings of the human mind.
wrong	Taking into account the uncertainty as to the initial temperature of the beaker, the results are not conclusive.
poor	Taking into account the uncertainty as to the initial temperature of the beaker necessitates that the results be deemed inconclusive.
better	Since the initial temperature of the beaker was not recorded, the results are inconclusive.

Notice that in each case the best way to eliminate the problem is to dispense with the participial phrase entirely. More often than not one's writing is improved by using active verbs rather than participial phrases. Many people seem to feel that writing which is filled with participial phrases somehow sounds more important; in fact, such phrases tend to obscure the writer's meaning under unnecessary padding. This is true even when the participles are not dangling:

wrong	Another significant characteristic having a significant impact on animal populations is the extreme diurnal temperature range on the desert surface.
	(Can a characteristic have an impact? A small point is here buried in a morass of meaningless abstraction.)
better	The extreme diurnal temperature range on the desert surface also affects animal populations.
wrong	Referring generally to the social stratification systems of the city as a whole, we can see clearly that types of accommodation, varying throughout in accordance with income levels and other socio-economic factors, display an extraordinary diversity.
	(Is there anything either clear or extraordinary about this?)
better	In this city rich people and poor people live in different neighborhoods and rich people live in larger houses than poor people.

Common Errors in English # 13.

By cutting out the padding in this way the writer may occasionally find to his surprise that instead of saying something rather weighty and important as he had thought he was doing he is in fact saying little or nothing. But he should not be discouraged if this happens; the same is true for all writers. The best response is simply to chuckle and scratch out the sentence!

---

14. Dangling past participles (e.g., *considered, developed, regarded*): The same sorts of problems that occur with present participles are frequent with past participles as well:

wrong	Considered from a cost point of view, Combarp Capital Corporation could not really afford to purchase Skinflint Securities.
	(Combarp is not being considered; the purchase is.)
poor	Considered from the point of view of cost, the purchase of Skinflint Securities was not a wise move by Combarp Capital Corporation..
better	Combarp Capital Corporation could not really afford to buy Skinflint Securities.
wrong	Once regarded as daringly modern in its portrayal of fashionable *fin de siecle* decadence, Wilde draws on traditional patterns to create a powerful new Gothic tale. (*The Cambridge Guide to Literature in English*)
	(The novel is an 'it'; Oscar Wilde was a 'he.')
right	*The Picture of Dorian Gray* was once regarded as daringly modern in its portrayal of fashionable *fin de siecle* decadence. In the novel Wilde draws on traditional patterns to create a powerful new Gothic tale.
wrong	Used with frequency, a man will feel refreshed and rejuvenated. (aftershave advertisment)
right	Used with frequency, this product will help a man feel refreshed and rejuvenated.

---

15. Dangling infinitive phrases:

wrong	To conclude this essay, the French Revolution was a product of many interacting causes.
	(The French Revolution concluded no essays.)
poor	To conclude this essay, let me say that the French Revolution was a product of many causes.
better	The explanations given for the French Revolution, then, are not mutually exclusive; it was a product of many interacting causes.

[A good writer does not normally need to tell her readers that she is concluding an essay; they can see the space at the bottom of the page. A little word such as *then*, set off by commas, is more than enough to signal that this is a summing-up.]

Common Errors in English # 14.

wrong	To receive a complimentary copy, the business reply card should be returned before June 30.
	(The card will not receive anything.)
right	To receive a complimentary copy, you should return the business reply card before June 30.
wrong	To appreciate the full significance of the Meech Lake Accord, a range of factors need to be considered.
	(A factor cannot appreciate.)
poor	To appreciate the full significance of the Meech Lake Accord, we need to consider many things.
better	The Meech Lake Accord was important in many ways.

16. Dangling gerund (*of going, in doing,* etc.) phrases:

wrong	In reviewing the evidence, one point stands out plainly.
	(A point cannot review evidence.)
poor	In reviewing the evidence, we can see one point standing out plainly.
better	One point stands out plainly from this evidence.
wrong	When analyzing the figures, ways to achieve substantial savings can be discerned.
	(The ways cannot analyse.)
poor	When we analyse the figures we can see ways to achieve substantial savings.
better	The figures suggest that we can greatly reduce our expenses.

Other sorts of phrases can be caught dangling too. But almost all writers are capable of attaching them properly if they re-read and revise their work carefully.

wrong	On behalf of City Council and the people of Windsor, it gives me great pleasure to welcome you to our city.
	(Mayor David A Burr, *Windsor Guide*, Winter 1988)
	[The Mayor, not a faceless *it*, is acting on behalf of the others.]
right	On behalf of City Council and the people of Windsor, I am pleased to welcome you to our city.

SEQUENCE OF TENSES

If the main verb of a sentence is in the past tense, other verbs must also express a past viewpoint (except when a general truth is being expressed). Some writers have trouble keeping the verb tenses they use in agreement, particularly when indirect speech is involved, or when a quotation is incorporated into a sentence.

---

17. Agreement of tenses in indirect speech — past plus subjunctive:

wrong   He said that he will fix the engine before the end of July, 1999.

right   He said that he would fix the engine before the end of July, 1999.

("He said that he will fix the engine" implies that the fixing has not yet occurred but may still occur.)

---

18. Agreement of tenses in indirect speech — past plus past perfect:

wrong   He claimed that he smoked drugs many years earlier, but that he never inhaled.

right   He claimed that he had smoked drugs many years earlier, but that he had never inhaled.

---

19. Agreement of tenses — quoted material:

wrong   Prime Minister Blair admitted that "such a policy is not without its drawbacks."

(The past tense *admitted* and the present tense *is* do not agree.)

There are two ways of dealing with a difficulty such as this:

(a) Change the sentence so as to set off the quotation without using the connecting word, *that*. Usually this can be done with a colon. In this case the tense you use does not have to agree with the tense used in the quotation. The words before the colon, though, must be able to act as a complete sentence in themselves.

(b) Use only that part of the quotation that can be used in agreement with the tense of the main verb.

right 	Prime Minister Blair did not claim perfection: "such a policy is not without its drawbacks," he admitted.
or 	Prime Minister Blair admitted that such a policy was "not without its drawbacks."

Here are some other examples:

wrong 	Churchill promised that "we shall fight on the beaches, . . . we shall fight in the fields and in the streets, we shall fight in the hills; we shall never surrender."

(This suggests that you, the writer, will be among those fighting.)

right 	Churchill made the following promise: "We shall fight on the beaches, . . . we shall fight in the fields and in the streets, we shall fight in the hills; we shall never surrender."

(Notice that the word *that* is now removed.)

or 	Churchill promised that the British people would "fight on the beaches,...in the fields and in the streets,... in the hills," and that they would "never surrender."

wrong 	In the 1974 election campaign the Liberals' claimed that "the Land is strong."
right 	In the 1974 election campaign the Liberals' slogan was, "The Land is Strong."
or 	In the 1974 election campaign the Liberals' asserted that the Land was strong.

IRREGULAR OR DIFFICULT VERBS

The majority of verbs in English follow a regular pattern—*I open* in the simple present tense, *I opened* in the simple past tense, *I have opened* in the present perfect tense, and so forth. However, most of the more frequently used verbs are in some way or another irregular. To pick an obvious example, we say *I went* instead of *I goed*, and *I have gone* instead of *I have goed*. What follows is a list of the main irregular or difficult verbs in English. The past participle (column 3) is used in tenses such as the present perfect (e.g., *I have grown, He has found*) and the past perfect (*I had grown, I had found*).

The verbs that most frequently cause problems are given special treatment in the following list.

Note: In both regular and irregular verbs, the present tense is formed by using the infinitive without the preposition *to*.

Present and infinitive	Simple past	Past participle
20. arise	arose	arisen
wrong	A problem had arose even before the discussion began.	
right	A problem had arisen even before the discussion began.	
awake	awoke/awaked (passive: was awakened)	awoken/awaked/woken
be	was/were	been
21. bear	bore	borne
wrong	It was heartbreaking for her to lose the child after having bore it for so long.	
right	It was heartbreaking for her to lose the child after having borne it for so long.	
22. beat	beat	beaten
wrong	The Yankees were badly beat by the Blue Jays.	
right	The Yankees were badly beaten by the Blue Jays.	

Present and infinitive	Simple past	Past participle
become	became	become

23. begin began begun

wrong He had already began treatment when I met him.
right He had already begun treatment when I met him.

bend	bent	bent
bite	bit	bitten
bleed	bled	bled
blow	blew	blown
break	broke	broken
bring	brought	brought
build	built	built
burn	burned/burnt	burned/ burnt

24. burst burst burst

wrong The pipes bursted while we were on holiday.
right The pipes burst while we were on holiday.

buy	bought	bought
can	could	been able
catch	caught	caught

25. choose chose chosen

wrong In 1949 Newfoundlanders choose to join Confederation.
right In 1949 Newfoundlanders chose to join Confederation.

cling	clung	clung
come	came	come
cost	cost	cost
dig	dug	dug
do	did	done

26. dive dived dived

wrong He dove into the shallow water.
right He dived into the shallow water.

27. drag dragged dragged

wrong The newspapers drug up a lot of scandal about her.
right The newspapers dragged up a lot of scandal about her.

draw	drew	drawn

Common Errors in English # 23.

Present and infinitive	Simple past	Past participle
dream	dreamed/dreamt	dreamed/dreamt

28.

	drink	drank	drunk
wrong		He has drank more than is good for him.	
right		He has drunk more than is good for him.	

Habs Should Have Drank A Toast To Discipline
(headline, *The Globe and Mail*, Dec. 19, 1990)

Short on Education
(letters to the editor, *The Globe and Mail*, Dec. 27, 1990)

Re Habs Should Have Drank A Toast To Discipline (Dec. 19): Whoever wrote this headline should have went to school longer.

Simon Farrow, North Vancouver

---

drive	drove	driven
eat	ate	eaten
fall	fell	fallen
feel	felt	felt
fight	fought	fought
find	found	found

29.

	fit	fitted or fit (US)	fitted
wrong		That dress has fit her since she was married.	
right		That dress has fitted her since she was married.	

flee	fled	fled

30.

	fling	flung	flung
wrong		George flinged his plate across the room.	
right		George flung his plate across the room.	

fly	flew	flown

31.

	forbid	forbade	forbidden
wrong		Yesterday he forbid us to climb the fence.	
right		Yesterday he forbade us to climb the fence.	

Common Errors in English # 28.

Present and infinitive	Simple past	Past participle
32. forecast	forecast	forecast

wrong   The Weather Office has forecasted more rain.
right   The Weather Office has forecast more rain.

forget	forgot	forgotten
forgive	forgave	forgiven
freeze	froze	frozen
get	got	got
give	gave	given
go	went	gone
grind	ground	ground

(e.g., I have ground the coffee.)

grow	grew	grown

---

33. hang	hanged/hung	hanged/hung

Note: *Hanged* is used only when referring to a person being killed by hanging. Say, "The criminal has been hanged," but "We have hung the picture on the wall."

wrong   No one has been hung in Canada since 1962.
right   No one has been hanged in Canada since 1962.

have	had	had
hear	heard	heard
hide	hid	hidden
hit	hit	hit
hold	held	held
hurt	hurt	hurt
keep	kept	kept
kneel	knelt	knelt
know	knew	known

---

34. lay	laid	laid

Note: Although many authorities feel that the distinction is not worth troubling over in informal English, formal English still distinguishes between *lay* and *lie*; you *lay* something on a table, and a hen *lays* eggs, but you *lie* down to sleep. In other words, *lie* is an intransitive verb; it should not be followed by a direct object. *Lay*, by contrast, is transitive.

wrong   That old thing has been laying around for years.
right   That old thing has been lying around for years.

Common Errors in English # 32.

Present and infinitive	Simple past	Past participle
lead	led	led
lean	leaned/leant	leaned/leant
leap	leaped/leapt	leaped/leapt
learn	learned/learnt	learned/learnt
leave	left	left
lend	lent	lent
let	let	let

35. | lie | lay | lain |

wrong He asked if I would like to lay down and rest.
right He asked if I would like to lie down and rest.

See also above, number 34.

light	lighted/lit	lighted/lit
lose	lost	lost
make	made	made
may	might	
mean	meant	meant
meet	met	met
must	had to	
pay	paid	paid

36. | prove | proved | proven |

wrong We have proved the hypothesis to be correct.
right We have proven the hypothesis to be correct.

put	put	put
read	read	read

37. | ride | rode | ridden |

wrong The actor had never rode a horse before.
right The actor had never ridden a horse before.

38. | ring | rang | rung |

wrong I rung the bell three times, but no one answered.
right I rang the bell three times, but no one answered.

Common Errors in English # 35.

Present and infinitive	Simple past	Past participle
rise	rose	risen
run	ran	run
saw	sawed	sawed/sawn
say	said	said
see	saw	seen
seek	sought	sought
sell	sold	sold
sew	sewed	sewed/sewn
shake	shook	shaken
shall	should	

39.

	shine	shone	shone
wrong	The moon shined almost as brightly as the sun.		
right	The moon shone almost as brightly as the sun.		

shoot	shot	shot
show	showed	showed/shown

40.

	shrink	shrank	shrunk
wrong	The Government's majority shrunk in the election.		
right	The Government's majority shrank in the election.		

shut	shut	shut
sing	sang	sung

41.

	sink	sank	sunk
wrong	The *Edmund Fitzgerald* sunk on Lake Superior.		
right	The *Edmund Fitzgerald* sank on Lake Superior.		

sit	sat	sat
sleep	slept	slept
slide	slid	slid
smell	smelled/smelt	smelled/smelt
sow	sowed	sowed/sown
speak	spoke	spoken
speed	speeded/sped	speeded/sped
spell	spelled/spelt	spelled/spelt

Common Errors in English # 39.

Present and infinitive	Simple past	Past participle
spend	spent	spent
spill	spilled/spilt	spilled/spilt
spin	spun	spun
spit	spat	spat
split	split	split
spread	spread	spread

42.

	spring	sprang	sprung

wrong The soldiers hurriedly sprung to their feet.
right The soldiers hurriedly sprang to their feet.

stand	stood	stood
steal	stole	stolen
stick	stuck	stuck
sting	stung	stung
strike	struck	struck
swear	swore	sworn
sweep	swept	swept

43.

	swim	swam	swum

wrong Pictures were taken while the royal couple swum in what they thought was a private cove.

right Pictures were taken while the royal couple swam in what they had thought was a private cove.

swing	swung	swung
take	took	taken
teach	taught	taught
tear	tore	torn
tell	told	told
think	thought	thought
throw	threw	thrown
tread	trod	trodden/trod
understand	understood	understood
wake	waked/woke	waked/woken
wear	wore	worn
weep	wept	wept

Common Errors in English # 42.

Present and infinitive	Simple past	Past participle
win	won	won
wind	wound	wound
wring	wrung	wrung

e.g.   She wrings out her clothes if they are wet.

write	wrote	written

INFINITIVES, GERUNDS, OBJECTS: "TO BE OR NOT TO BE"?

There are no rules in English to explain why some words must be followed by an infinitive (*to go, to do, to be,* etc.), while others must be followed by a gerund (*of going, in doing,* etc.), and still others by a direct object. Here are some of the words with which difficulties of this sort most often arise.

---

44. **accept** something (not accept to do something) — needs a direct object

wrong	The Committee accepted to try to improve the quality of the postal service.
right	The Committee accepted the task of trying to improve the postal service.
or	The Committee agreed to try to improve the postal service.

---

45. **accuse** someone of doing something (not to do)

wrong	Klaus Barbie was accused to have killed thousands of innocent civilians in WW II.
right	Klaus Barbie was accused of having killed thousands of innocent civilians in WW II.

---

46. **appreciate** something: When used to mean *be grateful*, this verb requires a direct object.

wrong	I would appreciate if you could respond quickly.
right	I would appreciate it if you could respond quickly.
or	I would appreciate a quick response.

(The verb *appreciate* without an object means *increase in value*.)

---

47. **assist** in doing something (not to do)

wrong	He assisted me to solve the problem.
right	He assisted me in solving the problem.
or	He helped me to solve the problem.

---

48. **capable** of doing something (not to do)

wrong	He is capable to run 1500 metres in under four minutes.

Common Errors in English # 44.

right	He is capable of running 1500 metres in under four minutes.
or	He is able to run 1500 metres in under four minutes.

49. **confident** of doing something

wrong	She is confident to be able to finish the job before dusk.
right	She is confident of being able to finish the job before dusk.
or	She is confident that she will finish the job before dusk.

49. **consider** something or someone to be something *or* consider them something (not as something)

wrong	According to a recent policy paper, the Party now considers a guaranteed annual income as a good idea.
right	According to a recent policy paper, the Party now considers a guaranteed annual income to be a good idea.
or	According to a recent policy paper, the Party now regards a guaranteed annual income as a good idea.

51. **discourage** someone from doing something (not to do)

wrong	The new Immigration Act is intended to discourage anyone who wants to come to Canada to enter the country illegally.
right	The new Immigration Act is intended to discourage anyone who wants to come to Canada from entering the country illegally.

52. **forbid** someone to do something (not from doing)

wrong	The witnesses were forbidden from leaving the scene of the crime until the police had completed their preliminary investigation.
right	The witnesses were forbidden to leave the scene of the crime until the police had completed their preliminary investigation.

53. **insist** on doing something *or* insist that something be done (but not insist to do)

wrong	The customer has insisted to wait in the front office until she receives a refund.
right	The customer has insisted on waiting in the front office until she receives a refund.

54. **intention:** Have an intention of doing something *but* someone's intention is/was to do something

wrong	Hitler had no intention to keep his word.
right	Hitler had no intention of keeping his word.
or	Hitler did not intend to keep his word.
or	Hitler's intention was to break the treaty.

Common Errors in English # 49.

55. justified <u>in doing</u> something (<u>not</u> to do something)

wrong He is not justified to make these allegations.
right He is not justified in making these allegations.

56. look forward <u>to doing</u> something (<u>not</u> to do something)

wrong I am looking forward to receive your reply.
right I am looking forward to receiving your reply.

57. opposed <u>to doing</u> something (<u>not</u> to do something)

wrong He was opposed to set up a dictatorship.
right He was opposed to setting up a dictatorship.
or He was opposed to the idea of setting up a dictatorship.

58. organize <u>something</u> (<u>not</u> organize to do something)

wrong We organized to meet at ten the next morning.
right We organized a meeting for ten the next morning.
or We arranged to meet at ten the next morning.

59. persist <u>in doing</u> something (<u>not</u> to do something)

wrong Despite international disapproval and the will of Congress, the Reagan administration persisted to help the contras in Nicaragua.
right Despite international disapproval and the will of Congress, the Reagan administration persisted in helping the contras in Nicaragua.

60. plan to do (<u>not</u> on doing)

wrong They planned on closing the factory in Windsor.
right They planned to close the factory in Windsor.

61. prohibit someone <u>from doing</u> something

wrong Members of the public were prohibited to feed the animals.
right Members of the public were prohibited from feeding the animals.

62. regarded <u>as</u> (<u>not</u> regarded to be)

wrong He is commonly regarded to be one of Canada's best musicians.
right He is commonly regarded as one of Canada's best musicians.

63. responsible <u>for doing</u> (<u>not</u> to do)

wrong Mr Dumphy is responsible to market the full line of the company's pharmaceutical products.
right Mr Dumphy is responsible for marketing the full line of the company's pharmaceutical products.

---

64. **sacrifice** <u>something</u>: The use of *sacrifice* without a direct object may have crept into the language through the use of the verb as a baseball term (*Martinez sacrificed in the ninth to bring home Womack.*).

wrong	He sacrificed to work in an isolated community with no electricity or running water.
right	He sacrificed himself to work in an isolated community with no electricity or running water.
or	He sacrificed a good deal; the isolated community he now works in has no electricity or running water.

---

65. **seem** <u>to be</u> (<u>not</u> as if)

wrong	The patient seemed as if he was in shock.
right	The patient seemed to be in shock.

Exception: When the subject is *it*, *seem* can be followed by *as*. (e.g., It seemed as if he was sick, so we called the doctor.)

---

66. **suspect** someone <u>of doing</u> something (<u>not</u> to do)

wrong	His wife suspected him to have committed adultery.
right	His wife suspected him of committing adultery.
or	His wife suspected that he had committed adultery.

---

68. **tendency** <u>to do</u> something (<u>not</u> of doing)

wrong	Some Buick engines have a tendency of over-revving.
right	Some Buick engines have a tendency to over-rev.
or	The engine has a habit of over-revving.

PREPOSITION PROBLEMS "UP WITH WHICH I WILL NOT PUT"

The prepositions used in English often make little or no sense. What good reason is there for saying *inferior to* but *worse than*? None whatsoever, but over the centuries certain prepositions have come to be accepted as going together with certain verbs, nouns etc. There are no rules to help one learn the combinations; here are some of the ones that most commonly cause difficulty.

---

69. **agree** with someone / with what someone says; agree to do something, to something; agree on a plan, proposal, etc.

wrong	The union representatives did not agree with the proposed wage increase.
right	The union representatives did not agree to the proposed wage increase.
or	The union representatives did not agree with management about the proposed wage increase.

---

70. **angry** with someone; angry at or about something

wrong	He was angry at me for failing to keep our appointment.
right	He was angry with me for failing to keep our appointment.

---

71. **annoyed** with someone; annoyed by something

wrong	The professor is often annoyed with the attitude of the class.
right	The professor is often annoyed by the attitude of the class.

---

72. **appeal** to someone for something

wrong	The Premier appealed for the residents to help.
right	The Premier appealed to the residents for help.

---

73. **argue** <u>with</u> someone <u>about</u> something

wrong	They argued against each other for half an hour.
right	They argued with each other for half an hour.

---

74. **arrive** <u>in</u> a place / <u>at</u> a place (<u>not</u> arrive a place, <u>except</u> arrive home). Airlines are perhaps to blame for the error of using both *arrive* and *depart* without prepositions.

wrong	He won't join the Yankees until tomorrow night when they arrive Milwaukee.
	(*The Globe and Mail*, April 13, 1988)
right	He won't join the Yankees until tomorrow night when they arrive in Milwaukee.

---

75. **attach** two or more things (<u>not</u> attach together)

wrong	The Siamese twins were attached together at the hip.
right	The Siamese twins were attached at the hip.

---

76. **borrow** something <u>from</u> someone

wrong	I borrowed him a pair of trousers.
right	I borrowed a pair of trousers from him.

---

77. **cancel** something (<u>not</u> cancel out, except when the verb is used to mean *counterbalance* or *neutralize*)

wrong	She cancelled out all her appointments.
right	She cancelled all her appointments.

---

78. **care** <u>about</u> something (meaning to think it worthwhile, or important to you)

wrong	George does not care for what happens to his sister.
right	George does not care what happens to his sister.
or	George does not care about what happens to his sister.

---

79. **centre:** centred <u>on</u> something (<u>not</u> around something); for one thing to be centred <u>around</u> another is physically impossible.

wrong	The novel is centred around the conflict between British imperialism and native aspirations.
right	The novel centres on the conflict between British imperialism and native aspirations.

---

80. **chase** someone/something <u>away</u> for doing something; despite the way the word is misused in baseball slang, the verb *chase* with no preposition means *run after*, not *send away*.

wrong	Starting pitcher Greg Maddux was chased in the fifth inning.
right	Starting pitcher Greg Maddux was pulled from the game in the fifth inning.

Common Errors in English # 73.

---

81. **collide** <u>with</u> something (<u>not</u> against something)
wrong   The bus left the road and collided against a tree.
right   The bus left the road and collided with a tree.

---

82. **compare** <u>to</u> / compare <u>with</u>: To compare something <u>to</u> something else is to liken it, especially when speaking metaphorically (e.g., "Can I compare thee to a summer's day?"). To compare something <u>with</u> something else is to judge how the two are similar <u>or different</u> ("If you compare one brand with another you will notice little difference."). Use *compare with* when noting differences.

wrong   The First World War was a small conflict compared to the Second World War, but it changed humanity even more profoundly.
right   The First World War was a small conflict compared with the Second World War, but it changed humanity even more profoundly.

---

83. **concerned** <u>with</u> something (meaning having some connection with it, having something to do with it) and concerned <u>about</u> something (meaning being interested in it, or worried about it)
wrong   The Ministry is very concerned with the level of pollution in this river.
right   The Ministry is very concerned about the level of pollution in this river.

---

84. **conform** <u>to</u>
wrong   The building does not conform with current standards.
right   The building does not conform to current standards.
or   The contractors did not comply with current standards.

---

85. **congratulate** someone <u>on</u> something
wrong   The Opposition leaders congratulated the Prime Minister for his success.
right   The Opposition leaders congratulated the Prime Minister on his success.

---

86. **connect** two things / connect one thing <u>with</u> another (<u>not</u> connect up with)
wrong   As soon as he connects up these wires, the system should work.
right   As soon as he connects these wires, the system should work.

---

87. **conscious of** something

wrong   He was not conscious that he had done anything wrong.

right   He was not conscious of having done anything wrong.

(Note: unlike *conscious*, *aware* can be used with *of* or with a *that* clause.)

---

88. **consist in** / consist **of**: *Consist in* means to exist in, to have as the essential feature; *consist of* means to be made up of.

wrong   Success consists of hard work.
                     (i.e. The essence of success is hard work.)

right   Success consists in hard work.

wrong   The U.S. Congress consists in two houses – the House of Representatives and the Senate.

right   The U.S. Congress consists of two houses – the House of Representatives and the Senate.

---

89. **consult someone** (**not** consult with someone)

wrong   She will have to consult with the Board of Directors before giving us an answer.

right   She will have to consult the Board of Directors before giving us an answer.

or   She will have to talk to the Board of Directors before giving us an answer.

---

90. **continue** something, **with** something, **to** a place (**not** continue on)

wrong   We were told to continue on with our work.

right   We were told to continue with our work.

---

91. **convenient for** someone, **for** a purpose / convenient **to** a place

wrong   This house is very convenient to me; it is only a short walk to work.

right   This house is very convenient for me; it is only a short walk to work.

---

92. **cooperate with** someone (**not** cooperate together)

wrong   The Provinces should cooperate together to break down inter-provincial trade barriers.

right   The Provinces should cooperate with one another to break down inter-provincial trade barriers.

---

93. **correspond to** (be in agreement with); **correspond with** (exchange letters with)

wrong   The fingerprints at the scene of the crime corresponded with those of the suspect.

right   The fingerprints at the scene of the crime corresponded to those of the suspect.

---

94. **couple of** things/times/people, etc.)

wrong	The body had been partially hidden under a pier on Lake Union, a couple hundred feet from the Aurora Avenue Bridge.
	(*The Seattle Post-Intelligencer, April 6, 1996*)
right	The body had been partially hidden under a pier on Lake Union, a couple of hundred feet from the Aurora Avenue Bridge.
or	The body had been partially hidden under a pier on Lake Union, approximately two hundred feet from the Aurora Avenue Bridge.

(In formal writing it is best to use *two* rather than *a couple of*.)

95. criticism of something/somebody

wrong	His criticisms against her were completely unfounded.
right	His criticisms of her were completely unfounded.

96. depart from a place

wrong	One woman was heard saying to a friend as they departed SkyDome...
	(*The Toronto Star*, Nov. 29, 1989)
right	One woman was heard saying to a friend as they departed from the SkyDome...
or	One woman was heard saying to a friend as they left the SkyDome...

97. die of a disease / of old age; die from injuries, wounds

wrong	My grandfather died from cancer when he was only forty-two years old.
right	My grandfather died of cancer when he was only forty-two years old.

98. different from, to, than. *Different to* and *different from* are both acceptable British usage; *different from* is the preferred form in Canada; *different than* is a common and entirely acceptable form in the United States.

US usage	These results are different than those we obtained when we did the same experiment yesterday.
UK usage	These results are different to those we obtained when we did the same experiment yesterday.

99. discuss something (not discuss about something; no preposition is needed)

wrong	They discussed about what to do to ease tensions in the Middle East.
right	They discussed what to do to ease tensions in the Middle East.

Common Errors in English # 95.

100. divide something (no preposition necessary)

wrong	Lear wants to divide up his kingdom among his three daughters.
right	Lear wants to divide his kingdom among his three daughters.

101. do something <u>for</u> someone (meaning something that will help); do something <u>to</u> someone (meaning something that will hurt)

wrong	Norman Bethune did a lot to the people of China.
right	Norman Bethune did a lot for the people of China.

102. end: At the end <u>of</u> something; in the end (no additional preposition). *In the end* is used when the writer does not say <u>which</u> end he means, but leaves this to be understood by the reader. *At the end <u>of</u>* is used when the writer mentions the end he is referring to.

wrong	In the end of *Things Fall Apart*, we both admire and pity Okonkwo.
right	At the end of *Things Fall Apart*, we both admire and pity Okonkwo.
or	In the end, we both admire and pity Okonkwo.

103. end <u>at</u> a place (<u>not</u> end up at)

wrong	We do not want to end up at the same place we started from.
right	We do not want to end at the same place we started from.

104. fight <u>someone</u> or <u>with</u> someone (<u>not</u> against; fight means *struggle against*, so to add *against* is redundant)

wrong	They fought against each other for almost an hour.
right	They fought with each other for almost an hour.
or	They fought each other for almost an hour.

105. frightened <u>by</u> something (when it has just frightened you); frightened <u>of</u> something (when talking about a constant condition)

wrong	He was suddenly frightened of the sound of a door slamming.
right	He was suddenly frightened by the sound of a door slamming.

106. graduate <u>from</u> a school

wrong	He graduated McGill in 1999.
right	He graduated from McGill in 1999.

---

107. help doing [i.e. be unable to refrain from doing], <u>not help from doing</u>

wrong	She could not help from agreeing to his suggestion.
right	She could not help agreeing to his suggestion.

---

108. hurry (<u>not</u> hurry up)

wrong	She told me to hurry up if I didn't want to miss the train.
right	She told me to hurry if I didn't want to miss the train.

---

109. identical <u>with</u> (<u>not</u> to)

wrong	This hotel is identical to the Holiday Inn we stayed in last week.
right	This hotel is identical with the Holiday Inn we stayed in last week.

---

110. in: Do not use *in* where *throughout* is meant; particularly when using such words as *whole* or *entire*, be careful to use *throughout*.

wrong	Political repression is common in the whole world.
right	Political repression is common throughout the world.

---

111. independent <u>of</u> something/someone

wrong	I would like to live entirely independent from my parents.
right	I would like to live entirely independent of my parents.

---

112. inferior <u>to</u> someone/something

wrong	Most people think that margarine is inferior than butter.
right	Most people think that margarine is inferior to butter.

(Inferior and superior are the only two comparative adjectives which are not followed by than.)

---

113. inside or **outside** something (<u>not</u> of something)

wrong	Within thirty minutes a green scum had formed inside of the beaker.
right	Within thirty minutes a green scum had formed inside the beaker.

---

114. interested <u>in</u> something/ <u>in</u> doing something

wrong	She is very interested to find out more about plant genetics.
right	She is very interested in finding out more about plant genetics.

---

115. investigate something (<u>not</u> investigate about or into something)

Common Errors in English # 107.

wrong	The police are investigating into the murder in Brandon last week.
right	The police are investigating the murder in Brandon last week.

116. **join** someone (<u>not</u> join up with)

wrong	Conrad Black joined up with his brother Montagu in making the proposal to buy the company.
right	Conrad Black joined his brother Montagu in making the proposal to buy the company.

117. **jump** (<u>not</u> jump up)

wrong	Unemployment has jumped up to record levels recently.
right	Unemployment has jumped to record levels recently.

118. **lift** something (<u>not</u> lift up)

wrong	I twisted my back as I was lifting up the box.
right	I twisted my back as I was lifting the box.

119. **lower** something (<u>not</u> lower down something)

wrong	They lowered the coffin down into the grave.
right	They lowered the coffin into the grave.

120. **mercy**: have mercy <u>on</u> someone; show mercy to/towards someone

wrong	We should all have mercy for anyone who is suffering.
right	We should all have mercy on anyone who is suffering.

121. **meet / meet with**: *Meet with* in the sense of *attend a meeting with* is a recent addition to the language. If one is referring to a less formal or less prolonged encounter, however, there is no need for the preposition.

wrong	Stanley finally met with Livingstone near the shores of Lake Victoria.
	(The meaning here is "came face to face with for the first time.")
right	Stanley finally met Livingstone near the shores of Lake Victoria.

122. **near** something (<u>not</u> near to something)

wrong	The village of Battle is very near to the place where The Battle of Hastings was fought in 1066.
right	The village of Battle is very near the place where the Battle of Hastings was fought in 1066.

123. **object** <u>to</u> something.

wrong	Some people have objected against being required to wear a seat belt.
right	

Common Errors in English # 116.

Some people have objected to being required to wear a seat belt.

---

124. **off** something (<u>not</u> off of)

wrong   The man stepped off of the platform into the path of the moving train.

right   The man stepped off the platform into the path of the moving train.

---

125. **opposite:** When used as a noun, *opposite* is followed by *of*; when used as an adjective, it is followed by *to* or *from*, or by no preposition.

wrong   His conclusion was the opposite to mine.
             (Here, *opposite* is a noun.)

right   His conclusion was the opposite of mine.

---

126. **partake** of something/ **participate** in something

wrong   They have refused to partake in a new round of talks on the subject of free trade.

right   They have refused to participate in a new round of talks on the subject of free trade.

---

127. **prefer** one thing/person <u>to</u> another (<u>not</u> more than another)

wrong   They both prefer tennis more than squash.

right   They both prefer tennis to squash.

---

128. **protest** something (<u>not</u> protest against). *To protest* means to argue against; the preposition is redundant.

wrong   The demonstrators were protesting against the Government's decision to allow missile testing.

right   The demonstrators were protesting the Government's decision to allow missile testing.

---

129. **refer** <u>to</u> something (<u>not</u> refer back to something)

wrong   If you are confused, refer back to the diagram on page 24.

right   If you are confused, refer to the diagram on page 24.

---

130. **regard:** <u>With</u> regard <u>to</u> something/ <u>as</u> regard<u>s</u> something

wrong   I am writing in regards to the balance owing on your account.

Common Errors in English # 124.

| *fair* | I am writing with regard to the balance owing on your account. |
| *better* | I am writing about the balance owing on your account. |

---

131. **rejoice** <u>at</u> something (<u>not</u> for something)

| *wrong* | He rejoiced for his good fortune when he won the lottery. |
| *right* | He rejoiced at his good fortune when he won the lottery. |

---

132. **repeat** something (<u>not</u> repeat again)

| *wrong* | If you miss an answer you must repeat the whole exercise again. |
| *right* | If you miss an answer you must repeat the whole exercise. |

---

133. **request** something *or* request that something be done (but <u>not</u> request for something unless one is using the noun — <u>a</u> request <u>for</u> something)

wrong	He has requested for two more men to help him.
right	He has requested two more men to help him.
or	He has put in a request for two more men to help him.

---

134. **retroactive** <u>to</u> a date

| *wrong* | The tax changes are retroactive from July 1. |
| *right* | The tax changes are retroactive to July 1. |

---

135. **return** <u>to</u> a place (<u>not</u> return back)

| *wrong* | He wanted to return back to Edmonton as soon as possible. |
| *right* | He wanted to return to Edmonton as soon as possible. |

---

136. **seek** something/someone (<u>not</u> seek for something)

| *wrong* | She suggested that we seek for help from the police. |
| *right* | She suggested that we seek help from the police. |

---

137. **sight:** <u>in</u> sight (near enough to be seen); <u>out of</u> sight (too far away to be seen); <u>on</u> sight (immediately after being seen)

| *wrong* | The general ordered that deserters be shot in sight. |

Common Errors in English # 131.

right   The general ordered that deserters be shot on sight.

---

138. **speak** <u>to</u> someone (when one speaker is giving information to a listener); speak <u>with</u> someone (when the two are having a discussion)

wrong   She spoke harshly with the secretary about his spelling mistakes.

right   She spoke harshly to the secretary about his spelling mistakes.

---

139. suffer <u>from</u> something

wrong   He told me that he was suffering with the flu.

right   He told me that he was suffering from the flu.

---

140. **superior** <u>to</u> someone / something (<u>not</u> than someone / something)

wrong   The advertisements claim that this detergent is superior than the others.

right   The advertisements claim that this detergent is superior to the others.

---

141. **surprised** <u>at / by</u> something: *At* is used to suggest that the person is disappointed or scandalized; unless one wishes to suggest this, *by* is the appropriate preposition.

wrong   I was surprised at the unexpected arrival of my sister.

right   I was surprised by the unexpected arrival of my sister.

---

142. **type** <u>of</u> person/thing

wrong   This type carburetor is no longer produced.

right   This type of carburetor is no longer produced.

---

143. **underneath** something (<u>not</u> underneath of)

wrong   When we looked underneath of the table, we found what we had been looking for.

right   When we looked underneath the table, we found what we had been looking for.

---

144. **until** a time or an event (<u>not</u> up until)

wrong   Up until 1967 the National Hockey League was made up of only six teams.

Common Errors in English # 138.

| *right* | Until 1967 the National Hockey League was made up of only six teams. |

145. **warn** someone <u>of</u> a danger/<u>against</u> doing something/<u>not</u> to do something

| *wrong* | She warned me about the danger involved in the expedition. |
| *right* | She warned me of the danger involved in the expedition. |

146. **worry** <u>about</u> something (<u>not</u> at something / for something)

| *wrong* | He is always worried at what will happen if he loses his job. |
| *right* | He is always worried about what will happen if he loses his job. |

147. **Prepositions in pairs or lists:** If a sentence includes two or more nouns or verbs that take different prepositions, make sure to include <u>all</u> the necessary words.

| *wrong* | The fire was widely reported in the newspapers and television. |
| *right* | The fire was widely reported in the newspapers and on television. |

148. **Ending a sentence with a preposition:** Some authorities have argued that it is poor English to end a sentence with a preposition. The best answer to them is Winston Churchill's famous remark upon being accused of ending with a preposition: "This is the sort of pedantic nonsense up with which I will not put." Obviously such awkwardness as this can only be avoided by ending with a preposition. It is surely true that in many other cases ending sentences with prepositions is awkward. In practice, however, these are situations that we are already likely to avoid.

The following dialogue (a version of which was passed on to me by Prof. A. Levey of the University of Calgary) provides in dramatic form another demonstration of the absurdity of strictures against ending with prepositions.

"Where do you come from?"

"From a place where we don't end sentences with prepositions."

"Let me rephrase. Where do you come from, you stupid pedant?"

SINGULAR & PLURAL DIFFICULTIES

149. A number of nouns are unusual in the way that a **plural** is formed. Here is a list of some that frequently cause mistakes. The most troublesome — as well as a few pronouns that cause **similar** difficulties — are also given individual entries below:

appendix	appendices
attorney general	attorneys general
bacterium	bacteria
basis	bases
court martial	courts martial
crisis	crises
criterion	criteria
curriculum	curricula
datum	data
ellipsis	ellipses
emphasis	emphases
erratum	errata
father-in-law	fathers-in-law
focus	foci
governor general	governors general
index	indexes or indices
matrix	matrixes or matrices
medium	media
millennium	millennia
nucleus	nuclei
parenthesis	parentheses
referendum	referenda or referendums
runner-up	runners-up
stratum	strata
symposium	symposia
synthesis	syntheses
thesis	theses

150. accommodation: The plural form is not normally used.

wrong My family and my friend's family were both unable to

Common Errors in English # 149.

	find accommodations downtown.
right	My family and my friend's family were both unable to find accommodation downtown.

151. **anyone/anybody/no one/none/nobody:** All are singular. It is often necessary to spend a few moments puzzling over how to phrase one's ideas before one finds a way to get all the verbs and subjects to agree, and at the same time avoid awkwardness. Ironically, however, the 'correct' solution may in this case not be the best one. (See **Bias-free Language** , pp. 180-81.)

not in agreement	Anyone may visit when they like.
in agreement	Anyone may visit when he or she likes.
in agreement	Anyone may visit at any time.
not in agreement	No one likes to leave a place that they have grown fond of.
in agreement	No one likes to leave a place that he or she has grown fond of.
in agreement	No one likes to leave a place that has fond memories attached to it.

152. **bacteria:** A plural word; the singular is *bacterium.*

wrong	There were many bacterias in the mouldy bread.
right	There were a lot of bacteria in the mouldy bread.

153. **behavior:** Although social scientists speak of *a behavior* or of *behaviors* in technical writing, in other disciplines and in conversational English the word is uncountable (i.e. it cannot form a plural or be used with the indefinite article). Say *types of behavior,* not *behaviors.*

wrong	He has a good behavior.
right	His behavior is good.
or	He behaves well.

154. **between/among:** It is often supposed that *between* should always be used for two, *among* for more than two. As the *Oxford English Dictionary* points out, however, "in all senses *between* has been, from its earliest appearance, extended to more than two." Perhaps the most important difference is that *between* suggests a relationship of things or people to each other as individuals, whereas *among* suggests a relationship that is collective and vague. Thus we say "the ball fell among the hollyhocks" where we are expressing the relationship of the ball to many flowers collectively, and where the

precise location of the ball is unspecified. But we should <u>not</u> say, as we watch a baseball game, "the ball fell among the three fielders"; here we know the precise location of the ball and are expressing the relationship between it and the three individuals.

wrong	The ball fell among the three fielders.
right	The ball fell between the three fielders.

155. both/all: Use *both* to refer to two, and *all* to refer to more than two.

wrong	Harris and Waluchow were the chief speakers in the debate yesterday. They all spoke very well.
right	Harris and Waluchow were the chief speakers in the debate yesterday. They both spoke very well.

156. brain: One person can only have <u>one</u> *brain.* The use of the plural to refer to the *brain* of one person (e.g., "He blew his brains out") is slang, and should not be used in formal written work.

wrong	He used his brains to solve the problem.
right	He used his brain to solve the problem.

157. children: Be careful when forming the possessive; the apostrophe should come before the *s*.

wrong	All the childrens' toys had been put away.
right	All the children's toys had been put away.

158. confusion: Uncountable — we do not normally speak of *a confusion* or of *confusions*.

wrong	The misunderstanding about his time of arrival caused a confusion.
right	The misunderstanding about his time of arrival caused confusion.

159. criteria: Plural; the singular is *criterion*.

wrong	The chief criteria on which an essay should be judged is whether or not it communicates clearly.
right	The chief criterion on which an essay should be judged is whether or not it communicates clearly.

160. damage: In its usual meaning, this noun has no plural, since it is uncountable. We speak of *damage*, <u>not</u> *a damage*, and of *a lot of damage*, <u>not</u> *many damages*. The word *damages* means <u>money</u> paid to cover the cost of any damage one has caused.

wrong	The crash caused many damages to his car, but he was unhurt.
right	The crash caused a lot of damage to his car, but he was unhurt.

161. **data:** Like *bacteria, media,* and *phenomena,* the noun *data* is plural. The singular form, which is rarely used, is *datum.*

wrong	This data proves conclusively that the lake is badly polluted.
right	These data prove conclusively that the lake is badly polluted.

162. **each/every/none:** All three are singular. The same problems experienced with *anyone* and *no one* (see above) are common here as well. Even experienced writers often have difficulty phrasing sentences involving these words so as to have the parts agree. (Ironically, however, the 'correct' solution may in this case not always be the best one. See **Bias-Free Language,** pp. 180-81.)

not in agreement	Each person applying for the job must fill out this form before they will be granted an interview.
in agreement	Each person applying for the job must fill out this form before he or she will be granted an interview.
in agreement	Each person applying for the job must fill out this form before being granted an interview.

163. **each other/one another:** Use *each other* for two, *one another* for more than two.

wrong	The three brothers always tell stories to each other before going to sleep.
right	The three brothers always tell stories to one another before going to sleep.
wrong	The two men had long since begun to get on one another's nerves. (Alan Moorehead, *The White Nile*)
right	The two men had long since begun to get on each other's nerves.

164. **either/neither:** *Either* and *neither* are both singular. This can create considerable awkwardness in structuring sentences. (See also **Bias-Free Language,** pp. 180-81 on this point.)

wrong	Somehow, neither Sally nor Great Uncle Magnus were as tidy as they had been when they set out. (Margaret Mahy, *Ultra-Violet Catastrophe*)

Trying to correct the error here by simply changing *were* to *was,* creates a new problem with the *they* in the second half of the sentence; a further change is also necessary.

right	Somehow, neither Sally nor Great Uncle Magnus was as tidy as both had been when they set out.
wrong	So far neither the Liberal rank and file nor the electorate seem satisfied with Jean Chretien's performance.
	(*The Globe and Mail*, Sept. 20, 1990)
right	So far neither the Liberal rank and file nor the electorate seems satisfied with Jean Chretien's performance.

---

165. either/any; neither/none: Use *either* and *neither* for two, *any* and *none* for more than two.

wrong	Shirley has six sisters, but she hasn't seen either of them since Christmas.
right	Shirley has six sisters, but she hasn't seen any of them since Christmas.

---

166. government: A <u>singular</u> noun.

wrong	The government are intending to build a new terminal at this airport before 2006.
right	The government is intending to build a new terminal at this airport before 2006.

---

167. graffiti: A plural noun; the singular form is *graffito*.

wrong	Graffiti covers most of the subway cars in the city.
right	Graffiti cover most of the subway cars in the city.

---

168. media: Plural; the singular is *medium*.

wrong	The media usually assumes that the audience has a very short attention span.
right	The media usually assume that the audience has a very short attention span.

---

169. money: Some people seem to think that *monies* has a more official ring to it than *money* when they are talking of business affairs, but there is no sound reason for using this plural form in good English.

wrong	The Council has promised to provide some monies for this project.
right	The Council has promised to provide some money for this project.

---

170. news: Despite the *s*, this is a <u>singular</u> collective noun. Make sure to use a singular verb with it.

wrong	Today's news of troubles in the Middle East are very disturbing.

right	Today's news of troubles in the Middle East is very disturbing.

---

171. **phenomena:** Plural; the singular is phenomenon.

wrong	The great popularity of 'disco' music was a short-lived phenomena.
right	The great populaity of 'disco' music was a short-lived phenomenon.

---

172. **police:** a <u>plural</u> noun. Be sure to use a plural verb with it.

wrong	The police is investigating the case, and hope to make an arrest soon.
right	The police are investigating the case, and hope to make an arrest soon.

---

173. **someone/somebody:** Both are singular. Be careful with sentences involving one of these pronouns and the pronoun *they*; getting the phrasing right is not always easy.

wrong	Someone has forgotten to turn off the stove; they should be more careful.
fair	Someone has forgotten to turn off the stove; he or she should be more careful.
or	Some careless person has forgotten to turn off the stove.

PRONOUN PROBLEMS: WHO CARES ABOUT WHOM?

Those unfamiliar with the territory may also wish to refer to the section on pronouns in the **Reference Guide to Basic Grammar** at the back of the book. Readers may also wish to refer to the discussion of *y'all* and *youse* in the Preface.

---

174. **extra pronoun:** It is easy to add an extra pronoun, particularly if the subject of the sentence is separated from the verb by a long adjectival clause.

wrong	The countries which Hitler wanted to conquer in the late 1930s they were too weak to resist him.
right	The countries which Hitler wanted to conquer in the late 1930s were too weak to resist him.
wrong	The line that is longest in a triangle it is called the hypotenuse.
right	The line that is longest in a triangle is called the hypotenuse.

---

175. **first person:** In formal writing it is customary to use *I* and *me* infrequently or not at all. The object of a formal piece of writing is normally to present an argument, and writers realize that they can best argue their case by presenting evidence rather than by stating that such and such is what they think. Thus many teachers advise their students always to avoid using the first personal singular (*I* and *me*) in their writing.

This guideline should not be regarded as a firm and fast rule. George Orwell, often praised as this century's finest essayist, uses *I* and *me* frequently. As the following example illustrates, however, he employs the first person to guide the reader through his argument, not to make the points in the argument:

> If one gets rid of these habits one can think more clearly, and to think more clearly is a necessary first step towards political

Common Errors in English # 174.

regeneration: so that the fight against bad English is not frivolous and is not the exclusive concern of professional writers. I will come back to this presently, and I hope that by that time the meaning of what I have said will become clearer.

('Politics and the English Language')

Phrases such as *I think* and *I feel*, on the other hand, will not help you convince the reader of the strength of your main points.

wrong	Many authorities assume inflation to be a cause of high interest rates, but I think that high interest rates are a cause of inflation. This essay will prove my argument through numerous examples.
right	Many authorities assume inflation to be a cause of high interest rates; in fact, high interest rates are often a cause of inflation. Let us take the years 1978 to 1983 in the US as an example.

176.   **I** and **me:** Perhaps as a result of slang use of *me* as a subject pronoun ("Me and him got together for a few beer last night"), the impression seems to have lodged in many minds that the distinction between *I* and *me* is one of degree of politeness or formality rather than one of subject and object.

wrong	There is no disagreement between you and I.
right	There is no disagreement between you and me.

(Both *you* and *I* are here objects of a preposition — *between*. "Between you and I" is no more correct than is "I threw the ball at he.")

177. **than:** Does *than* take a subject or an object pronoun? Purists argue that we should say "She's brighter than *I* [am]", and "He's louder than she [is]" — that the verb is always understood in such sentences, even when we do not say it or write it, and that the unspoken verb requires a subject. It's hard to argue, however, that the increasingly widespread use of object pronouns after *than* is either ugly or confusing.

less formal	She always sleeps later than him.
more formal	She always sleeps later than he [does].

178. **unreferenced or wrongly referenced pronoun:** Normally a pronoun must refer to a noun in the previous sentence or clause. In the following sentence, for example, the pronoun *she* clearly refers to the noun *Charity*, which is the subject of the first clause in the sentence:

e.g.	Charity told Alfred that she would start work at nine.

Common Errors in English # 176.

Notice how confusing the sentence becomes, however, if there are two possible *shes* in the first part of the sentence:

e.g. Charity told Mavis that she would start work at nine.

Does this mean that Charity will start work at nine, or that Mavis will? From the sentence it is impossible to tell. In cases like this, where it is not absolutely clear who or what a pronoun refers to, use the noun again instead:

clear Charity told Mavis that she (Charity) would start work at nine.

In the following case the writer has gone astray by mentioning two things — one singular, one plural — and then matching only one of the two with a pronoun. In this instance the best remedy is to substitute a noun for the pronoun.

wrong Shields's characters are so exquisitely crafted and her plot so artfully conceived that it keeps the reader rivetted until the final page.
(*The Globe and Mail*)

right Shields's characters are so exquisitely crafted and her plot so artfully conceived that the book keeps the reader rivetted until the final page.

wrong My father and my brother visited me early this morning. He told me that something important had happened in Regina.

right My father and my brother visited me early this morning. Father told me that something important had happened in Regina.

Similar mistakes are often made in writing about a general class of people, such as police officers, or doctors, or football players. When writing in this way one can use either the third person singular (e.g. "A doctor helps patients. He...") or the third person plural ("Doctors help patients. They..."). Mixing the two in such situations often leads people to write unreferenced pronouns.

wrong A herbalist knows a lot about herbs and other plants. They can often cure you by giving you medicine.
(Here the pronoun *they* is presumably meant to refer to the plural noun, *herbalists*, but the writer has only referred to a herbalist.)

right A herbalist knows a lot about herbs and other plants. He can often cure you by giving you medicine.

or Herbalists know a lot about herbs and other plants.

Common Errors in English # 178.

They can often cure you by giving you medicine.

It may also not be clear what or who a pronoun refers to if it is placed too far away from the noun:

wrong	The Finance Minister increased corporation taxes by an average of 43 percent. Other measures in the budget included $100 million in student assistance and a 2 per cent increase in sales taxes. He also introduced a variety of measures to help small businesses.
right	The Finance Minister increased corporation taxes by an average of 43 percent. Other measures in the budget included $100 million in student assistance and a 2 per cent increase in sales taxes. The Minister also introduced a variety of measures to help small businesses.

Be particulrly careful when using *this* as a pronoun; if the preceding sentence is a long one, it may not be at all clear what *this* refers to:

wrong	The deficit was forecast to be $200 million, but turned out to be over $2 billion. This reflected the government's failure to predict the increase in interest rates and the onset of a recession. (This <u>what</u>?)
right	The deficit was forecast to be $200 million, but turned out to be over $2 billion. This vast discrepancy reflected the government's failure to predict the increase in interest rates and the onset of a recession.

Sometimes the meaning may be clear, but the omission of a pronoun may create unintended and humorous ambiguity:

wrong	She visited a doctor with a bad case of the flu. (Did the doctor have the flu?)
right	She visited a doctor when she had a bad case of the flu.

wrong	The Cougar was a sporty car aimed at the youthful-feeling who wanted luxury in their automobiles. Its buyers were similar to Mustangs, but more affluent.
right	The Cougar was a sporty car aimed at the youthful-feeling who wanted luxury in their automobiles. Its buyers were similar to those who bought Mustangs, but more affluent.

---

179. who, whom. The subject and the object pronoun, but of course it's not as simple as that. Nor is it — as those who don't feel it worth keeping *whom* around might have us believe — merely a matter of stuffiness or pedantry on the part of linguistic purists. Sound has a great deal to do with it. Even purists must sometimes find themselves saying, "I didn't know who I was talking to," even though the rules say it should be *whom* (subject — I; object — to whom). In similar fashion the enemies of *whom* must surely be tempted to sacrifice principle rather than attempt such an owlish mouthful as "To who was he talking?" They would do so not on the grammatical grounds of *whom*, the object pronoun, being correct since it is acting as the object of the preposition *to*, but on the grounds of *whom*, the word with an *m* on the end, being in that sentence a lot easier to say. In such circumstances it's hard to make a good case against allowing formality to accommodate itself occasionally to convenience of pronunciation.

less formal	Scott Fitzgerald never cared who he irritated.
more formal	Scott Fitzgerald never cared whom he irritated.

PART OF SPEECH CONVERSIONS: A QUESTION OF PRINCIPLE?

A 1994 Calvin and Hobbes cartoon strip nicely conveys the amusement that part of speech conversions may engender:

- I like to verb words.
- What?
- I take nouns and adjectives and use them as verbs. Remember when "access" was a thing? Now it's something you **do**. It got verbed. . . . Verbing weirds language.
- Maybe we can eventually make language a complete impediment to understanding.

In fact, however, there is no good reason why a word that has become established as one part of speech should not be used as another; the language has always been changing and growing in this way. As Tom Shippey asks:

> What can be the matter with using nouns as adjectives? Everyone does it; how about "stone wall"? It has been built into the language since before English settlers found Ireland, let alone America. . . . As for converting nouns to verbs, what about "water"? "Watering the horses" is recorded from before the Conquest. (*Times Literary Supplement*, October 19-25, 1990)

For that matter, what about *chair, table, paper, shelf, bottle, cup, knife, fork, eye, mouth, finger*? The list of nouns that have also become verbs is a very long one, and it includes many of the most basic nouns in the language. The point in being aware of the conversion of one part of speech to another, then, is not that the practice is always a bad one. Rather it is to keep oneself aware of whether or not one is saying something in the best possible way. If the new creation fills a need, saying something more clearly and concisely than it is possible to do otherwise, then it deserves to survive. But if it fulfils no useful purpose — if clearer and more concise ways of saying the same thing already exist — then it's better to avoid it.

Common Errors in English # 179.

---

180. **access:** Except in the vocabulary of computers, *access* is probably best kept as a noun, not a verb; alternatives such as *enter* and *reach* are usually more precise.

worth checking	The cafeteria may be accessed from either the warehouse or the accounts department.
better	The cafeteria may be reached through the warehouse or the accounts department.

---

181. **adjective for adverb:** If a word is modifying a verb, it should as a general rule be an adverb rather than an adjective. This is normally the case when the descriptive word comes directly after the verb. We say, "The boy laughed quietly," for example (rather than "The boy laughed quiet"), because the descriptive word *quietly* refers to the verb *laughed*, not the noun *boy*. Similarly, in the sentence "The quiet boy laughed" we use the adjective *quiet* to refer to the noun *boy*. The verb *to be*, however, which of course does not name an action in the way that other verbs do, is normally followed by adjectives rather than adverbs. (Verbs such as *taste, smell* and *feel* resemble *be* in this respect.) Thus we say "The boy is quiet," not "The boy is quietly;" we use the adjective rather than the adverb because we are again describing the boy, not the action of being. Very few would make the mistake of saying "He laughed quiet," but almost everyone occasionally chooses an adjective where the adverb should be used.

wrong	I did good on the test yesterday.
right	I did well on the test yesterday.
wrong	She asked us not to talk so loud.
right	She asked us not to talk so loudly.
wrong	The premiers thought it should be worded different.
right	The premiers thought it should be worded differently.
wrong	According to Mr Adams, "most books will go heavier into evolution, which is a good thing." (*The Washington Post*, June 1987)
right	According to Mr Adams, "most books will go more heavily into evolution, which is a good thing."
wrong	He performs bad whenever he is under pressure.
right	He performs badly whenever he is under pressure.

The pragmatists may have a point when it comes to the propriety of using comparative adjectives such as *easier* in place of more long winded adverbs such as *more easily*. Should the *Financial Post* editor have corrected the headline in the October 1987 issue that read "Northern Miners Breathe Easier"? Certainly it's easier to use the adjective here in place of the two-part adverb, *more easily*. Whether or not it's better is less clear; certainly many purists are not pleased by the practice.

less formal	The purpose of desktop publishing is to do the same old thing cheaper, easier, and quicker. (*The Globe and Mail*, July 1987)
more formal	The purpose of desktop publishing is to do the same old thing more cheaply, more easily, and more quickly.

182. advice/advise: *Advice* is the noun, *advise* is the verb.

wrong	They refused to take our advise.
right	They refused to take our advice.

183. affect/effect: *Effect* is normally used as a noun meaning *result*. (It can also be used as a verb meaning *put into effect*, as in "The changes were effected by the Committee.") *Affect* is a verb meaning *cause a result*.

wrong	When the acid is added to the solution, there is no visible affect.
right	When the acid is added to the solution, there is no visible effect.
wrong	"The issues that effect us here on the reserve are the same issues that effect the whole constituency," Mr. Littlechild said. (*The Globe and Mail*)
right	"The issues that affect us here on the reserve are the same issues that affect the whole constituency," Mr. Littlechild said.

184. author: A noun, not a verb; there is no need to find a substitute for *write*.

wrong	Smith is a member of the Appeals Court, and has authored two books on the judicial system.
right	Smith is a member of the Appeals Court, and has written two books on the judicial system.

185. breath/breathe: *Breath* is the noun, *breathe* the verb.

wrong	When you breath, your lungs take in oxygen.
right	When you breathe, your lungs take in oxygen.

186. dependent/dependant: *Dependent* is the adjective, *dependant* the noun. You are dependent on someone or something, and your young children are your dependants; they are dependent on you.

Common Errors in English # 182.

wrong	Emily is still dependant on her parents for financial support.
right	Emily is still dependent on her parents for financial support.

---

187. dialogue: As a verb, *talk* serves perfectly well, even after all these years.

awkward	The two department heads should dialogue with each other more frequently.
better	The two department heads should talk to each other more frequently.

---

188. enthuse/enthusiastic: *Enthuse* is the verb; *enthused* is its past participle. The adjective is *enthusiastic*.

wrong	In 1968 almost everyone was enthused about Pierre Trudeau.
right	In 1968 almost everyone was enthusiastic about Pierre Trudeau.
or	In 1968 almost everyone enthused over Pierre Trudeau.

---

189. first/firstly: *Firstly* is now generally thought of as archaic, though it is not incorrect. Be sure to be consistent, though, in the use of *first, second,* etc. in lists.

wrong	There were several reasons for France's reluctance to commit more resources to the New World. First, she was consumed with the battle for supremacy in Europe. Secondly, the returns on previous investments had been minimal.
right	There were several reasons for France's reluctance to commit more resources to the New World. First, she was consumed with the battle for supremacy in Europe. Second, the returns on previous investments had been minimal.

---

190. good/well: The most common of the adjective-for-adverb mistakes.

wrong	As the manager put it, "He pitched good, but not real good."
	(*The Toronto Star*, August 11, 1987)
fair	He pitched well, but not really well.
better	He did not pitch very well.

---

191. impact: The use of *impact* as a verb has become widespread even in formal English, but *affect* remains an attractive option.

awkward	The government's decision will impact upon wholesalers in all areas of the country.
better	The government's decision will affect wholesalers in all

areas of the country.

192. like/as: *Like* is a preposition, not a conjunction. If introducing a clause, use *as* in formal writing.

e.g.	He looks like his father.
	(*Like* introduces the noun *father*.)
	He looks as his father did at his age.
	(*As* introduces the clause *as his father did at his age.*)
	He is acting like a drunkard.
	(*Like* introduces the noun *drunkard*.)
	He is acting as if he were drunk.
	(*As* introduces the clause *as if he were drunk.*)

wrong	Like I said before, smoking is forbidden.
right	As I said before, smoking is forbidden.

wrong	He runs like I do — with short, choppy strides.
right	He runs as I do — with short, choppy strides.
or	He runs like me. We both take short, choppy strides.

wrong	Baby Doc ran Haiti like his father had done.
right	Baby Doc ran Haiti the way his father had.

The attempt is also sometimes made to use *like what* in place of *as.*

wrong	Bush wanted to appear tough, like what Reagan did when he ordered the invasion of Grenada.
right	Bush wanted to appear tough, as Reagan did when he ordered the invasion of Grenada.

193. its/it's: *Its* is an adjective meaning *belonging to it.* *It's* is a contraction of *it is* — a pronoun plus a verb. (Similarly, *whose* is an adjective meaning *belonging to whom*, whereas *who's* is a contraction of *who is.*)

wrong	Its important to remember that the population of North America in this period was less than 10 million.
right	It is important to remember that the population of North America in this period was less than 10 million.

wrong	A coniferous tree continually sheds it's leaves.
right	A coniferous tree continually sheds its leaves.

194. lend/loan: In formal English *loan* should be used only as a noun; *lend* is the verb.

wrong	He was unwilling to loan his sister any money.
right	He was unwilling to lend his sister any money.

195. loath/loathe: *Loath* is the adjective; *loathe* is the verb.

wrong	He told me he is beginning to loath his job.

Common Errors in English # 192.

right   He told me he is beginning to loathe his job.

---

196. loose/lose: *Loose* is normally used as an adjective meaning *not tight*; as a verb it means *to make loose* (e.g., "He loosed the reins"). *Lose* is of course always a verb.

wrong	As soon as it became dark she began to loose control of herself.
right	As soon as it became dark she began to lose control of herself.
wrong	If this movie doesn't bring the song back to the hit parade, then you know it's flopped — and that Spielberg is loosing his touch. (*The Toronto Star*)
right	If this movie doesn't bring the song back to the hit parade, then you know it's flopped — and that Spielberg is losing his touch.

---

197. maybe/may be: *Maybe* is an adverb that should be replaced by *perhaps* in formal writing. *May be* is a compound verb.

wrong	May be he will come, but I doubt it.
right	Maybe he will come, but I doubt it.
or	Perhaps he will come, but I doubt it.
wrong	The prototype maybe ready by 2005.
right	The prototype may be ready by 2005.

---

198. meantime/meanwhile: *Meantime* is a noun, used most frequently in the phrase *in the meantime*. *Meanwhile* is an adverb.

wrong	The Germans were preparing for an attack near Calais. Meantime, the Allies were readying themselves for the invasion of Normandy.
right	The Germans were preparing for an attack near Calais. Meanwhile, the Allies were readying themselves for the invasion of Normandy.

---

199. practice/practise: In Canada and Britain *practise* (verb) and *practice* (noun) should also be distinguished; in the U.S. *practice* serves as both noun and verb.

USA	The team's first practise will be held on Thursday.
UK / CDA	The team's first practice will be held on Thursday.

---

200. predominate/predominant: *Predominate* is the verb, *predominant* the adjective. (Either *predominately* or *predominantly* may be used as adverbs.)

wrong	The Social Credit movement was predominate only in

	Alberta and British Columbia.
right	The Social Credit movement was predominant only in Alberta and British Columbia.

201. principal/principle: *Principal* can be either a noun or an adjective. As a noun it means *the person in the highest position of authority in an organization* (e.g., a school *principal*) or *an amount of money*, as distinguished from the interest on it. As an adjective it means *first in rank or importance* ("The *principal* city of northern Nigeria is Kano"). *Principle* is always a noun, and is never used of a person; a *principle* is a *basic truth or doctrine*, a *code of conduct*, or a *law describing how something works*.

wrong	We feel this is a matter of principal.
right	We feel this is a matter of principle.

wrong	Up went the shares of the two principle players in our emerging mobile telephone field. *(Financial Post, June 12, 1989)*
right	Up went the shares of the two principal players in our emerging mobile telephone field.

202. prophecy/prophesy: *Prophecy* is the noun, *prophesy* the verb.

wrong	His comment should be regarded as a prediction, not a prophesy.
right	His comment should be regarded as a prediction, not a prophecy.

203. quality: Although in colloquial English *quality* is frequently used as a replacement for *good* or *worthwhile*, in formal writing it should be used as a noun, not an adjective. It should also be remembered that something may as easily be of poor quality as of good quality.

wrong	The salesman claims that this is a quality product.
right	The salesman claims that this is a product of high quality.

or	The salesman claims that this is a good product.
wrong	"It was Mother's Day. I was trying to spend some quality time with my wife."
	(An NHL vice-president explaining why he had not attended an important playoff game, as quoted in *The Toronto Star*)
right	"It was Mother's Day. I was trying to spend some time with my wife."

204. quote/quotation: In formal English *quote* is the verb, *quotation* the noun.

wrong	The following quote shows just how determined she is to change the Constitution.

right	The following quotation shows just how determined she is to change the Constitution.

---

205. **real/really:** One of the most commonly made adjective-for-adverb mistakes.

wrong	Some of the fish we caught were real big.
fair	Some of the fish we caught were really big.
better	Some of the fish we caught were very big.

---

206. **verb-noun confusion:** Where verbs and nouns have similar forms, be careful not to confuse them. Some of the most common examples are: *advice* (noun) and *advise* (verb); *extent* (noun) and *extend* (verb); *device* (noun) and *devise* (verb); *revenge* (noun) and *avenge* (verb); *loan* (noun) and *lend* (verb).

wrong	Jimmy Carter has now to a large extend been forgotten.
right	Jimmy Carter has now to a large extent been forgotten.

wrong	She wanted to revenge the harm he had caused her.
right	She wanted to avenge the harm he had caused her.

---

207. **whose/who's:** *Whose* means *belonging to whom*; *who's* is a contraction of *who is*.

wrong	Kennedy is not normally remembered as the President who's policies embroiled the US in the Vietnam conflict, but several scholars have suggested that he was as much responsible as was Johnson.
right	Kennedy is not normally remembered as the President whose policies embroiled the US in the Vietnam conflict, but several scholars have suggested that he was as much responsible as was Johnson.

WORD MEANINGS: ARE CARS EVER STATIONERY?

208. accept/except: These two words are often confused because of their similar sounds. *Accept* is a verb meaning *to receive something favourably (or at least without complaining)*. Examples:

We accepted the invitation to his party.

We will have to accept the decision of the judge.

Except, on the other hand, is a conjunction (or sometimes a preposition) which means *not including* or *but*.

wrong	All the permanent members of the Security Council accept China voted to authorize the use of force against Iraq.
right	All the permanent members of the Security Council except China voted to authorize the use of force against Iraq.

209. adapt/adopt/adept: To *adapt* something is to alter or modify it; to *adopt* something is to approve it or accept responsibility for it; *adept* is an adjective meaning *skilful*.

wrong	The Board adapted the resolution unanimously.
right	The Board adopted the resolution unanimously.

210. adverse/averse: *Adverse* means *unfavourable*; *averse* means *reluctant or unwilling*.

wrong	The plane was forced to land because of averse weather conditions.
right	The plane was forced to land because of adverse weather conditions.

211. affect/effect: *Effect* is normally used as a noun meaning *result*. (It can also be used as a verb meaning *put into effect*, as in "The changes were effected by the Committee.") *Affect* is a verb meaning *cause a*

Common Errors in English # 208.

result.

wrong	When the acid is added to the solution, there is no visible affect.
right	When the acid is added to the solution, there is no visible effect.
wrong	"The issues that effect us here on the reserve are the same issues that effect the whole riding," Mr. Littlechild said. (*The Globe and Mail*)
right	"The issues that affect us here on the reserve are the same issues that affect the whole riding," Mr. Littlechild said.

212. **aggravate/annoy/irritate:** *Aggravate* means *make worse.*

e.g.	The injury was aggravated by the bumpy ride in the ambulance.

In formal English *aggravate* should not be used to mean *annoy* or *irritate.*

wrong	She found his constant complaints very aggravating.
right	She found his constant complaints very irritating.

213. **alliterate/illiterate:** *Alliterate* is a verb meaning *to use consecutively two or more words that begin with the same sound.*

e.g.	The big, burly brute was frighteningly fat.

Illiterate is an adjective meaning either *unable to read* or *unable to read and write well.* Those who confuse the two are sometimes, if unfairly, accused of being illiterate.

wrong	Over forty percent of the population of Zambia is functionally alliterate.
right	Over forty percent of the population of Zambia is functionally illiterate.

214. **alternately/alternatively:** *Alternately* means *happening in turn, first one and then the other*; *alternatively* means *instead of.* Be careful as well with the adjectives *alternate* and *alternative.*

wrong	An alternate method of arriving at this theoretical value would be to divide the difference between the two prices by the number of warrants.
right	An alternative method of arriving at this theoretical value would be to divide the difference between the two prices by the number of warrants. (*or* "Another method of...")
wrong	Professor Beit-Hallahmi seems to have trouble alternatively in reading his own book accurately and in reading my review of it correctly. (Stanley Hoffman, *The New York Review of Books*)
right	Professor Beit-Hallahmi seems to have trouble alternately in reading his own book accurately and in reading my review of it correctly.

Common Errors In English # 212.

215. ambiguity: There are many types of ambiguity; for other references see the chapters on Pronoun Problems and Word Order, and the entries below for such words as *flammable*. But see the adjacent box too.

BRITISH LEFT WAFFLES ON FALKLAND ISLANDS

The following are all examples of ambiguity in newspaper headlines. In some cases it may take several moments to decipher the intended meaning.

- TWO PEDESTRIANS STRUCK BY BRIDGE
- MAN HELD OVER GIANT L.A. BRUSH FIRE
- ILLEGAL ALIENS CUT IN HALF BY NEW LAW
- PASSERBY INJURED BY POST OFFICE
- RED TAPE HOLDS UP NEW BRIDGE
- BRITISH LEFT WAFFLES ON FALKLAND ISLANDS
- VILLAGE WATER HOLDS UP WELL
- JERK INJURES NECK, WINS AWARD
- BISHOP THANKS GOD FOR CALLING

(The above examples come courtesy of columnist Bob Swift of Knight-Ridder Newspapers, and of Prof. A. Levey of the University of Calgary.)

And, from the Global News weather telecast, September 13, 1990, the following gem:

- "OUT WEST TOMORROW, THEY'RE GOING TO SEE THE SUN, AS WELL AS ATLANTIC CANADA."

---

216. amiable/amicable: *Amiable* is used to describe someone's personality; *amicable* describes the state of relations between people.

wrong   Michibata said that the split with his former tennis partner had been an amiable one. (Associated Press story, 1994)

right   Michibata said that the split with his former tennis partner had been an amicable one.

---

217. amoral/immoral: *Amoral* means *not based on moral standards*;

immoral means *wrong according to moral standards.*

wrong	The modern reader is unlikely to share Alexander Pope's views as to what constitutes amoral behavior.
right	The modern reader is unlikely to share Alexander Pope's views as to what constitutes immoral behavior.

---

218. anti/ante: If you remember that *anti* means *against* and *ante* means *before* you are less likely to misspell the many words that have one or the other as a prefix.

wrong	The UN had many anticedents — most notably the League of Nations formed after World War I.
right	The UN had many antecedents — most notably the League of Nations formed after World War I.

---

219. anxious/eager: The adjective *anxious* means *uneasy, nervous, worried*; it should not be used in formal writing to mean *eager.*

wrong	He was anxious to help in any way he could.
right	He was eager to help in any way he could.

---

220. appraise/apprise: To *appraise* something is to estimate its value; to *apprise* someone of something is to inform him or her of it.

wrong	The house has been apprised at $120,000.
right	The house has been appraised at $120,000.

---

221. assure/ensure/insure: To *assure* someone of something is to tell them with confidence or certainty; to *insure* (or *ensure*) that something will happen is to make sure that it does; to *insure* something is to purchase insurance on it so as to protect yourself in case of loss.

wrong	Our inventory is ensured for $1,000,000.
right	Our inventory is insured for $1,000,000.

---

222. attitude: In colloquial English in recent years *attitude* has undergone a considerable transformation, becoming first a synonym for *bad attitude* and then a word more broadly denoting strength of character. In conversational English "She's got attitude" is more likely to be intended as a compliment than a criticism. But in formal written English such colloquial usages should be used sparingly, if at all.

---

223. be/become: The difference between the two is that *to be* simply indicates existence, while *to become* indicates a process of change. Whenever you are talking about a <u>change</u>, use *become* instead of *be.*

wrong	I had been quite contented, but as time went by I was

	unhappy.
right	I had been quite contented, but as time went by I became unhappy.
wrong	After years of struggle, Zimbabwe finally was independent in 1980.
right	After years of struggle, Zimbabwe finally became independent in 1980.

---

224. beg the question: The original meaning of *beg the question* is *take for granted the very thing to be argued about* — **not** *invite the question.* In the words of Thomas Hurka, the former *Globe and Mail* 'Principles' columnist, "'begging the question' is *not* what Alex Trebek does on *Jeopardy.*" The extension of the phrase to mean *invite the question* has become so widespread in recent years that it may be vain to think of the tide being reversed, but the original concept of question begging is a useful one, and we should be reluctant to allow it to disappear.

wrong:	This sort of sexual abuse case begs the question as to how such behavior could be hidden for so many years.
	(The Calgary Herald, January 4, 1997)
right:	This sort of sexual abuse case makes us wonder how such behavior could be hidden for so many years.

---

225. bored, boring: *Bored* is the opposite of *interested* and *boring* is the opposite of *interesting.* In other words, one is quite likely to be bored when someone reads out what one has already read in the newspaper, or when one is watching a football game when the score is 38-0, or when one is doing an uninteresting job. To be bored, however, is <u>not</u> the same as being sad, or depressed, or irritated, or angry.

wrong	She was so bored with her husband that she tried to kill him.
right	She was so angry with her husband that she tried to kill him.

---

226 breach / breech: To *breach* a wall or a contract is to break or break through it, and the breach is the breaking. *Breech* refers to a part of a cannon or rifle — or to the buttocks (hence a "breech birth" in which the buttocks or feet emerge before the head.

wrong	The lawyers claimed that her actions constituted a breech of contract.

right   The lawyers claimed that her actions constituted a
                 breach of contract.

227. **brusque / brisk:** To be *brusque* is to be abrupt or slightly rude in
speech or manner; *brisk* means quick or lively.

wrong   He didn't say anything rude to me, but his manner was
                 rather brisk.
right   He didn't say anything rude to me, but his manner was
                 rather brusque.

228. **can/may:** In formal writing *can* should be used to refer to ability,
may to refer to permission.

wrong   He asked if he could leave the room.
                 (This only makes literal sense if you are talking about an injured person
                                conversing with his doctor.)
right   He asked if he might leave the room.

229. **capital/capitol:** As a noun, *capital* can refer to wealth, to the city
from which the government operates, to an upper case letter, or to
the top of a pillar. It can also be used as an adjective to mean *most
important* or *principal*. *Capitol* is much more restricted in its
meaning — a specific American legislative building or Roman temple.

wrong   The prosecution alleged that he had committed a
                 capitol offence.
right   The prosecution alleged that he had committed a
                 capital offence.

230. **career/careen:** As a verb, *career* means to swerve wildly. *Careen*
originally meant to tilt or lean, but now in North America especially
is often treated as a synonym for *career*. Since *careen* has other
specifically nautical meanings some authorities resist the conflation
of the two verbs.

231. **careless/uncaring:** *Careless* means *negligent* or *thoughtless*; you
can be careless about your work, for example, or careless about your
appearance. Do not use *careless*, however, when you want to talk
about not caring enough about other people.

wrong   He acted in a very careless way towards his mother
                 when she was sick.
right   He acted in a heartless way towards his mother when
                 she was sick.

232. censor/censure: To *censor* something is to prevent it, or those parts of it that are considered objectionable, from being available to the public. To *censure* someone is to express strong criticism or condemnation.

wrong	The Senate censored the Attorney General for his part in the scandal.
right	The Senate censured the Attorney General for his part in the scandal.

233. classic/classical: As an adjective *classic* means of such a high quality that it has lasted or is likely to last for a very long time. *Classical* is used to refer to ancient Greece and Rome, or, particularly when speaking of music, to refer to a traditional style.

wrong	Sophocles was one of the greatest classic authors; his plays are classical.
right	Sophocles was one of the greatest classical authors; his plays are acknowledged classics.

234. childish/childlike: The first is a term of abuse, the second a term of praise.

wrong	Her writing expresses an attractive childish innocence.
right	Her writing expresses an attractive childlike innocence.

235. climatic/climactic: Weather is not the most exciting part.

wrong	Difficulties in predicting long-term trends are inherent in any climactic projections.
right	Difficulties in predicting long-term trends are inherent in any climatic projections.

236. collaborate/corroborate: To *collaborate* is to work together, whereas to *corroborate* is to give supporting evidence.

wrong	He collaborated her claim that the Americans had corroborated with the Nazi colonel Klaus Barbie.
right	He corroborated her claim that the Americans had collaborated with the Nazi colonel Klaus Barbie.

237. compliment/complement: To *compliment* someone is to praise him, and a *compliment* is the praise; to *complement* something is to add to it to make it better or complete, and a *complement* is the number or amount needed to make it complete.

Common Errors in English # 232.

wrong	None of the divisions had its full compliment of troops.
right	None of the divisions had its full complement of troops.
wrong	Gretzky's mission in New York will be to compliment Mark Messier, the team's captain and franchise player. (Associated Press story, Oct. 1, 1996)
right	Gretzky's mission in New York will be to complement Mark Messier, the team's captain and franchise player.

---

238. **comprise/compose:** The whole *comprises* or includes the various parts; the parts *compose* the whole.

wrong	The British government is comprised of far fewer ministries than is the Canadian government.
right	The British government comprises far fewer ministries than does the Canadian government.
or	The British government is composed of far fewer ministries than is the Canadian government.

---

239. **conscience/conscious/consciousness:** To be *conscious* is to be awake and aware of what is happening, whereas *conscience* is the part of our mind that tells us it is right to do some things and wrong to do other things (such as steal or murder). *Conscience* and *consciousness* are both nouns; the adjectives are *conscientious* (aware of what is right and wrong) and *conscious* (aware).

wrong	She was tempted to steal the chocolate bar, but her conscious told her not to.
right	She was tempted to steal the chocolate bar, but her conscience told her not to.

---

240. **contemptuous/contemptible:** We are *contemptuous* of anyone or anything we find *contemptible*.

wrong	The judge called the delinquent's behavior utterly contemptuous.
right	The judge called the delinquent's behavior utterly contemptible.

---

241. **continual/continuous:** If something is *continuous* it never stops; something *continual* is frequently repeated but not unceasing. The same distinction holds for the adverbs *continually* and *continuously*.

wrong	He has been phoning me continuously for the past two weeks. (Surely he stopped for a bite to eat or a short nap.)

| *right* | He has been phoning me continually for the past two weeks. |

242. **copyright:** *Copyright* is the right to make copies of something. The fact that these are often of written material has encouraged a confusion of spelling.

| *wrong* | The software company plans to copywrite some of the advances it will introduce this year.
(*The Financial Post*, March, 1989) |
| *right* | The software company plans to copyright some of the advances it will introduce this year. |

243. **council/counsel; councillor/counsellor:** A *council* is an assembled group of officials, and a *councillor* is a member of that group. *Counsel* is advice, or in the special case of a lawyer, the person offering advice. In other situations the person offering *counsel* is a *counsellor*.

wrong	The city counsel met to discuss the proposed bylaw.
right	The city council met to discuss the proposed bylaw.
wrong	The lawyer offered sound council as to the advisability of launching a suit.
right	The lawyer offered sound counsel as to the advisability of launching a suit.
wrong	Overall, she enjoyed summer camp, but she did not like her councillor.
right	Overall, she enjoyed summer camp, but she did not like her councsellor.

244. **credible/credulous:** Someone *credulous* (believing) is likely to believe anything, even if it is not *credible* (believable).

| *wrong* | "Maybe I'm too credible," she said. "I believe everything my husband tells me." |
| *right* | "Maybe I'm too credulous," she said. "I believe everything my husband tells me." |

245. **decimate:** Most etymologists agree that originally this word meant *kill one of every ten*. It has come to be used more loosely to mean *destroy a considerable number of*, and sometimes *kill nine of every ten*, but it is best not to use it in a way that some authorities feel, as H.W. Fowler puts it, "expressly contradicts the proper sense."

wrong	The regiment was decimated; less than 40 per cent survived.
right	The regiment suffered extreme losses; less than 40 per cent survived.

---

246. **deduce/deduct:** *Deduction* is the noun stemming from both these verbs, which is perhaps why they are sometimes confused. To *deduce* is to draw a conclusion, whereas to *deduct* is to subtract.

wrong	Sherlock Holmes deducted that Moriarty had committed the crime.
right	Sherlock Holmes deduced that Moriarty had committed the crime.

---

247. **definite/definitive:** If something is *definite* then there is no uncertainty about it; a *definitive* version of something fixes it in its final or permanent form — just as a dictionary definition attempts to fix the meaning of a word. Often a sentence is better with neither of these words.

wrong	Glenn Gould's recording of Bach's *Brandenburg Concertos* is often thought of as the definite modern version.
right	Glenn Gould's recording of Bach's *Brandenburg Concertos* is often thought of as the definitive modern version.

wrong	Once we have completed our caucus discussion I will be making a very definitive statement.
right	Once we have completed our caucus discussion I will be making a statement.
or	Once we have completed our caucus discussion I will have something definite to say.

---

248. **degradation/decline:** *Degradation* carries the connotation of shame and disgrace; certain military spokespeople have been making every attempt to corrupt it. To *degrade* something is not to reduce it, or downgrade it, or destroy it.

wrong	Among those units in which women played a combat role there was no degradation in operational effectiveness.
right	Among those units in which women played a combat role there was no decline in operational effectiveness.
or	...there was no reduction in operational effectiveness.
wrong	According to US authorities, the Iraqi threat has now been significantly degraded.

(Global news, January 24, 1991)
right   According to US authorities, the Iraqi threat has now
                        been significantly reduced.

---

249. **deny/refute:** To *deny* something is to assert that it is not true; to
refute it is to prove conclusively that it is not true.

wrong   During yesterday's press conference the President
                        angrily refuted the allegations: "There has been no
                        improper relationship," he said. (Associated Press,
                        January 20, 1998)

right   During yesterday's press conference, the President
                        angrily denied the allegations: "There has been no
                        improper relationship," he said.

---

250. **deprecate/depreciate:** To *deprecate* something is to suggest that it
is not valuable or worthy of praise; something that *depreciates* loses
its value.

wrong   Robert Stanfield is a very self-depreciating man.
right   Robert Stanfield is a very self-deprecating man.

---

251. **discrete/discreet:** *Discrete* means *separate* or *distinct*, whereas
discreet means *prudent and tactful; unwilling to give away secrets.*

wrong   David Letterman is not renowned for being discrete.
right   David Letterman is not renowned for being discreet.

---

252. **disinterested/uninterested:** A *disinterested* person is unbiased;
uninfluenced by self-interest, especially of a monetary sort. It is thus
quite possible for a person who is entirely *disinterested* in a particular
matter to be completely fascinated by it. If one is *uninterested* in
something, on the other hand, one is bored by it.

wrong   He was so disinterested in the game that he left after
                        the fifth inning with the score at 2-2.
right   He was so uninterested in the game that he left after
                        the fifth inning with the score at 2-2.

wrong   It was vintage Ronald Reagan: stumbling over his text,
                        unsure of his facts, disinterested in the topic at hand.
                        (*The Toronto Star*, Nov. 15, 1987)
right   It was vintage Ronald Reagan: stumbling over his text,
                        unsure of his facts, uninterested in the topic at hand.

---

253. **disorient/disorientate:** Both are considered correct by many
authorities, but the extra syllable of the second grates on the ear.

Poor   I was entirely disorientated in the darkness.
Better   I was entirely disoriented in the darkness.

Common Errors in English # 249.

---

254. **dissemble/disassemble:** To *dissemble* is to disguise your feelings — a mild form of lying. To *disassemble* is to take apart.

wrong   For the test we are required to first assemble and then dissemble a V-8 engine.

right   For the test we are required to first assemble and then disassemble a V-8 engine.

---

255. **dissociate/disassociate:** There is no need for the extra syllable.

poor   T.S. Eliot speaks of the disassociation of sensibility that began in the seventeenth century.

better   T.S. Eliot speaks of the dissociation of sensibility that began in the seventeenth century.

---

256. **distinct/distinctive:** *Distinct* means *able to be seen or perceived clearly; easily distinguishable from those around it.* *Distinctive* means *unusual; not commonly found.* There is a similar contrast between the adverbs *distinctly* and *distinctively,* and the nouns *distinction* and *distinctiveness.*

wrong   I distinctively heard the sound of a car engine.

right   I distinctly heard the sound of a car engine.

---

257. **economic/economical:** *Economic* means pertaining to economics, or sufficient to allow a reasonable return for the amount of money or effort put in. *Economical* is a word applied to people, which means thrifty. The difference applies as well to *uneconomic* and *uneconomical.*

wrong   Controversy over whether it would be economical to develop the vast Hibernia oilfield continued through to 1997.

right   Controversy over whether it would be economic to develop the vast Hibernia oilfield continued through to 1997.

---

258. **effective/efficacious/effectual/efficient:** *Effective, efficacious* and *effectual* all mean sufficient to produce the desired effect. *Efficacious,* however, applies only to things: a person cannot be efficacious. *Effectual* was once applied only to actions, but is now sometimes applied to people as well. *Effective* can apply to actions or people. *Efficient* has an added connotation: producing results with

Common Errors In English # 254.

little waste of money or effort. Thus a promotional campaign to persuade people to buy a product by giving away free samples to every man, woman, and child in the country might be *effective*, but it would certainly not be *efficient*; a good deal of waste would be involved. The same difference applies to the nouns *effectiveness* and *efficiency*. (*Efficacy* is a rather pretentious noun that is usually best avoided.)

wrong	The Board wants to increase the efficacy of the machinery we use.
right	The Board wants to increase the efficiency of the machinery we use.
poor	It would not be efficacious to launch a direct mail campaign with a product of this sort.
better	It would not be effective to launch a direct mail campaign with a product of this sort.

259. **e.g./i.e.:** The abbreviation *e.g.* is short for *exempli gratia* ('examples given'). It is sometimes confused with the abbreviation *i.e.*, which is short for *id est* ('that is to say').

wrong	Those citizens of India who speak Hindi (e.g. the vast majority of the population) are being encouraged by the government to learn a second language.
right	Those citizens of India who speak Hindi (i.e. the vast majority of the population) are being encouraged by the government to learn a second language.

260. **elemental/elementary:** A thing is *elemental* if it forms an important or essential element of the whole; it is *elementary* if it is easy to understand, or at a relatively simple level.

wrong	He lacked even the most elemental understanding of the problem.
right	He lacked even the most elementary understanding of the problem.

261. **elicit/illicit:** *Elicit* is a verb; one *elicits* information about something. *Illicit* is an adjective meaning *illegal* or *not approved*.

wrong	She has been dealing in elicit drugs for some time.
right	She has been dealing in illicit drugs for some time.

262. **eligible/illegible:** One is *eligible* for a job or for membership in an

organization if one meets the standard set for applicants. One of the requirements might be that one's handwriting not be *illegible*.

wrong	He regretted that I was not illegible to join his club.
right	He regretted that I was not eligible to join his club.

263. **emigrant/immigrant:** To *migrate* is to move from one place to another. The prefix *ex*, shortened to *e*, means *out of*, so an *emigrant* from a country is someone who is moving out of it. The prefix *in* or *im* means *in* or *into*, so an *immigrant* to a country is someone moving into it. Similarly, *emigration* is the movement of people out of a country, while *immigration* is the movement of people into a country. Notice the spelling in both cases; e-migrant (one *m*), im-migrant (two *m*s)

wrong	More than 100,000 emigrants entered America last year.
right	More than 100,000 immigrants entered America last year.

264. **eminent/imminent/immanent:** A person is *eminent* if she is well-known and well-respected; an event is *imminent* if it is about to happen; a quality (or a god) is *immanent* if it pervades everything.

wrong	Even those working for the party in the 1999 campaign did not believe that a majority victory was immanent.
right	Even those working for the party in the 1999 campaign did not believe that a majority victory was imminent.

265. **enervate/invigorate:** Because of the similarity in sound between *enervate* and *energy*, it is often thought to mean *make more energetic*. In fact it means just the opposite — *to lessen the strength of*. If something makes you more energetic it *invigorates* you.

wrong	She found the fresh air quite enervating; I haven't seen her so lively in months.
right	She found the fresh air quite invigorating; I haven't seen her so lively in months.

266. **enormity/enormousness:** Originally the adjective *enormous* simply meant *deviating from the norm*, but by the early nineteenth century it had also come to mean *abnormal, monstrous*, or *extraordinarily wicked*. Today the only meaning is of course *vast* in size or quantity, but the connotation of wickedness is preserved in

the noun *enormity*. We may speak of the *enormity* of a person's crime, but if we want a noun to express vast size we should use *enormousness* or *vastness*.

wrong	What most impresses visitors to the Grand Canyon is usually its sheer enormity.
right	What most impresses visitors to the Grand Canyon is its sheer enormousness.
better	What most impresses visitors to the Grand Canyon is its vastness.

---

267. **epithet/epigraph/epitaph/epigram:** four words often confused. Here are their meanings:

Epithet	an adjective or short phrase describing someone (*"The Golden Brett*, the epithet often used to describe Brett Hull, involves an allusion to the nickname of his famous father.")
Epigraph	an inscription, especially one placed upon a building, tomb, or statue to indicate its name or purpose
Epitaph	words describing a dead person, often the words inscribed on the tomb
Epigram	a short, witty or pointed saying
wrong	His epigram will read, "A good man lies here."
right	His epitaph will read, "A good man lies here."

---

268. **equal/equitable/equable:** Things that are *equal* have the same value. Arrangements that are *equitable* are fair and just. An *equable* person is one who is moderate and even-tempered.

wrong	The distribution of Commons and Senate seats is an equable one; in almost every case the percentage of combined seats allocated to a province closely approximates the percentage of the Canadian population made up by its inhabitants.
right	The distribution of Commons and Senate seats is an equitable one; in almost every case the percentage of combined seats allocated to a province closely approximates the percentage of the Canadian population made up by its inhabitants.

---

269. **explicit/implicit:** If something is *explicit* it is *unfolded* — stated in precise terms, not merely suggested or implied. Something that is *implicit* is *folded in* — not stated overtly. By extension *implicit* has also

come to mean *complete* or *absolute* in expressions such as *implicit trust* (i.e., trust so complete that it does not have to be put into words).

wrong	I told you implicitly to have the report on my desk first thing this morning.
right	I told you explicitly to have the report on my desk first thing in the morning.

---

270. financial/fiscal/monetary/economic: The terms used in personal, business, and government finance are not always the same. Here are four that are often not clearly understood:

Financial	having to do with finance or the handling of money.
Fiscal	having to do with public revenue.
Monetary	having to do with the currency of a country. (Only in very limited circumstances, such as the expression *monetary value*, can monetary have the more general meaning of *having to do with money*.)
Economic	having to do with the economy. Thus a government's *economic* program embraces both *fiscal* and *monetary* policies.
wrong	My brother is a nice person, but he has no monetary ability.
right	My brother is a nice person, but he has no financial ability.

---

271. finish/be finished/have finished: In slang usage to *be finished* means *to be at the end of one's life or career* ("If that player's knee is seriously injured again, he is finished"). This special use should not be extended to the verb *finish* in its normal meaning.

wrong	Are you finished your work?
right	Have you finished your work?

---

272. flammable/inflammable: The two words share the same meaning; *flammable* may have originated because of the possibility for confusion over the word *inflammable*, which looks like a negative but isn't. *Non-flammable* should be used to mean *difficult or impossible to burn*.

wrong	Asbestos is an inflammable material.
right	Asbestos is a non-flammable material.

---

273. flout/flaunt: To *flout* is to disobey or show disrespect for; to *flaunt* is to display very openly.

wrong	Aggressive policing seems to have increased the number of people flaunting the law.
right	Aggressive policing seems to have increased the number of people flouting the law.

274. **formerly/formally:** The similarity of sound often leads to confusion.

wrong	In August Mr. Laurel formerly broke with Mrs. Aquino. *(The Globe and Mail*, Feb. 9, 1989)
right	In August Mr. Laurel formally broke with Mrs. Aquino.

275. **fortunate/fortuitous:** *Fortunate* means lucky; *fortuitous* means happening by chance.

wrong	This combination of circumstances is not a fortuitous one for our company; we shall have to expect reduced sales in the coming year.
right	This combination of circumstances is not a fortunate one for our company; we shall have to expect reduced sales in the coming year.

276. **forward/foreword:** You find a *foreword* before the other words in a book.

wrong	The author admits in the forward to her book that the research was not comprehensive.
right	The author admits in the foreword to her book that the research was not comprehensive.

277. **founder/flounder:** As a verb, *founder* means *to get into difficulty; to stumble or fall, to sink* (when speaking of a ship), or *to fail* (when speaking of a plan). To *flounder* is *to move clumsily or with difficulty,* or *to become confused* in an effort to do something.

wrong	He foundered about in a hopeless attempt to solve the problem.
right	He floundered about in a hopeless attempt to solve the problem.

278. **further/farther:** *Farther* refers only to physical distance.

wrong	Eisenhower argued that the plan should receive farther study.
right	Eisenhower argued that the plan should receive further study.

279. **historic/historical:** *Historic* means *of sufficient importance that it is likely to become famous in history; historical* means *having to do*

with history (historical research, historical scholarship, etc.).

wrong	We are gathered here for a historical occasion – the opening of the city's first sewage treatment plant.
right	We are gathered here for a historic occasion – the opening of the city's first sewage treatment plant.

280. **hopefully:** one of the greatest causes of disagreement among grammarians. Traditionalists argue that the correct meaning of the adverb *hopefully* is *filled with hope,* and that the use of the word to mean *it is to be hoped that* is therefore incorrect. On the other side it is plausibly argued that many adverbs can function as independent comments at the beginning of a sentence. ("Finally, let me point out that..."; "Clearly, we have much to do if we are to..."; "Obviously, it will not be possible to..."). Why should *hopefully* be treated differently? Why indeed? Using *hopefully* for this purpose may not make for beautiful English, but it should not be regarded as a grievous error.

poor	Hopefully, it will be possible to finish before tomorrow.
	(As usually happens, "hopefully" is here used with the passive, making for a wordy sentence.)
better	We hope we can finish before tomorrow.

poor	Hopefully, we will arrive before dusk.
	(This sentence should be rewritten in order to ensure that the sentence does not suggest the meaning, "we will arrive filled with hope before dusk.")
better	I hope we will arrive before dusk.

281. **human/humane:** Until the eighteenth century there was no distinction made between the two in either meaning or pronunciation; they were simply alternative ways of spelling the same word. In recent centuries *humane* has come to be used to refer exclusively to the more attractive human qualities – kindness, compassion and so forth.

wrong	Their group is campaigning for the human treatment of animals.
right	Their group is campaigning for the humane treatment of animals.

282. **idioms:** Similarity in sound and meaning between words often leads to the mixing-up of idioms.

wrong	He acts as if he were to the manner born.
right	He acts as if he were to the manor born.

wrong	Authorities termed it a democratic transition, but for all intensive purposes it was a coup d'etat.
right	Authorities termed it a democratic transition, but for all intents and purposes it was a coup d'etat.

wrong	The new recruits were reminded that they would have to tow the line.
right	The new recruits were reminded that they would have to toe the line.

---

283. **illusion/allusion:** An *allusion* is an indirect reference to something; an *illusion* is something falsely supposed to exist.

wrong	Joyce is making an illusion in this passage to a Shakespearean sonnet.
right	Joyce is making an allusion in this passage to a Shakespearean sonnet.

---

284. **imply/infer:** To *imply* something is to suggest it without stating it directly; the other person will have to *infer* your meaning. It may be a comfort to the many who have confused the two to know that the mistake goes back at least as far as Milton:

wrong	Great or Bright infers not Excellence.
	(*Paradise Lost* viii, 91)
right	Great or Bright implies not Excellence.
	(The fact that a thing is great or bright does not imply that it is also excellent.)

wrong	I implied from his tone that he disliked our plan.
right	I inferred from his tone that he disliked our plan.

---

285. **in/into:** The difference is that *into* is used to indicate movement from outside to inside.

wrong	Writers in Britain generally expressed sympathy for Rushdie's decision, although some said he was caving into pressure.
right	Writers in Britain generally expressed sympathy for Rushdie's decision, although some said he was caving in to pressure.

Common Errors in English # 283.

---

286. **incidents/incidence:** *Incidents* is the plural of *incident* (happening), whereas *incidence* is a singular noun meaning the rate at which something occurs.

wrong	The incidents of lung cancer is much lower in Zambia than it is in North America.
right	The incidence of lung cancer is much lower in Zambia than it is in North America.

---

287. **ingenious/ingenuous:** *Ingenious* means *clever*; *ingenuous* means *pleasantly open and unsophisticated.*

wrong	Her manner was completely ingenious; I cannot imagine she was trying to deceive us.
right	Her manner was completely ingenuous; I cannot imagine she was trying to deceive us.

---

288. **innumerable:** so numerous that it is impossible to count; do not use as synonym for *many*.

wrong	Scholars have advanced innumerable explanations for the dinosaurs' disappearance.
right	Scholars have advanced many explanations for the dinosaurs' disappearance.

---

289. **insist/persist:** To *insist* (that something be done, *or* on doing something) is to express yourself very forcefully. To *persist* in doing something is to keep on doing it, usually despite some difficulty or opposition.

wrong	Even after he had been convicted of the crime, he persisted that he was innocent.
right	Even after he had been convicted of the crime, he insisted that he was innocent.

---

290. **instinctive/instinctual:** There is no difference in meaning; it is thus better to stay with the older (and more pleasant sounding) *instinctive*.

poor	Biologists disagree as to what constitutes instinctual behavior.
better	Biologists disagree as to what constitutes instinctive behavior

---

291. **judicial/judicious:** *Judicial* means *having to do with law courts and the administration of justice. Judicious* means *having good*

judgment.

wrong	He made one or two judicial comments about the quality of the production.
right	He made one or two judicious comments about the quality of the production.

---

292. **know:** When one *knows* something, that piece of knowledge has been in one's mind for some time. The process of gathering or acquiring knowledge is called *discovering.*

wrong	Although I noticed the new employee on Monday, I did not know her name until today.
right	Although I noticed the new employee on Monday, I did not discover her name until today.

---

293. **later/latter:** *Later* means *afterwards in time*, whereas the *latter* is the last mentioned (of two things).

wrong	I looked up the battle of Stalingrad in both the *World Book* and the *Encyclopaedia Britannica*. The later provided much more information.
right	I looked up the battle of Stalingrad in both the *World Book* and the *Encyclopaedia Britannica*. The latter provided much more information.

---

294. **laudable/laudatory:** *Laudable* means worthy of praise; *laudatory* means *expressing praise.*

wrong	His efforts to combat poverty are very laudatory.
right	His efforts to combat poverty are very laudable.

---

295. **liable/likely:** *Liable* means obliged by law ("You will be *liable* for any damage caused when you are driving the vehicle"), or in danger of doing or suffering from something undesirable ("That chimney is *liable* to fall"). Since in the latter meaning *likely* can often be used in place of *liable,* it is often assumed that there is really no distinction between the two. Careful writers, however, do not use *liable* unless they are referring to possible consequences of an <u>undesirable</u> nature.

poor	Last Sunday Woods won the Colonial Open. He's liable to win again before the Canadian Open.
better	Last Sunday Woods won the Colonial Open. He's likely to win again before the Canadian Open.

Common Errors in English # 292.

---

296. libel/slander: *Libel* is written (and published); *slander* is oral.

wrong	He was careful in his speech to avoid making any libellous remarks.
right	He was careful in his speech to avoid making any slanderous remarks.

---

297. lightning/lightening: One is not likely to see the sky *lightening* until after the thunder and *lightning* are over.

wrong	Three of the men were severely injured by the lightening.
right	Three of the men were severely injured by the lightning.

---

298. literally: *Literal* means *by the letter* — in exact agreement with what is said or written. A literal meaning is thus the opposite of a figurative or metaphorical meaning. Do not use the adverb *literally* simply to emphasize something.

wrong	As silviculturalists we are — literally — babes in the woods.

(Ken Drushka, *Stumped: The Forest Industry in Transition*)
[Silviculturalists may be literally in the woods, but they are not literally babes.)

right	As silviculturalists we are babes in the woods.

---

299. make/allow/make possible: To *make* someone do something is to force them to do it (often against their wishes); to *allow* someone to do something is to permit them or *make it possible* for them to do something that they want to do.

wrong	A new hospital wing is being built; this will make many more people come for treatment.
right	A new hospital wing is being built; this will allow many more people to come for treatment.
or	A new hospital wing is being built; this will make it possible for many more people to come for treatment.

---

300. masterful/masterly: *Masterful* means *domineering*; *masterly* means *exhibiting mastery or great skill*.

wrong	Once again last night, Liona Boyd gave the audience a masterful performance.
right	Once again last night, Liona Boyd gave the audience a masterly performance.

Common Errors In English # 296.

301 **mitigate/militate:** To *mitigate* something is to make it less harsh or severe; thus *mitigating* circumstances are those that make a criminal offence less serious. To *militate* against something is to act as a strong influence against it.

wrong	The natural history orientation of early anthropology also mitigated against studies of change. (Bruce G. Trigger in *Natives and Newcomers*)
right	The natural history orientation of early anthropology also militated against studies of change.

302. **momentarily:** *Momentarily* means *lasting only a moment* ("He was *momentarily* confused"). Common usage also allows the word to mean *in a moment* or *soon*; in formal writing it is best to avoid this use.

poor	Ms. Billings has informed me that she will join us momentarily.
better	Ms. Billings told me that she will join us soon.

303. **need/want:** The verb *need* conveys the idea that it would be difficult or impossible for you to do without the needed thing. If you are talking about acquiring something that is not necessary or essential, use *want* instead; everyone *needs* water and food, but no one really *needs* a television. Be careful too not to commit to paper the slang use of *need to* for *should*.

wrong	I need to marry a woman who is very beautiful, very intelligent, very kind, and very rich.
right	I want to marry a woman who is very beautiful, very intelligent, very kind, and very rich.
wrong	The government needs to improve the roads in this area.
right	The government should improve the roads in this area.

304. **non sequitur:** A *non sequitur* is a statement that has no clear relationship with what has preceded it. There may be some connection within the mind of the speaker or writer, but it has not

been expressed in words.

wrong   The company should purchase computers immediately. This office is completely untidy.

THAT'S WHY SO MUCH RICE IS CONSUMED IN CHINA

Reporting the possibility of mean old George Bell's being traded to the Philadelphia Phillies, Marty York asks, "is it a *non sequitur* for George Bell to exist in the city of Brotherly Love? "
The answer, if he really wants one, is no.
It may be an irony, a contradiction, an inconsistency, or even *nihil ad rem*. But it is not a *non sequitur*. That's why so much rice is consumed in China.

(Robertson Cochrane, letter to the *Globe & Mail*, Oct. 1990)

---

right   The company should purchase computers immediately. Even aside from the efficiencies that we can expect to gain, a computerized system should greatly reduce the amount of paperwork — and paper clutter — around this office. For years now piles of paper in a restricted space have created an unacceptable level of untidiness.

---

305. **obligate/oblige:** These two words share the same Latin root but have different shades of meaning and are used rather differently. One feels a sense of obligation, but feels obliged to do something.

wrong   She felt obligated to finish the book her friend had lent her.

right   She felt obliged to finish the book her friend had lent her.

---

306. **of/have:** The difference in meaning is obvious, but the similarity in sound consistently leads people to write sentences involving such meaningless expressions as *should of, would of, could of, may of, might of* and *must of*.

wrong   The experiment would of succeeded if the solution had been prepared correctly.

right   The experiment would have succeeded if the solution had been prepared correctly.

Common Errors In English # 305.

| *wrong* | Hitler believed that Rommel should of been able to defeat Montgomery at El Alamein. |
| *right* | Hitler believed that Rommel should have been able to defeat Montgomery at El Alamein. |

---

307. **other:** if one uses the words *the other* it suggests that the thing or person one is about to mention is the only *other* one is going to write about. If there are several *others* to be mentioned, *another* is the word to choose.

| *wrong* | One reason why Germany lost the Second World War was that she underestimated the importance of keeping the United States out of the conflict. The other reason was that her intelligence network was inferior to that of the Allies. Moreover, Hitler's decision to invade Russia was a disastrous mistake. |

(Here the use of *the other* in the second sentence leads the reader to believe this is the only other reason. When a third reason is mentioned in the next sentence, the reader is taken by surprise.)

| *right* | One reason why Germany lost the Second World War was that she underestimated the importance of keeping the United States out of the conflict. Another reason was that her intelligence network was inferior to that of the Allies. Moreover, Hitler's decision to invade Russia was a disastrous mistake. |

---

308. **our/are:** Like the substitution of *of* for *have*, the confusion of *our* and *are* should never survive the rough draft stage. Unfortunately, it very frequently does.

| *wrong* | Almost all are time is spent together. |
| *right* | Almost all our time is spent together. |

---

309. **partake/participate:** *Partake* refers to things (especially food and drink), *participate* to activities.

| *wrong* | The Governor General made a brief appearance, but did not partake in the festivities. |
| *right* | The Governor General made a brief appearance, but did not participate in the festivities. |

---

310. **per cent/percentage:** If you use *per cent,* you must give the number. Otherwise, use *percentage.*

Common Errors in English # 307.

wrong	The per cent of people surveyed who reported any change of opinion was very small.
right	The percentage of people surveyed who reported any change of opinion was very small.
or	Only six per cent of the people surveyed reported any change of opinion.

Note: *Percentage* is always one word; authorities differ as to whether *per cent* should always be written as as two words, or whether it also may be written as one word.

---

311. **persecute/prosecute:** To *persecute* someone is to treat them in a harsh and unfair manner, especially because of their political or religious beliefs. To *prosecute* someone is to take legal action against them in the belief that they have committed a crime.

wrong	Catholics began to be prosecuted in England in the sixteenth century.
right	Catholics began to be persecuted in England in the sixteenth century.

---

312. **persuade:** To *persuade* someone of something is to make them believe that it is true. To persuade them to do something is to lead them, through what one says, to do the desired thing. If one does not succeed in making them believe or do what one wants, then one has not persuaded or convinced them, but only <u>tried</u> to persuade them. (The confusion of *refute* with *deny* [above, number 249] is a parallel mistake.)

wrong	After all Portia's persuasion Shylock still refuses to change his mind.
right	After all Portia's attempts to persuade him, Shylock still refuses to change his mind.

---

313. **phase:** an overused word; remember that it refers only to time; it should not be thought of as a synonym for *part*.

wrong	The federal bureaucracy has a bewildering number of phases.
right	The federal bureaucracy has a bewildering number of levels and departments.

---

314. **pore/pour:** As *The Globe and Mail Style Book* puts it, one should "not write of someone pouring over a book unless the tome in question is getting wet."

wrong	After pouring over the evidence, the committee could find no evidence of wrongdoing.

right	After poring over the evidence, the committee could find no evidence of wrongdoing.

---

315. **practical/practicable:** *Practical* means *suitable for use,* or *involving activity rather than theory.* *Practicable* means *able to be done.* Changing the railway system back to steam locomotives would be *practicable* but extremely *impractical.* In most cases *practical* is the word the writer wants; excessive use of *practicable* will make writing sound pretentious rather than important.

wrong	We do not feel that the construction of a new facility would be practicable at this time.
right	It would not be practical to construct a new facility now.

---

316. **prescribe/proscribe:** To *prescribe* something is to recommend or order its use; to *proscribe* something is to forbid its use.

wrong	One local physician has already proscribed this new drug for a dozen of her patients, and in every case their condition has improved after taking i.t.
right	One local physician has already prescribed this new drug for a dozen of her patients, and in every case their condition has improved after taking it.

---

317. **presently:** The subject of much disagreement among grammarians; should *presently* be restricted to its original meaning of *soon,* or should common usage of the word to mean *now* be allowed to spread unopposed? Traditionalists argue that the acceptance of both meanings encourages ambiguity, but in fact the verb tense usually makes clear whether the speaker means *soon* or *now* ("I will be there presently," "I am presently working on a large project," etc.). Perhaps the best solution is to avoid the rather pompous *presently* altogether, and stick to those fine Anglo-Saxon words *soon* and *now.*

poor	I am seeing Mr. Jones presently.
better	I am seeing Mr. Jones now.
or	I will be seeing Mr. Jones soon.

---

318. **proposition/proposal:** The only formally correct meaning of *proposition* is a statement that expresses an idea, as in "This country is dedicated to the proposition that all men are created equal." It is better not to use it to mean *proposal.*

Common Errors in English # 315.

poor	The department has put forward a proposition for increasing sales.
better	The department has put forward a proposal for increasing sales.

---

319. **prove:** To *prove* something is to eliminate any doubt whatsoever as to its truth. Outside of mathematics, science or philosophical logic *proof* is rarely possible; what one is doing when writing about history or political science or English is presenting an argument, not a *proof*. Be cautious in the claims you make in formal writing.

poor	The following passage proves that T.S. Eliot was anti-Semitic.
better	The following passage strongly suggests that T.S. Eliot was anti-Semitic.

---

320. **raise/rise:** *Raise* means *to lift*; *rise* means *to come up*.

wrong	They rose the curtain at 8 o'clock.
right	They raised the curtain at 8 o'clock.
or	The curtain rose at 8 o'clock.

---

321. **rational/rationale:** *Rational* is an adjective meaning *logical* or *sensible*. A *rationale* is an explanation for something.

wrong	The underlying rational for the proliferation of soaps and detergents is not to make our skin or clothes any cleaner, but to increase the profits of the manufacturers.
right	The underlying rationale for the proliferation of soaps and detergents is not to make our skin or clothes any cleaner, but to increase the profits of the manufacturers.

---

322. **ravish/ravage:** *Ravish* has two quite unrelated meanings — to rape, or to fill with delight. To *ravage* is to damage or destroy.

wrong	The tree had been ravished by insects.
right	The tree had been ravaged by insects.

---

323. **real/genuine:** The basic meaning of *real* is *existing*; the opposite of *fake* or *forged* is *genuine*.

poor	The buyer had thought the painting was a Cézanne, but he soon discovered it was not real.
better	The buyer had thought the painting was a Cézanne, but

he soon discovered it was not genuine.

---

324. **respectively/respectfully:** *Respectively* means *in the order mentioned*; *respectfully* means *done with respect.*

wrong	Green Bay, Denver and San Francisco were, respectfully, the three best teams in the NFL last season.
right	Green Bay, Denver and San Francisco were, respectively, the three best teams in the NFL last season.

---

325. **reticent/reluctant:** *Reticent* means *reluctant to speak; reserved about speaking.* A country may be *reluctant* to go to war; it cannot be *reticent* to go to war. And to say " reticent to speak" is to repeat oneself:

wrong	She was reticent to speak up, even when her family's reputation had been attacked.
right	She was reluctant to speak up, even when her family's reputation had been attacked.
or	She remained reticent, even when her family's reputation had been attacked.

---

326. **sensory/sensuous/sensual:** Advertising and pornography have dulled the distinction among these three adjectives. The meanings of *sensory* and *sensuous* are similar — *sensual* is the sexy one:

Sensory	having to do with the senses
Sensuous	having to do with the senses, or appealing to the senses
Sensual	offering physical pleasure, especially of a sexual sort
wrong	Boswell suggested they go to a house of ill repute, but Johnson had no desire for sensuous pleasures.
right	Boswell suggested they go to a house of ill repute, but Johnson had no desire for sensual pleasures.

---

327. **set/sit:** *Set* means *to place something somewhere.*

wrong	I could remember everything, but I had difficulty sitting it down on paper.
right	I could remember everything, but I had difficulty setting it down on paper.
wrong	He asked me to set down on the couch.
right	He asked me to sit down on the couch.

---

328. **simple/simplistic:** *Simplistic* is a derogatory word meaning *too simple* or *excessively simplified.*

wrong	The questions were so simplistic that I was able to answer all but one correctly.
right	The questions were so simple that I was able to answer all but one correctly.

---

329. **somehow:** *Somehow* means *by some method* ("Somehow I must repair my car so that I can arrive in time for my appointment"). It does not mean *in some ways, to some extent,* or *somewhat.*

wrong	His brother is somehow mentally disturbed.
right	His brother is mentally disturbed in some way.
or	His brother is somewhat disturbed mentally.

---

330. **specially/especially:** *Specially* means *for a particular purpose* ("These utensils are specially designed for left-handed people"). *Especially* means *particularly* or *more than in other cases.*

wrong	The entire system pleased her, but she was was specially happy to see that the computer program had been especially created for small business users.
right	The entire system pleased her, but she was especially happy to see that the computer program had been specially created for small business users.

---

331. **stationary/stationery:** *Stationary* means *not moving*; *stationery* is what you write on.

wrong	As Mr. Blakeney remembered it, Lord Taylor "would always park his car in the no-parking zone outside the Bessborough Hotel, leaving House of Lords stationary on the windshield." (*The Toronto Star*, June 1987)
right	As Mr. Blakeney remembered it, Lord Taylor "would always park his car in the no-parking zone outside the Bessborough Hotel, leaving House of Lords stationery on the windshield."

---

332. **stimulant/stimulus:** *Stimulus* (plural *stimuli*) is the more general word for anything that produces a reaction; *stimulant* normally refers to a drink or drug that has a *stimulating* effect.

wrong	The shocks were intended to act as stimulants to the rats that we used as subjects for the experiment.
right	The shocks were intended to act as stimuli to the rats that we used as subjects for the experiment.

333. **tack/tact:** *Tack* is a sailing term; a different tack means *a different direction relative to the wind. Tact* is skill in saying or doing the right or polite thing.

wrong	We will have to exercise all our tack in the coming negotiations.
right	We will have to exercise all our tact in the coming negotiations.

334. **than/that:** The difference in meaning is obvious, but slips of the pen or typewriter too often allow this error to make it to the final draft.

wrong	It turns out that the company needs more money that we had expected.
right	It turns out that the company needs more money than we had expected.

335. **they/their/there/they're:** Four words that are confused perhaps more frequently than any others. *They* is a pronoun used to replace any plural noun (e.g., books, people, numbers). *There* can be used to mean *in* (or *at*) *that place*, or can be used as an introductory word before various forms of the verb *to be* (*There is, There had been*, etc.). *Their* is a possessive adjective meaning *belonging to them*. Beware in particular of substituting *they* for *there*:

wrong	They were many people in the crowd.
right	There were many people in the crowd.

The easiest way to check whether one is making this mistake is to ask if it would make sense to replace *they* with a noun. In the above sentence, for example, it would obviously be absurd to say, "The people were many people in the crowd."

The confusion of *they, there,* and *their* is the sort of mistake that all writers are able to catch if they check their work carefully before writing the final draft.

wrong	Soviet defenceman Mikhail Tatarinov is considered to be there enforcer.
	(*Peterborough Examiner*)
right	Soviet defenceman Mikhail Tatarinov is considered to be their enforcer.
wrong	There all going to the dance this Saturday.
right	They're all going to the dance this Saturday.

Common Errors in English # 333.

or They are all going to the dance this Saturday.

---

336. **tiring/tiresome:** Something that is *tiring* makes you feel *tired*, though you may have enjoyed it very much. Something that is *tiresome* is tedious and unpleasant.

wrong Although it is tiresome for him, my father likes to play tennis at least twice a week.

right Although it is tiring for him, my father likes to play tennis at least twice a week.

---

337. **to/too/two:** *Too* can mean *also* or be used (*too many, too heavy*) to indicate excess; *two* is of course the number.

wrong She seemed to feel that there was to much to do.

right She seemed to feel that there was too much to do.

---

338. **to/towards:** *Towards* indicates motion.

wrong The deer moved slowly to me through the tall grass.

right The deer moved slowly towards me through the tall grass.

---

339. **unexceptional/unexceptionable:** *Unexceptional* means ordinary, not an exception; *unexceptionable* means you do not object (or *take exception*) to the thing or person in question.

wrong One way Reagan pays for this is in the confusion and controversy that surround the unexceptional White House plan to reflag 11 Kuwaiti tankers with the Stars and Stripes. It is a modest proposal that in itself should not cause the handwringing now being observed on Capitol Hill.

(*The Washington Post*, July 20 1987)

(The plan to reflag the tankers clearly <u>was</u> an exception; the U.S. had not done anything similar for years. What the writer means to say is that the plan is unexceptionable — that no one should have any objection to it.)

right One way Reagan pays for this is in the confusion and controversy that surround the unexceptionable White House plan to reflag 11 Kuwaiti tankers with the Stars and Stripes. It is a modest proposal that in itself should not cause the handwringing now being observed on Capitol Hill.

---

340. **unique/universal/perfect/complete/correct:** None of these can be

a matter of degree. Something is either unique or not unique, perfect or imperfect, and so on.

wrong	Fathers may have a relatively unique contribution to make to family functioning and the development of the child.
right	Fathers may have a unique contribution to make to family functioning and the development of the child.

341. **valid/true/accurate:** An *accurate* statement is one that is factually correct. A combination of *accurate* facts may not always give a *true* picture, however. For example, the statement that former Canadian Prime Minister Mackenzie King often visited prostitutes is entirely *accurate*, but gives a false impression; in fact King visited prostitutes to try to convince them of the error of their ways, not to use their services. *Valid* is often used carelessly and as a consequence may seem fuzzy in its meaning. Properly used it can mean *legally acceptable*, or *sound in reasoning*; do not use it to mean *accurate, reasonable, true,* or *well-founded*.

poor	Churchill's fear that the Nazis would become a threat to the rest of Europe turned out to be valid.
better	Churchill's fear that the Nazis would become a threat to the rest of Europe turned out to be well-founded.
poor	Bergson (1998) makes a valid point about the motives of the French government being suspect in its dealings with African nations.
better	Bergson (1998) has shown conclusively that the motives of the French government in its dealings with African nations were deeply suspect.

342. **vein/vain:** *Veins* run through your body; to be *vain* is to be conceited; an effort that brings no results is in *vain*.

wrong	Shakespeare portrays Sir John Oldcastle — or Falstaff, as he is usually known — as vein and irresponsible but immensely amusing and likeable.
right	Shakespeare portrays Sir John Oldcastle — or Falstaff, as he is usually known — as vain and irresponsible but immensely amusing and likeable.

343. **verbal/oral:** *Oral* means *spoken rather than written*, whereas *verbal* means *having to do with words*. A person who is unable to speak may have a high level of *verbal* skill.

wrong	I can write well enough, but I have difficulty in expressing ideas verbally.
right	I can write well enough, but I have difficulty in expressing ideas orally.

---

344. **were/where:** *Were* is of course a past tense form of the verb *to be*, while *where* refers to a place.

wrong	This is the place were Dante met Beatrice.
right	This is the place where Dante met Beatrice.

WORD ORDER PROBLEMS

Word order problems are of many sorts. See also, for example, the discussions elsewhere in this book of syntax; of ambiguity; of split infinitives; of indefinite pronouns such as *each, every,* and *anyone*; and of *not only...but also.*

345 ambiguity/confusion: Inappropriate word order is one of the most common sources of ambiguity and confusion. Often a change in punctuation may also be required to correct the problem.

wrong	The liner tilted dramatically after fire broke out in the engine room, 50 miles south of Cyprus. *(The Observer,* October 5, 1997)
right	The liner tilted dramatically after fire broke out in the engine room. At the time the ship was 50 miles south of Cyprus.
wrong	He has not come under any pressure to make way for a new leader, despite the failure of any tangible benefits from his government's economic policies.
right	He has not come under any pressure to make way for a new leader, despite the failure of his government's economic policies to bring any tangible benefits.
wrong	Proportion of overweight people between 18 and 64 years trying to lose weight by sex in Alberta 1990 (Heading on chart, Alberta Heart Health Survey, reprinted in *The Calgary Herald,* June 3, 1994)
right	Proportion in Alberta of overweight people between 18 and 64 years, by sex, who were trying to lose weight, 1990

346. amounts: For no good reason, adjectives having to do with amounts or quantities (e.g. *much, few, many*) normally precede the noun or pronoun to which they refer, even when the verb *to be* is used. In this way such adjectives differ from other adjectives. For example, we can talk about "a happy man," putting the adjective *happy* before the noun *man,* or we can use the present tense of the verb *to be* and say "The man is happy," in which case the adjective *happy* comes after the noun *man.* In contrast, it is not correct to say, "We were many at the meeting," or "The people here are few". Instead the sentence must be changed around, and the adjectives put before the nouns. The easiest way to do this is by using *there* and the verb *to be.* The revised versions of the above sentences are,

right   There were many of us at the meeting.
right   There are few people here.

A further example:
wrong   The students at the football game were many.
right   There were many students at the football game.

---

347. **balance:** Often paired connectives ("if...then," "either... or" [given a separate entry below], "not only...but also", "both...and") can help in achieving balance. But here, as always, the writer must be careful that the words are in the right places; otherwise the fragile element of balance is lost:

wrong   Hardy was not only a prolific novelist but wrote poetry too, and also several plays.
right   Hardy was not only a prolific novelist but also a distinguished poet and a dramatist.
(The noun "novelist"is balanced by the later nouns "poet" and "dramatist".)

wrong   To subdue Iraq through sanctions, the United Nations felt, was better than using military force.
right   To subdue Iraq through sanctions, the United Nations felt, was better than to use military force.
(The infinitive "to subdue" is balanced by the infinitive "to use".)

wrong   In 1972 there was a stop-McGovern movement and a stop-Carter movement in 1976.   (*The Globe and Mail,* July, 1988)
right   In 1972 there was a stop-McGovern movement and in 1976 a stop-Carter movement.
or   In 1972 there was a stop-McGovern movement and in 1976 there was a stop-Carter movement.

---

348. **direct object position:** The normal position for direct objects is after the verb. When the direct object is put at the beginning of a

sentence it sounds awkward, and the word order may lead students to include an extra, unwanted pronoun later in the sentence. It is therefore best to always keep the direct object after the verb.

wrong	Some of the money I put it in the bank.
	(Notice the extra pronoun *it*.)
right	I put some of the money in the bank.
	(*I* is the subject, *some of the money* is the direct object.)

---

349. either . . . or: These words should directly precede the pair of things to which they refer. The same applies to *neither...nor*.

wrong	I will either pick an apple or a banana.
	(*Either* and *or* refer to *apple* and *banana*. Therefore they must come immediately before those words.)
right	I will pick either an apple or a banana.
wrong	He will go either to New York for the holiday or remain here.
	(The choice is between going and remaining.)
right	He will either go to New York for the holiday or remain here.
wrong	The experiment can either be performed with hydrogen or with oxygen.
right	The experiment can be performed with either hydrogen or oxygen.
	(The choice is between the two gasses, not between performing and doing some other thing.)

---

350. except: A phrase beginning with *except* should appear directly after the noun or pronoun to which *except* refers.

wrong	We all had to wait except for those who had bought tickets in advance.
right	All except those who had bought tickets in advance had to wait.

---

351. first person last rule: When speaking about both yourself and another person (or other people), always mention the other person first. The first person pronoun (*I, me*) should come last.

wrong	I and my brother decided to go shopping yesterday.
right	My brother and I decided to go shopping yesterday.

---

352. only: The adverb *only* should come directly before the word or words it refers to. "She could only see him" implies that she could not hear, smell or touch him; "She could see only him" implies that she had eyes for no one else.

Common Errors in English # 349.

wrong	She only asked six people to the party.
right	She asked only six people to the party.

---

353. **questions in indirect speech:** In a question we normally reverse the order of the subject and the verb. For example, to change the statement "She was sad" to a question, we reverse the order of *she* and *was* and ask, "Was she sad?" The same rule does not apply, however, to questions in indirect speech. These are considered to be part of a statement and, as in any other statement, the entire verb should come after the subject. For example, to turn the above sentence into indirect speech we would say, "I asked her whether she was sad" (<u>not</u> "I asked her was she sad.")

wrong	I asked him how was he.
right	I asked him how he was.

wrong	She asked her brother where was he going.
right	She asked her brother where he was going.

Notice as well that these sentences are statements, not questions. They therefore do not end with a question mark.

---

354. **relative pronouns:** Relative pronouns (*who, which, whom, whose* etc.) normally refer to the word that has come immediately before them. This may sometimes turn out to be difficult, in which case the word order may have to be changed.

wrong	He purchased his friend's shop, whom he had known for many years.
	(The relative pronoun *whom* refers to *friend*, not *shop*. Change the word order to put *whom* directly after *friend*.)
right	He purchased the shop from his friend, whom he had known for many years.

wrong	On Saturday I went to my brother's wedding, whose new wife is a senior government official.
right	On Saturday I went to the wedding of my brother, whose new wife is a senior government official.

TOO MANY WORDS / TOO FEW WORDS

Wordiness is perhaps the most persistent disease afflicting modern writing; references to it permeate this book. The mistake of including too few words in a sentence is much less common; most of the following entries, therefore, are instances of too many words rather than too few.

---

355. actual/actually: Usually redundant.

wrong	Many people assume that Switzerland is made up entirely of bankers and watchmakers. In actual fact, the Swiss economy is very diversified.
right	Many people assume that Switzerland is made up entirely of bankers and watchmakers. In fact, the Swiss economy is very diversified.

---

356. as regards: Use *about*, or rephrase.

wrong	As regards your request for additional funding, we have taken the matter under advisement.
right	We are considering your request for more money.

---

357. as stated earlier: If so, why state it again?

wrong	The Venus flytrap, which as stated earlier is an insectivorous plant, grows only in a restricted area of New Jersey.
right	The Venus flytrap grows only in a restricted area of New Jersey.

---

358. as you know, as we all know: Usually better omitted.

wrong	As we all know, Bill Clinton was elected President in 1992, and again in 1996.
right	Bill Clinton was elected President in 1992, and again in 1996.

---

359. aspect: Often a pointer to an entire phrase or clause that can be cut.

wrong	The logging industry is a troubled one at the present time. One of the aspects of this industry that is a

	cause for concern is the increased production of cheaper timber in South America.
right	The logging industry is now a troubled one. Increased production of cheaper timber in South America has reduced the market for North American wood.

360. **at a later date:** Later

wrong	We can decide this at a later date.
right	We can decide this later.

361. **at the present time:** *Now*, or nothing.

wrong	At the present time the company has ten employees.
right	The company has ten employees.

362. **attention:** *It has come to my attention that* is almost always unnecessarily wordy.

wrong	It has come to my attention that shipments last month were 15 per cent below targeted levels.
right	Shipments last month were 15 per cent below targeted levels.

363. **basis/basically:** Both are often pointers to wordiness.

wrong	On the basis of the information we now possess it is possible to see that William Bligh was not the ogre he was once thought to be. Basically, he was no harsher than most captains of the time.
right	Recent research suggests that William Bligh was not the ogre he was once thought to be. He was no harsher than most captains of the time.

364. **cause:** Sentences using *cause* as a verb can often be rephrased more concisely; try to think of other verbs.

wrong	The increased sales tax caused the people to react with fury.
right	The increase in sales tax infuriated the people.
wrong	The change in temperature caused the liquid to freeze within seventeen minutes.
right	The liquid froze within seventeen minutes of the temperature change.

365. **close proximity to:** *Near.*

wrong	The office is situated in close proximity to shops and transportation facilities.
right	The office is near a shopping centre and a bus stop.

Common Errors in English # 360.

366 e.g. . . . etc.: If you begin by saying 'for example,' it is redundant to add 'and others' at the end of your list. See also immediately below, and under *such as* in the chapter on joining ideas together.

wrong	In several African nations (e.g. Rwanda, Malawi, Zaire etc.) tyrannical or murderous regimes have been overthrown in the 1990s.
right	In several African nations (e.g. Rwanda, Malawi, Zaire) tyrannical or murderous regimes have been overthrown in the 1990s.

367. etc.: The Latin *et cetera*, or *etc.* for short, means *and the rest* or *and others*. To say *and etc.* is really to say *and and others*. Beware as well of combining *etc.* with expressions such as *such as*.

wrong	During recent years several countries (Mexico, Argentina and etc.) have amassed huge debts, which they are now unable to pay.
right	During recent years several countries (Mexico, Argentina, etc.) have amassed huge debts, which they are now unable to pay.
wrong	Plants such as venus flytraps, pitcher plants, etc. feed on insects.
right	Plants such as venus flytraps and pitcher plants feed on insects.
or	Some plants (venus flytraps, pitcher plants, etc.) feed on insects.

368. exists: Often a pointer to wordiness.

wrong	A situation now exists in which voters suspect the government's motives, regardless of whether or not they approve of its actions.
right	Voters now suspect the government's motives even if they approve of its actions.

369. fact: Be wary of *the fact that*.

wrong	Due to the fact that we have discontinued this product, we are unable to provide spare parts.
right	Because we have discontinued this product we are unable to provide spare parts.
wrong	The fact that every member nation has one vote in the General Assembly does not give each one equal influence.
right	Each member nation has one vote in the General Assembly, but some have more influence than others.
wrong	Despite the fact that virtually no one in those days could foresee the end of American surpluses, Jones

| | could. |
| *right* | Jones was one of the few to foresee the end of American surpluses. |

---

370. **factor:** Heavily overused, and a frequent cause of wordiness.

| *wrong* | An important factor contributing to the French Revolution was the poverty of the peasantry. |
| *right* | The poverty of the peasantry was a major cause of the French Revolution. |

---

371. **from my point of view, according to my point of view, in my opinion:** All three expressions are usually redundant.

wrong	From my point of view, basic health care is more important than esoteric and expensive machines or procedures that benefit few.
fair	I think that basic health care is more important than esoteric and expensive machines or procedures that benefit few.
better	Basic health care is more important than esoteric and expensive machines or procedures that benefit few.

---

372. **I myself:** In almost all cases the addition of *myself* is needlessly repetitive.

| *wrong* | I myself believe in freedom of speech. |
| *right* | I believe in freedom of speech. |

---

373. **in all probability:** *Probably.*

| *wrong* | In all probability we will be finished tomorrow. |
| *right* | We will probably be finished tomorrow. |

---

374. **include:** Often a needed word or two is omitted after this verb. The best solution may be to rephrase or find another verb.

wrong	The report includes both secondary and post-secondary education.
right	The report includes material on both secondary and post-secondary education.
or	The report deals with both secondary and post-secondary education.
wrong	The Thirty Years War included most countries in Europe.
right	The list of countries that fought in the Thirty Years War includes almost every European nation.
right	Almost every European country fought in the Thirty Years War.

Common Errors in English # 370.

375. **interesting:** In most cases the writer should not have to tell the reader that what he is saying is interesting.

wrong	It is interesting to observe that illiteracy affects almost as high a proportion of native-born Americans as it does immigrants.
right	Illiteracy affects almost as high a proportion of native-born Americans as it does immigrants.

376. **mean for:** The preposition is unnecessary.

wrong	I did not mean for him to do it all himself.
right	I did not mean that he should do it all himself.

377. **nature:** Often contributes to wordiness.

wrong	The nature of the brain is to process information incredibly swiftly.
right	The brain processes information extremely swiftly.

378. **personally:** It is safe to let your reader take it for granted that you are a person.

wrong	Personally, I feel that the Supreme Court has too much power.
right	I feel that the Supreme Court has too much power.

379. **point in time:** *Now* or *then.*

wrong	At that point in time central Africa was very sparsely populated.
right	Central Africa was then very sparsely populated.

380. **really:** If an intensifier must be used, *very* is preferable.

wrong	It is really important that this be done today.
right	It is very important that this be done today.
or	This must be done today.

381. **regard, with regard to, as regards:** Try *about, over,* or rephrase.

wrong	I am writing with regard to your proposal to centralize production.
right	I am writing about your proposal to centralize production.
wrong	As regards the trend in interest rates, it is likely to continue to be upward.
right	Interest rates are likely to continue to increase.
wrong	This Act gave the government powers with regard to the readjustment of industry.
right	This Act gave the government powers over the readjustment of industry.

382. **redundancy:** Redundancies are words or expressions that repeat in different words a meaning already expressed. Commonly used expressions that involve redundancy include *end result, plans for the future, general public, nod your head, optimistic about the future, a personal friend of mine, mutual cooperation.* Sometimes a case may be made for using a phrase of this sort in order to emphasise a point. What is to be avoided is thoughtless and purposeless wordiness.

wordy	This property will appreciate greatly in value.
better	This property will appreciate greatly.
wordy	The house is very large in size.
better	The house is very large.
wordy	"It was decided it would be mutually beneficial to both of us if he left."
	(*The Globe and Mail*, Sept. 20, 1990)
better	"It was decided it would be mutually beneficial if he left."
or	"We agreed it would be better for both of us if he left."

383. **situation:** By avoiding this word you will usually make your sentence shorter and better.

wrong	This treaty created a situation in which European countries gave up a degree of autonomy in return for greater security.
right	Through this treaty European countries gave up a degree of autonomy in return for greater security.

384. **There is/are/was/were:** These constructions often produce sentences that are needlessly long.

wrong	There were many factors which undermined the government's popularity in this period.
right	Many things undermined the government's popularity in this period.
wrong	There are many historians who accept this thesis.
right	Many historians accept this thesis.

385. **too few words:** This mistake can happen anywhere in a sentence. One of the best tests of whether or not a writer has checked her work is whether or not there are missing words. In almost all cases, such omissions will be noticed through careful proofreading.

wrong	She rushed home to tell my family and about the accident.
right	She rushed home to tell my family and me about the accident.
wrong	Mrs. Gandhi reminded the Conference that just one

	intercontinental ballistic missile could plant 200 million trees, irrigate one million hectares of land, or build 6,500 health care centers. (United Nations official)
right	Mrs. Gandhi reminded the Conference that the money spent on just one intercontinental ballistic missile could be used to plant 200 million trees, irrigate one million hectares of land, or build 6,500 health care centers.

386. too many words: Many of the causes of this problem have been given separate entries.

wrong	So far as the purpose of this essay is concerned, it will concentrate on the expansion of Soviet power.
right	This essay will concentrate on the expansion of Soviet power.
wrong	Although the author does not claim to be writing a social study, the question arises whether the social implications of his analysis can be ignored.
right	Although the author does not claim to be writing a social study, his analysis does have social implications.

387. tragic/tragically: Unneccessary use of either the adjective or the adverb constitutes overkill.

redundant	Her husband, her child and more than a hundred others died in a tragic plane crash in 1997.
better	Her husband, her child and more than a hundred others died in a plane crash in 1997.

388. would like to take this opportunity to: *Would like.*

wrong	I would like to take this opportunity to thank my cousin in Peoria.
right	I am very grateful to my cousin in Peoria.

ONE WORD OR TWO?

A number of very commonly used English words have over many years become accepted as one word because they are combined so often. Other similar combinations, however, should still be written as two words. In a few cases one can see English usage changing on this point right now. A generation ago, for example, *alright* as one word could not have been found in any dictionary. Now a few authorities are beginning to regard *alright* as acceptable, and perhaps in another generation or two it will have completely replaced *all right*. For the moment, though, it is best to stick with *all right* rather than the more colloquial *alright*.

389. What has been written as two words should be one. Here are some common examples:

already: one word when used as an adverb ("He has finished already.")
altogether: one word when used as an adverb to mean *completely* or *entirely* ("He is not altogether happy with the result.")
awhile: one word when used as an adverb
another
anybody
anyone: one word unless it is followed by *of.*
bathroom
bloodshed
businessman (but see **Bias-free Language,** pp. 178, 184)
cannot: *can not* is less common, but still acceptable.
everybody
everyday: one word when used as an adjective (e.g., "Brushing your teeth should be part of your everyday routine"—here *everyday* is an adjective modifying the noun *routine*.)
everyone: one word unless it is followed by *of.*
everything
forever
furthermore
indeed
intact

into: one word except in the relatively few cases where the senses of *in* and *to* are clearly separate. (Fowler uses the example, "the Prime Minister took her in to dinner.")

maybe: when used as an adverb meaning *perhaps* (e.g., "Maybe I will join you later"—here the verb is *will join* and *maybe* is an adverb.)

nearby
nobody
onto: see *into*
ourselves
somebody
someone
straightforward
themselves
wartime
whatever
whenever

---

390. What has been written as one word should be two words. Here are some common examples:

a lot
all ready: two words when not used as an adverb ("We are all ready to go.")
all right
all together: two words when not used as an adverb (e.g., "They were all together when I left them.")
every day: two words when not used as an adjective (e.g., "We see each other every day.")
every time
in fact
in front
in order
in spite of
may be: two words when used as a verb (e.g., "He may be here later tonight" — *may be* is the verb in the sentence.)
no one

USAGE: WORD CONVENTIONS

---

391. according to: This expression normally is used only when one is referring to a <u>person</u> or to a group of people (e.g., "According to his lawyer, the accused was nowhere near the scene when the crime was committed," "According to Shakespeare, Richard III was an evil king").

wrong	According to geography, Congo is larger than all of Western Europe.
right	As we learn in geography, Congo is larger than all of Western Europe.
wrong	According to the story of *Cry the Beloved Country*, Stephen Kumalo has a quick temper.
right	The events of the story show that Stephen Kumalo has a quick temper.

---

392. age/aged: Do not use the noun *age* as a participle.

wrong	A woman age 35 was struck and killed by the car.
right	A woman aged 35 was struck and killed by the car.

---

393. all of: Many authorities advise that the expression *all of* should be avoided in the interests of economy. Perhaps so, but there is certainly no error involved, and in many cases the addition of the word *of* improves the rhythm of the sentence; Lincoln's famous maxim "You can not fool all the people all of the time" would not be improved by dropping the *of*.

---

394. amount: This word should only be used with things that are uncountable (sugar, goodwill, etc.).

wrong	A large amount of books were stolen from the library last night.
right	A large number of books were stolen from the library last night.

Common Errors In English # 391.

395. and: In most cases *or* rather than *and* should be used as a connective if the statement is negative.

wrong	Moose are not found in South America, Africa, and Australia.
right	Moose are not found in South America, Africa, or Australia.

396. anyways/anywheres: There is never a need for the *s*.

wrong	We were unable to find him anywheres.
right	We were unable to find him anywhere.

397. as: When this word is used to relate the times at which two actions happened, the actions must have happened <u>at the same time</u> (e.g., "As I got out of bed, I heard the sound of gunfire," where the hearing happens <u>during</u> the action of getting out; "As he was walking to work, he remembered that he had left the stove on," where the remembering happens <u>during</u> the walking). *As* should <u>not</u> be used in this way if the two actions happened at <u>different</u> times; if one action is completed before the other begins, always use *when*.

wrong	As I had finished my geography assignment, I started my history essay.
	(The finishing happens before the starting.)
right	When I had finished my geography assignment, I started my history essay.
wrong	As she discovered that the engine was overheating, she stopped the car immediately.
	(The discovering happens before the stopping.)
right	When she discovered that the engine was overheating, she stopped the car immediately.

Note: Since *when* can be used both when actions happen simultaneously and when they happen at different times, anyone who is at all uncertain about this point is wise to avoid using *as* to refer to time, and always stick to *when*. This has the added advantage of avoiding the possible ambiguity as to whether *as* is being used to mean *because* or to mean *when*.

398. as/that/whether: Do not use *as* to mean *that* or *whether*.

wrong	I don't know as how I can do the job in time.
right	I don't know whether I can do the job in time.

399 back formations: A back formation is the formation of a word from what one would expect to be its derivative. The verb *laze*, for example, is a back formation from the adjective *lazy*; a more recent

Common Errors in English # 395.

(and similar-sounding) back formation is the verb *liaise* from the noun *liaison*. Many back formations may be created from negatives that lack a positive form (*kempt, gruntled, couth, gainly, continent, wieldy, solent*, etc.). These should of course be avoided in formal written English.

wrong	Toronto is a pretty ruly place to watch a game.
	(Baseball Manager Lou Piniella, as quoted by Robertson Cochrane in *The Globe and Mail*, Oct. 29, 1994)
right	Toronto is a pretty civilized place to watch a game.

---

400. because of the following reasons/some reasons/many reasons: The word *because* makes it clear that a cause or reason is being introduced. The addition of a phrase such as *of the following reasons* is redundant. Either use *because* on its own, or use *for the following reasons/many reasons*, etc.

wrong	During her first few years in Canada, Susanna Moodie was unhappy because of several reasons.
right	During her first few years in Canada, Susanna Moodie was unhappy for several reasons.

---

401. both: The expressions *both alike, both equal*, and *both together* involve repetition.

poor	Macdonald and Cartier both arrived together at about eight o'clock.
better	Macdonald and Cartier arrived together at about eight o'clock.

---

402. can be able: *I can do it* and *I am able to do it* mean the same thing. Using both verbs together is redundant.

wrong	He thinks Dallas can be able to win the Cup.
right	He thinks Dallas can win the Cup.
or	He thinks Dallas will be able to win the Cup.

---

403. cannot help but: One too many negatives; use *can but* or *cannot help*.

wrong	He couldn't help but think he had made a mistake.
right	He couldn't help thinking he had made a mistake.
or	He could but think he had made a mistake.

---

404. change: You make a *change* (not do a *change*).

wrong	The manager did several changes to the roster before the match with Russia.
right	The manager made several changes to the roster before the match with Russia.

Common Errors In English # 400.

405. comment: We <u>make</u> comments (<u>not</u> say or do them).

wrong	Anyone who wishes to say any comments will have a chance to speak after the lecture.
right	Anyone who wishes to make any comments will have a chance to speak after the lecture.

406. compared to/than: The use of *compared to* as a participial phrase often leads to ambiguity and error. Unless one is speaking of one person *comparing* something to something else, it is usually better to use *than*.

wrong	There were many more trilliums in 1998 compared to previous years.
right	There were many more trilliums in 1998 than there had been in previous years.

407. convince: You *convince* people *that* they should do something, or *persuade* them *to* do it.

wrong	Reagan's advisers convinced him to approve the arms for hostages deal with Iran.
right	Reagan's advisers persuaded him to approve the arms for hostages deal with Iran.

408. elder/older: *Elder* can act as an adjective ("my *elder* son") or a noun ("the *elder* of the two"). *Older* can act only as an adjective. If using *than*, use *older*.

wrong	She is four years elder than her sister.
right	She is four years older than her sister.

409. for: One use of this preposition is to show purpose. Normally, however, *for* can only be used in this way when the purpose can be expressed in one word (e.g., *for safety, for security*). It is <u>not</u> usually correct to try to express purpose by combining *for* with a pronoun and an infinitive: expressions such as *for him to be happy, for us to arrive safely* are awkward and should be avoided. Instead, one can express purpose either by beginning with an infinitive (e.g., *in order to make life easier, in order to increase yield per hectare*), or by using *so that* (e.g., *so that life will be made easier, so that yield per hectare will be increased*).

wrong	Please speak slowly for me to understand what you say.
right	Please speak slowly so that I can understand what you say.

wrong	The team must work hard for it to have a chance at the Grey Cup.
right	The team must work hard if it is to have a chance at the Grey Cup.

---

410. forget: To *forget* something is to fail to remember it, <u>not</u> to leave it somewhere.

wrong	I forgot my textbook at home.
right	I left my textbook at home.
or	I forgot to bring my textbook from home.

---

411. had ought/hadn't ought: Use *ought* or *ought not* instead.

wrong	He hadn't ought to have risked everything at once.
right	He ought not to have risked everything at once.
or	He should not have risked everything at once.

---

412. hardly: *Hardly* acts as a negative; there is thus no need to add a second negative.

wrong	The advertisers claim that you can't hardly tell the difference.
right	The advertisers claim that you can hardly tell the difference.

---

413. how/what: One may talk about *how* something (or someone) *is*, or *what* something (or someone) is *like*, but <u>not</u> *how* they are *like*.

wrong	Tell me how it looks like from where you are.
right	Tell me how it looks from where you are.
or	Tell me what it looks like from where you are.
wrong	I do not know how the roads are like between St. John's and Cornerbrook.
right	I do not know what the roads are like between St. John's and Cornerbrook.
or	I do not know how the roads are between St. John's and Cornerbrook.

---

414. increase: Numbers can be *increased* or *decreased*, as can such things as *production* and *population* (nouns which refer to certain types of numbers or quantities). Things such as *houses*, however, or *books* (nouns which do not refer to numbers or quantities) cannot be *increased*; only the <u>number</u> of houses, books etc. can be *increased* or *decreased, raised* or *lowered*.

wrong	The government has greatly increased low-rent houses in the suburbs of Seattle.
right	The government has greatly increased the number of low-rent houses in the suburbs of Seattle.

---

415. information: One <u>gives</u> *information* (<u>not</u> tells it).

wrong	He told me all the information I wanted about how to apply.
right	He gave me all the information I wanted about how to apply.

---

416. investigation: We <u>make,</u> <u>carry out,</u> or <u>hold</u> an *investigation* (<u>not</u> do one).

wrong	The manager did a thorough investigation into the disappearance of funds from his department.
right	The manager made a thorough investigation into the disappearance of funds from his department.

---

417. irregardless: The result of confusion between *regardless* and *irrespective*. Use *regardless*.

wrong	She told us to come for a picnic, irregardless of whether it is rainy or sunny.
right	She told us to come for a picnic, regardless of whether it is rainy or sunny.

---

418. is when/is where: Many people use these phrases when attempting to define something. There is always a better way.

wrong	Osmosis is when a fluid moves through a porous partition into another fluid.
right	Osmosis occurs when a fluid moves through a porous partition into another fluid.
or	Osmosis is the movement of a fluid through a porous partition into another fluid.

---

419. journey: You <u>make</u> a journey (<u>not</u> do one).

wrong	If we do not stop along the way, we can do the journey in an hour.
right	If we do not stop along the way, we can make the journey in an hour.

---

420. law: A law is *passed, made,* or *put into effect* by the government, and *enforced* by the police. Laws are <u>not</u> *put* or *done*.

wrong	I think the government should put a law increasing the penalty for drunken driving.
right	I think the government should pass a law increasing the penalty for drunken driving.

---

421. less/fewer: When something can be counted (e.g., people, books, trees), use *fewer*. Use *less* only with <u>uncountable</u> nouns (e.g., *sugar, meat, equipment*).

wrong	As the modern economy spreads through the countryside, less will die of tropical diseases or infected wounds. (*The New York Times*, May 12, 1997)
right	As the modern economy spreads through the countryside, fewer will die of tropical diseases or infected wounds.
wrong	There are less steps and that means there is more room for error. (*Financial Post*, Nov. 20, 1989)
right	There are fewer steps and that means there is more room for error.

---

422. lie (meaning *speak falsely*): You *lie* <u>about</u> something, <u>not</u> that something.

wrong	He lied that he was eighteen years old.
right	He lied about his age, stating that he was eighteen.
or	He lied when he said he was eighteen years old.

---

423. mistake: *Mistakes* are <u>made</u> (<u>not</u> done).

wrong	He did seven mistakes in that short spelling exercise.
right	He made seven mistakes in that short spelling exercise.

---

424. more/most: To use *more* with a comparative adjective, or *most* with a superlative adjective is to repeat oneself.

wrong	The bride looked like the most happiest person in the world.
right	The bride looked like the happiest person in the world.
or	The bride looked like the most happy person in the world.
wrong	Gandalf is much more wiser than Frodo.
right	Gandalf is much wiser than Frodo.

---

425. nor: This word is usually used together with *neither*. Do <u>not</u> use it together with *not*; when using *not*, use *or* instead of *nor*.

wrong	She does not drink nor smoke.
right	She does not drink or smoke.
or	She neither drinks nor smokes.
wrong	[Liberal organizer Senator Al] Graham does not have the money nor the organization to work with that Atkins enjoys. (*The Toronto Star*, May 1987)
right	Graham does not have the money or the organization to work with that Atkins enjoys.

Common Errors In English # 422.

or Graham has neither the money nor the organization to work with that Atkins enjoys.

---

426. nothing/nobody/nowhere: These words should not be used with another negative word such as *not*. If one uses *not*, then one should use *anything* instead of *nothing, anybody* instead of *nobody, anywhere* instead of *nowhere.*

wrong He could not do nothing while he was in prison.
right He could not do anything while he was in prison.

---

427. opposed: You are opposed <u>to</u> something or someone (<u>not</u> with or against)

wrong Charles Darwin was opposed against the literal interpretation of the story of Creation, as found in *Genesis*.
right Charles Darwin was opposed to the literal interpretation of the story of Creation, as found in *Genesis*.

---

428. per cent/percentage: If you use *per cent,* you must give the number. Otherwise, use *percentage.*

wrong The per cent of people surveyed who reported any change of opinion was very small.
right The percentage of people surveyed who reported any change of opinion was very small.
or Only six per cent of the people surveyed reported any change of opinion.

Note: *Percentage* is always one word; authorities differ as to whether *per cent* should always be written as as two words, or whether it also may be written as one word.

---

429. preclude: To *preclude* something is to exclude any possibility of it happening; people cannot be *precluded.*

wrong Our cash flow problems preclude us from entering into any new commitments before 2003.
right Our cash flow problems preclude any new commitments before 2003.
or We do not have enough money to make a commitment to you now.

---

430. position/theory Positions and theories are held or argued; they do not hold or argue themselves.

wrong Devlin's position holds that a shared public morality is essential to the existence of society.
right Devlin's position is that a shared public morality is essential to the existence of society.

Common Errors in English # 426.

or	Devlin holds that a shared public morality is essential to the existence of society.

---

431. reason: The phrase "the reason is because" involves repetition; use *that* instead of *because*, or eliminate the phrase completely.

wrong	The reason ice floats is because it is lighter than water.
right	The reason ice floats is that it is lighter than water.
or	Ice floats because it is lighter than water.
wrong	The reason I have come is because I want to apply for a job.
right	I have come to apply for a job.

---

432. short/scarce: If a person is *short* of something, that thing is *scarce*.

wrong	Food is now desperately short throughout the country.
right	Food is now extremely scarce throughout the country.
or	The country is now desperately short of food.

---

433. since/for: Both these words can be used to indicate length (or duration) of time, but they are used in slightly different ways. *Since* is used to mention the <u>point</u> at which a period of time began (*since 6 o'clock, since 1980, since last Christmas*, etc.). *For* is used to mention the <u>amount</u> of time that has passed (*for two years, for six months, for centuries*, etc.).

wrong	She has been staying with us since three weeks.
right	She has been staying with us for three weeks.
or	She has been staying with us since three weeks <u>ago</u>.

---

434. so: When used to show degree or extent, *so* is normally used with *that*: "so big that...," "so hungry that...," etc. *So* should not be used as an intensifier in the way that *very* is used.

wrong	When she stepped out of the church she looked so beautiful.
right	When she stepped out of the church she looked very beautiful.
or	When she stepped out of the church she looked so beautiful that it was hard to believe she had once been thought of as plain.

---

435. some/any/someone/anyone: With negatives (*not, never*, etc.) *any* is used in place of *some*.

wrong	He never gives me some help with my work.

right   He never gives me any help with my work.

---

436. speech: You <u>make</u> a *speech* or <u>give</u> a *speech* (<u>not</u> do a *speech*).
wrong   The Dean was asked to do a speech at the
            Convocation.
right   The Dean was asked to give a speech at the
            Convocation.

---

437. start: If <u>both</u> the time at which an event begins <u>and</u> the time that it finishes are mentioned, it is not enough to use only the verb *start*.
wrong   The dance started from 9 p.m. till midnight.
right   The dance started at 9 p.m. and finished at midnight.
or   The dance continued from 9 p.m. until midnight.
or   The dance lasted from 9 p.m. until midnight.

---

438. suppose/supposed: Be sure to add the *d* in the expression *supposed to*.
wrong   We are suppose to be there by eight.
right   We are supposed to be there by eight.

---

439. supposed to/should: These two are very similar in meaning, and may often be used interchangeably; if a person is *supposed to* do something, then that is what she *should* do. In the <u>past</u> tense, however, the question of when and when not to use *supposed to* is quite tricky. You <u>may</u> use it when you are clearly talking about a <u>fixed plan</u> that has not been carried out (e.g., "He was supposed to arrive before two o'clock, but he is still not here"). You <u>should not</u> use it to apply to any action that you think was wrong, or you feel should not have been carried out. The safe solution to this problem is to always use *should* instead of *supposed to*.
wrong   What she said was impolite, but he was not supposed
            to hit her for saying it.
right   What she said was impolite, but he should not have hit
            her for saying it.

wrong   The National Party government was not supposed to
            keep Nelson Mandela in jail for so many years.
right   The National Party government should not have kept
            Nelson Mandela in jail for so many years.

---

440. thankful/grateful: We are *thankful* that something has happened, and *grateful* for something we have received.
wrong   I am very thankful for the kind thoughts expressed in
            your letter.

Common Errors in English # 436.

right   I am very grateful for the kind thoughts expressed in your letter.

---

441. too: The word *too* suggests that something is <u>more</u> than necessary, or <u>more</u> than desired. Do not use it indiscriminately to lend emphasis.

wrong   She looked too beautiful in her new dress.
right   She looked very beautiful in her new dress.

---

442. try/sure: Perhaps the most common error of all, in published books and articles as well as in less formal writing, is the use of *and* rather than *to* after *try* and *sure*.

wrong   No Montrealers stepped in to try and save the franchise.
                       (*The Toronto Star*)
right   No Montrealers stepped in to try to save the franchise.

wrong   Burton had agreed with the Sultan not to try and convert the Africans to Christianity.
                       (Alan Moorehead, *The White Nile*)
right   Burton had agreed with the Sultan not to try to convert the Africans to Christianity.

wrong   Be sure and take out the garbage before you go to bed.
right   Be sure to take out the garbage before you go to bed.

---

443. use/used: Be sure to add the *d* in the expression *used to*.

wrong   He use to be much more reckless than he is now.
right   He used to be much more reckless than he is now.

---

444. where: Do not use *where* for *that*.

wrong   I read in the paper where the parties are now tied in popularity.
right   I read in the paper that the parties are now tied in popularity.

Style, Structure, and Substance

PUTTING IDEAS TOGETHER

There are many ways of putting ideas together. Most of this chapter is concerned with the particulars of joining-words and how to use them; it may be useful, however, to begin with a brief look at some of the processes involved in putting ideas together.

Narration

The mode of thought involved in narratives is a very simple one: one thing happens, and then another thing happens, and then another thing happens.... Narration is particularly useful in an academic context when the writer is describing the steps in a procedure, such as a scientific experiment. (Normally, the body of a lab report is largely taken up by narration, though the most important sections — outlining the hypothesis, drawing conclusions, etc. — are not written in a narrative mode.)

Narrative is the most straightforward mode of thinking and of writing, and perhaps for that reason many of us tend to overuse it. Business people, for example, are sometimes tempted to rely too much on narrative rather than analysis in writing reports. And among students there is a special temptation to employ the narrative mode in writing history or literature essays. In a few cases this may be appropriate. If the writer is discussing the Whitewater affair during the administration of Bill Clinton, for example, the narrative mode may well be the best one to adopt; the sequence is a complex one, and getting it straight is crucial to establishing the degrees of guilt (who knew what when) of those involved. But the narrative should be introduced in support of the writer's argument. It must not overwhelm the ideas.

Common Errors in English # 445.

Cause and Effect

A great deal of writing involves discerning and analysing causes and effects. Whereas the natural connectives in narrative writing are "and" and "then," the natural connectives in writing about causes and effects are words such as "because," "since," and "therefore." These particular *connectives* — and how they relate to causes and effects — are treated fully below. But before turning to them it may be useful to understand something of the difference between *sequence* and *cause* — between "and ... then" and "since ... therefore".

sequences and causes: It is all too easy to confuse the fact that one thing happens after another thing with the notion that the first thing caused the second. Below, for example, are two arguments that were advanced against a provision in a piece of labour legislation introduced by an Ontario government in the 1990s that restricted the conditions under which employers would be permitted to hire outside workers during a strike. Both arguments drew comparisons with similar legislation passed by the Quebec government in the late 1970s. Here is the first argument:

> This provision would lead to the closing of newspapers in Ontario, just as happened in Quebec; the Montreal Star suffered a long strike and was forced to close down after the introduction of similar legislation.

The facts in this argument are right. The legislation went into effect, and then the Star suffered from a strike, and subsequently closed down. But was the first of these events primarily or even partially responsible for causing the third? The 1970s was a time of contraction in the newspaper business across Canada; newspapers also shut down in Ottawa, Winnipeg, and Vancouver. Moreover, the English population in Montreal — the market for the Star and its competitor, the Gazette — had been steadily shrinking for several years after the election of the Parti Québecois in 1976. With these facts in mind it is hard to feel convinced of any causal connection between the Quebec government's labour legislation and the closing of the Montreal Star. But let us look at the second argument:

Common Errors in English # 445.

> The provision will inevitably lead to an increase in the frequency and the duration of strikes. By 1980 in Quebec, two years after similar legislation was introduced in that province, the number of days lost to strikes had increased over fifty per cent.

The facts are right here too; days lost to strikes *were* much higher in 1980 than in 1976. But again, can we assume that the first event caused the second? Hardly. First, we should look at other possible causes. (For example, how was the overall economy performing in 1980 versus 1978?) Also, we should look at other years as a basis for comparison; why should the year 1980 be singled out? On doing so we will find that *on average*, in the years since the controversial legislation had been passed, the number and duration of strikes in Quebec had decreased. Another lesson in the care that deserves to be taken in making — and in responding to — arguments about cause and effect.

multiple causes: Events often have more than one cause, and claims must often be justified by more than one reason. This sounds straightforward enough, but it is easy to forget, as the following examples show.

Many of the arguments against military intervention in the Persian Gulf (both before the 1991 Gulf War and in 1998) took this form:

> The Americans are willing to fight Saddam Hussein because they believe the oil reserves of the Gulf region are of strategic and economic importance to them. This is not a good moral justification for going to war. Therefore we should not fight.

To begin with, this sort of argument confuses explanation with justification. To inquire into American motives is to ask *why* the Americans have been willing to go to war — a very different thing from asking *if they should* have been willing to go to war. It is always possible to do "the right deed for the wrong reason."

Beyond this, however, the argument assumes that if one explanation can safely be advanced for an action, it is also safe to conclude that it is the *only* explanation. In fact, of course, it is entirely possible for the US and its allies to have been willing to go to war *both* out of a self-interested desire to protect oil reserves *and* out of unselfish desires to resist aggression, to prevent the development of chemical and biological weapons, and so on.

Common Errors in English # 445.

Reasoning used by many on the opposite side of such debates may be equally flawed. The gist of the argument of the American, British and Canadian political leaders in 1991 was this:

> In an act of brutal aggression, Iraq invaded and annexed Kuwait, killing many of its citizens in the process. Aggression must be resisted. Therefore we should be willing to go to war.

And in 1998:

> In a flagrant flouting of UN resolutions, Iraq has refused to allow monitoring of strategic sites on which it has probably been developing chemical and biological weapons. Contempt for international law must be resisted. Therefore we should be willing to go to war.

As with the anti-war arguments above, the pro-war arguments here suffer from incomplete reasoning—reasoning that fails to allow for any multiplicity of causes, reasons, and effects. Did Iraq in 1991 have a legitimate historical claim on the territory of Kuwait (which, like Iraq, was carved out of what had been a part of the Ottoman Empire by the British)? What are the casualties likely to be in the event of war? Should aggression be resisted in all circumstances, and at any cost? These are some of the questions left unanswered.

And similarly in 1998: Should defiance of UN resolutions be resisted at any cost? Who is likely to suffer, and how much? Does military intervention carry with it the risk of sparking a larger conflict? Have other means short of military action been exhausted? Depending on the answers one provides to such questions, the appropriate course of action may become far less clear.

necessary and sufficient conditions: A useful distinction to use in sorting out the relative importance of multiple causes, effects, and reasons is the one between necessary and sufficient conditions. The presence of oxygen is a *necessary* condition for there to be fire; there can be no fire without oxygen. But it is not a *sufficient* condition; everything in the presence of oxygen does not automatically catch fire.

Similarly (in the argument discussed above), the 1991 political leaders were in effect arguing that the fact of Iraq having invaded and annexed another sovereign country was in itself a sufficient condition to justify going to war. Someone arguing against going to

Common Errors in English # 445.

war in the same circumstances might claim that the invasion of one country by another was a necessary condition for going to war, but not a sufficient one — that other, additional justification was required. And a third person might say that the invasion constituted neither a necessary nor a sufficient condition; that we should stay out of such affairs in any circumstances.

cause and correlation: Another useful distinction—particularly in the sciences and social sciences—is that between cause and correlation. Again, this may be made clear by example. A recent study has shown that the rate of breast cancer in women has increased markedly over the past twenty years. Over the same period, the average childbearing age has also increased dramatically. Now it is *possible* that the connection between those two occurrences may be causal in nature — that, for example, waiting until later in life to have children increases one's risk of breast cancer. But researchers caution that we should not assume this to be the case; more research needs to be done. As it stands, the connection is merely a correlation: an interrelationship of variable qualities. In this case, over the same period and under the same conditions, both variables increased.

When a correlation between two things exists,

- there may be a common cause or common causes for both;
- one may cause the other (or help to cause the other; again, more than one cause may be involved);
- the two may happen coincidentally as a result of quite separate causes.

Joining Words

The art of combining correct clauses and sentences logically and coherently is as much dependent on taking the time to think through what we are writing — and how the reader will respond to what we write — as it is on knowledge of correct usage. It is all too easy for most of us to assume that the flow of our thoughts will be as clear to the reader as it is to us. In practical terms this leads to the omission of links in the argument or of joining words that help the reader to see those links. Almost as common is the tendency to give too many or contradictory cues to the reader — a tendency that is often an

Common Errors in English # 445.

indication that ideas have not yet been thoroughly thought out. That in itself is nothing to be ashamed of; the key is to be willing to take the time to re-read and revise the work. Every good writer makes at least two and sometimes as many as five or six drafts of any piece of writing before considering it finished. Here are two examples, both taken from early drafts of books published by Broadview Press:

> At the end of World War II there was substantial optimism that the application of Keynesian analysis would lead to economic stability and security. Over the post-war period optimistic rationalism weakened in the face of reality.

> A short report in which you request an increase in your department's budget should be written in the persuasive mode. Most reports, however, do not have persuasion as their main objective. Persuasion, though, will often be one of their secondary objectives. In reports like these, some parts will be written in the persuasive mode.

445. **too few cues** (see also *non sequitur*): The first of these passages gives the reader too few cues. What is the connection between the idea of the first sentence and that of the second? One can figure it out without too much difficulty, but the flow of the argument is briefly interrupted while one does so. The problem is easily solved by the addition of one word to the second sentence:

right At the end of World War II there was substantial optimism that the application of Keynesian analysis would lead to economic stability and security. Over the post-war period, however, optimistic rationalism weakened in the face of reality.

446. **too many or contradictory cues:** The second passage suffers from the opposite problem; the use of *however* and *though* in consecutive sentences gives the reader the sense of twisting back on himself without any clear sense of direction. This sort of difficulty can be removed by rewording or rearranging the ideas:

right A short report in which you request an increase in your department's budget should be written in the persuasive mode. Most reports, however, do not have persuasion as their main objective. Persuasion will thus be at most a secondary objective. In reports like

Common Errors in English # 445.

these, some parts will be written in the persuasive mode.

The following pages list the chief words and expressions used in English to join ideas together, and discuss problems that are often experienced with them.

WORDS TO CONNECT IDEAS THAT ARE OPPOSED TO EACH OTHER

All these words are used to indicate that the writer is saying two things which seem to go against each other, or are different from each other. For example, in the sentence, "He is very rich, but he is not very happy," the fact that he is not happy is the <u>reverse</u> of what we might expect of a rich man. The word *but* indicates this opposition of ideas to the reader.

although	nevertheless
but	though
despite	whereas
even if	while
however	yet
in spite of	

Although

This word indicates that <u>in the same sentence</u> two things that seem to go against each other are being said. *Although* is usually used to introduce subordinate clauses, <u>not</u> phrases.

Although he has short legs, he can run very quickly.

Hume and Dr. Johnson, indeed, have a good deal in common, although Hume's attitude towards religion earned him Johnson's scorn.

---

447. Be careful not to use <u>both</u> *although* <u>and</u> *but* in the same sentence; one is enough:

| *wrong* | Although in most African countries the government is not elected by the people, but in Zimbabwe the government is democratically elected. |
| *right* | Although in most African countries the government is not elected by the people, in Zimbabwe the government is democratically elected. |

Common Errors in English # 447.

or   In most African countries the government is not
                     elected by the people, but in Zimbabwe the
                     government is democratically elected.

But

This word is usually used in the middle of a sentence to show that the
two ideas in the sentence oppose or seem to oppose each other. It
is also quite correct, however, to use *but* at the beginning of a
sentence, if what one is saying in the sentence forms a complete
clause and if the idea of the sentence seems to oppose the idea of
the previous sentence.

e.g.   The civilization of ancient Greece produced some of
                     the world's greatest works of art and gave birth to the
                     idea of democracy, but the Greeks also believed in
                     slavery.
or   The civilization of Greece produced some of the
                     world's greatest works of art and gave birth to the idea
                     of democracy. But the Greeks also believed in slavery.

448. When one is dealing with complex combinations of ideas it is
sometimes easy to forget which ideas are in fact in opposition and
which in support.

wrong   Brandy and bourbon, with the most "congenors," have
                     the highest hangover ratings. Red wine is a close
                     second, followed by dark rum, sherry, scotch, rye, beer,
                     white wine, gin, and vodka. Vintage red wines have 15
                     times as much histamine (it triggers allergic reactions)
                     as white wine, but vintage whites have fewer congenors.
                     (*The Globe and Mail*, Dec. 31, 1990)
          (The use of *but* is inappropriate here; that whites have both less
       histamine and fewer congenors is as one would expect; the two facts are
          both instances of white wines having fewer side effects than reds.)
right   Brandy and bourbon, with the most "congenors," have
                     the highest hangover ratings. Red wine is a close
                     second, followed by dark rum, sherry, scotch, rye,
                     beer, white wine, gin, and vodka. Vintage red wines
                     also have 15 times as much histamine (it triggers
                     allergic reactions) as white wine does.

449. Experienced writers are careful not to use *but* more than once in
a single sentence, or in consecutive sentences; they realize that doing
so tends to confuse the reader. (It is also unwise to use any
combination of *but* and *however* in this way.)

wrong   Chief Constable Smith said that Ryan had been legally
                     in possession of three handguns and two rifles, but he

thought it "incredible" that someone should be allowed to keep ammunition at his home. But he said any change in the firearms law was something which would not be discussed by him. (*The Guardian*, Aug. 30, 1987)

right　Chief Constable Smith said that Ryan had been legally in possession of three handguns and two rifles. Smith said he thought it "incredible" that someone should be allowed to keep ammunition at his home, but he would not comment directly on whether there should be a change in the firearms law.

Despite

This word means the same as *although*, but it is used to introduce phrases, not clauses.

Despite his old age, his mind is active and alert.

("Despite his old age" is a phrase; it has no verb.)

Although he is very old, his mind is active and alert.

("Although he is very old" is a clause, with *he* as a subject and *is* as a verb.)

Despite the rain, she wanted to go out to the park.

Although it was raining hard, she wanted to go to the park.

---

450. **despite:** Remember not to introduce clauses with *despite*.

wrong　Despite that the drink tasted very strong, there was very little alcohol in it.

right　Despite its strong taste, there was very little alcohol in the drink.

or　Although the drink tasted very strong, there was very little alcohol in it.

Even if

This expression is used when one is introducing a clause giving a condition. The word *even* emphasizes that the condition is surprising or unusual. Examples:

Even if I have to stay up all night, I am determined to finish the job.

(Staying up all night would be very unusual.)

Even if Bangladesh doubled its food production, some of its people would still be hungry.

(Doubling its food production would be very surprising.)

Common Errors in English # 450.

However

This word shows that what one is saying seems to go against what one has said in the previous sentence. It should normally be placed between commas in the middle of the sentence:

> The country suffered greatly during the three-year drought. This year, however, the rains have been heavy.

---

451. *However* should not be used to combine ideas within one sentence, unless a semi-colon is used.

wrong	Hitler attempted to conquer the Soviet Union however he was defeated.
right	Hitler attempted to conquer the Soviet Union; however, he was defeated.
or	Hitler attempted to conquer the Soviet Union. However, he was defeated.
or	Hitler attempted to conquer the Soviet Union but he was defeated.
wrong	There will not be regular mail pick-up from boxes this Friday, however regular mail pick-up will resume Saturday.
right	There will not be regular mail pick-up from boxes this Friday, but regular mail pick-up will resume Saturday.
or	There will not be regular mail pick-up from boxes this Friday. However, regular mail pick-up will resume Saturday.

(Note that *however* in the sense of *to whatever extent* may be used to introduce a clause: *However tired we are, we must finish the job tonight.*)

Nevertheless

Like *however*, *nevertheless* is normally used to show that the idea of one sentence seems to go against the idea of the previous sentence. It should not be used to join two clauses into one sentence. Example:

> According to the known laws of physics it is not possible to walk on water. Nevertheless, this is what the Bible claims Jesus did.

Whereas

This word is commonly used when one is comparing two things and showing how they differ. Like *although*, it must begin a subordinate

Common Errors in English # 451.

clause, and may be used either at the beginning or in the middle of a sentence.

e.g.   Whereas Americans are usually thought of as being loud and confident, Canadians tend to be more quiet and less sure of themselves.

or   Americans are usually thought of as being loud and confident, whereas Canadians tend to be more quiet and less sure of themselves.

---

452. Any sentence that uses *whereas* must have at least two clauses — a subordinate clause beginning with *whereas* <u>and</u> a main clause.

wrong   In 'The Rain Horse' a young person feels unhappy when he returns to his old home. Whereas in 'The Ice Palace' a young person feels unhappy when she leaves home for the first time.

right   In 'The Rain Horse' a young person feels unhappy when he returns to his old home, whereas in 'The Ice Palace' a young person feels unhappy when she leaves home for the first time.

While

---

453. **while:** *While* can be used in the same way as *although*. If there is any chance of confusion with the other meanings of *while*, however, it is better to use *although* in such circumstances.

wrong   While I support free trade in principle, I think it hurts this industry.

right   Although I support free trade in principle, I think it hurts this industry.

Yet

This word can be used either to refer to time (e.g., "He is not yet here"), or to connect ideas in opposition to each other. When used in this second way, it may introduce another word or a phrase, or a completely new sentence.

His spear was firm, yet flexible.

Barthes decries the language of "realism" — the pretence that one can represent on the page life as it really is. Yet it is difficult to see how following his prescriptions for an art of signs that "draw attention to their own arbitrariness" can entirely escape a tendency towards art that calls too much attention to its own surface, even art that is self-indulgent.

Common Errors in English # 452.

454. *Yet*, like the other words in this group, should not be paired with
another conjunction in such a way as to create too many twists and
turns in the argument.

wrong	Varying the pace, altering the tone, [director Joseph] Rubens keeps us off balance. Ultimately, though, that pedestrian script catches up with him, yet not before *Sleeping with the Enemy* has made its point.
	(The Globe and Mail, Feb. 8, 1991)

(The combination of *yet* and *though* is confusing for the reader.)

right	Varying the pace, altering the tone, [director Joseph] Rubens keeps us off balance. Ultimately, that pedestrian script catches up with him, yet not before *Sleeping with the Enemy* has made its point.

WORDS TO JOIN LINKED OR SUPPORTING IDEAS

also	indeed
and	in fact
as well	moreover
further	similarly
furthermore	: [colon]
in addition	; [semi-colon]
not only...but also	

Also, as well

These two are very similar both in meaning and in the way that they
are used. It is best not to use *also* to start sentences or paragraphs.
Examples:

He put forward his simplistic credo with enormous conviction. "To
do well at school," he assured us, "you must be willing to study. It
is also important to eat the right foods, exercise regularly, and get
plenty of sleep." While the one thing we all wanted, and none of us
had managed to get, was plenty of sex.

He put forward his simplistic credo with enormous conviction. "To
do well at school," he assured us, "you must be willing to study. It
is important as well to eat the right foods, exercise regularly, and
get plenty of sleep." While the one thing we all wanted, and none
of us had managed to get, was plenty of sex.

455. **also:** *Also* should not be used in the way that we often use *and* —
to join two clauses together into one sentence.

wrong	We performed the experiment with the beaker half full also we repeated it with the beaker empty.
right	We performed the experiment with the beaker half full and we repeated it with the beaker empty.
or	We performed the experiment with the beaker half full. We also repeated it with the beaker empty.

And

456. **and:** If this word appears more than once in the same sentence, it's worth stopping to ask if it would not be better to start a new sentence. Usually the answer will be yes.

wrong	All my family attended the celebration and most of my friends were there and we enjoyed ourselves thoroughly.
right	All my family attended the celebration and most of my friends were there too. We enjoyed ourselves thoroughly.
or	Recent studies indiocate that the average smoker is as much as three times as likely to develop cancer as is his non-smoking counterpart.

457. **as . . . as:** When making comparisons one may use the *as...as* combination **or** use a comparative adjective with *than*. But the two should not be combined.

wrong	Recent studies indicate that the average smoker is as much as three times as likely to develop cancer than his non-smoking counterpart. *(The Arizona Republic,* November 21, 1996)
right	Recent studies indicate that the average smoker is as much as three times more likely to develop cancer than his non-smoking counterpart.

458. **as well:** To avoid repetition, do not use *as well* in combination with *both*.

wrong	This method should be rejected, both because it is very expensive as well as because it is inefficient.
right	This method should be rejected, both because it is very expensive and because it is inefficient.

In addition, further, furthermore, moreover

All of these are commonly used to show that what the writer is saying gives additional support to an earlier statement she has made. An example:

> It is easy to see why many countries still trade with South Africa, despite their intense dislike of apartheid. For one thing, it is the richest country in Africa. Many of its resources, moreover, are of strategic importance.

Notice that all four expressions are often used after sentences that begin with words such as *for one thing* or *first*.

Indeed, in fact

Both of these are used to indicate that what the writer is saying is a restatement or elaboration of the idea he has expressed in the previous sentence. Notice that a colon or semi-colon may also be used to show this. Examples:

> Asia is the world's most populous continent. In fact, more people live there than in all the other continents combined.

> Asia is the world's most populous continent: more people live there than in all the other continents combined.

Not only...but also

459 **not only . . . but also:** This combination is used to join two pieces of supporting evidence in an argument. The combination can help to create balanced, rhythmic writing, but if it is to do so it must be used carefully. Notice that it is not necessary to use *but also* in all cases, but that if the phrase is omitted a semi-colon is normally required in order to avoid a run-on sentence.

wrong	Not only was Nirvana a commercial success, it was also among the first grunge bands to achieve musical respectability.
right	Not only was Nirvana a commercial success; it was also among the first grunge bands to achieve musical respectability.
or	Nirvana was not only a commercial success, but also a critical one; it was among the first grunge bands to achieve musical respectability.

Plus

460. **plus:** Do not use this word in the same way as *and* or *as well*.

wrong	For one thing, the Council did not much like the design for the proposed new City Hall. Plus, there was not enough money available to build it that year.
right	For one thing, the Council did not much like the design for the proposed new City Hall. As well, there was not enough money available to build it that year.

WORDS USED TO INTRODUCE CAUSES OR REASONS

The core of most arguments involves reasons why the writer's statements can be claimed to be true, and relationships of cause and effect. It is common to experience some difficulty at first in understanding such relationships clearly. The discussion below of the word *because* may be helpful in this respect. To begin with, though, here is a list of words that are used to introduce causes or reasons:

as	for
as a result of	on account of
because	since
due to	

As

This word can either be used to show the relationship between two events in time, or to indicate that one event is the cause of another. This sometimes leaves room for confusion about meaning (ambiguity). The following sentence is a good example:

As he was riding on the wrong side of the road, he was hit by a car.

This can mean either "When he was riding on the wrong side of the road..." or "Because he was riding on the wrong side of the road...." Unless the writer is absolutely certain that the meaning is clear, it may be better to use *while* or *when* instead of *as* to indicate relationships in time, and *because* instead of *as* to indicate relationships of cause and effect.

Common Errors in English # 460.

Because

This word creates many problems for writers. The first thing to remember is that any group of words introduced with *because* must state a cause or reason. It must *not* state a result or an example.

---

461. In the following sentences, *because* has been wrongly used:

wrong   The wind was blowing because the leaves were moving to and fro.

wrong   He had been struck by a car because he lay bleeding in the road.

A moment's reflection leads to the realization that both of these sentences are the wrong way round. The movement of the leaves is the <u>result</u> of the blowing of the wind, and the man's bleeding is the <u>result</u> of his having been hit. When the sentences are turned around, they become correct:

right   The leaves were moving to and fro because the wind was blowing.

right   He lay bleeding on the road because he had been struck by a car.

What leads many people to make mistakes like these is the sort of question that begins, "How do you know that..." or "Prove that..." or "Show that...." The person who is asked, "How do you know that the wind is blowing?" is likely to answer wrongly, "The wind is blowing because the leaves are moving to and fro." What he really means is, "I know the wind is blowing because I see the leaves moving to and fro." That answer is quite correct, since here the <u>seeing</u> is the cause of the <u>knowing</u>. Similarly, someone who is asked to show that the man in a story he has read has been hit by a car might answer wrongly, "He had been struck by a car because he lay bleeding in the road." What he really means is, "I <u>know</u> that he had been struck by a car because I <u>read</u> that he lay bleeding in the road."

It is of course awkward to use a lot of phrases such as "I know that" and "I see that." Here are some easier and better ways of answering such questions:

The movement of the trees shows that the wind is blowing.

The fact that the leaves are moving proves that the wind is blowing.

Since the man lay bleeding in the road, it seems likely that he had been hit by a car.

Common Errors in English # 461.

462. *Because* is also often used incorrectly to introduce examples. Look carefully at the following sentences:

wrong	The Suharto regime detained people in jail for long periods without ever bringing them to trial because it had little respect for the law.
wrong	In the story, 'The Hero,' Dora feels sorry for Julius because she sheds tears when he is expelled from school.

In these sentences the source of confusion may not be immediately clear. If we ask ourselves whether the fact that the regime did this <u>caused</u> it to have little respect for the law, however, we realize that the answer is no. Is the fact that Dora sheds tears a <u>cause</u> of her feeling sorry for Julius? Again, no. It may be a result of her feeling sorry, or an example chosen to show that she felt sorry, but it is certainly not a cause. Again, it is possible to correct these sentences as we did the ones above — by reversing the order of the ideas. But this may not always be an appropriate solution to the problem, particularly if what the writer is trying to show is an example or an illustration rather than a relationship of cause and effect. If, for example, one had been asked, "How do you know that Dora feels sorry for Julius?" or told to "Show that the Marcos regime had little respect for the law," one would not normally want to answer using *because*. Here are various ways of dealing with such difficulties:

> Dora feels sorry for Julius when he is expelled, as we can see when she sheds tears for him.

> It is clear that Dora feels sorry for Julius, since she sheds tears for him.

> We can see from the fact that Dora sheds tears for Julius that she feels sorry for him.

> The fact that the Suharto regime in Indonesia detained people for long periods without ever bringing them to trial shows that it had little respect for the law.

> The Suharto regime in Indonesia showed little respect for the law. It detained people for long periods, for example, without ever bringing them to trial.

> The Suharto regime in Indonesia had little respect for the law; it detained people for long periods without ever bringing them to trial.

Common Errors in English # 462.

Of all these examples the last is perhaps the best, since it is the most succinct.

---

463. It is best not to use *because* when listing several reasons for something; otherwise the writer gives the reader the impression that the first reason given is to be the only reason. The reader will then be surprised when others are mentioned.

wrong	He was happy because it was Friday. He was also happy because his team had won the game that morning and he had scored the winning goal. Finally, he was happy because he had done well on his exams.
right	He was happy for several reasons: it was Friday, he had scored the winning goal for his team that morning, and he had done well on his exams.
wrong	Frederick was able to enjoy such success because he was enormously adroit at waiting for the right opportunity, and seizing it when it was handed him. He was also successful because he created a military machine that had no equal.
right	One reason Frederick was able to enjoy such success was that he was enormously adroit at waiting for the right opportunity, and seizing it when it was handed him. But none of this would have been possible had he not also created a military machine that had no equal.

---

464. Some people like to answer "How...?" questions by using *because*. Instead, the word *by* should be used.

wrong	How did she help him? She helped him because she lent him some money.
right	How did she help him? She helped him by lending him some money.

Due to

---

465. **due to:** *Due* is an adjective and therefore should always modify a noun (as in the common phrase *with all due respect*). When followed by *to* it can suggest a causal relationship, but remember that the word *due* must in that case refer to the previous noun:

e.g.	The team's success is due to hard work.
	(*Due* refers to the noun *success*.)

Common Errors in English # 463.

It is not a good idea to begin a sentence with a phrase such as "Due to unexpected circumstances..." or "Due to the fact that...." To avoid such difficulties it is best to use *because*.

wrong	Due to the departure of our Sales Manager, the Marketing Director will take on additional responsibility for a short time.
right	Because our Sales Manager has resigned suddenly, the Marketing Director will take on additional responsibility for a short time.

Since

When used to introduce causes or reasons (rather than as a time word) *since* is used in essentially the same way as *because*.

WORDS USED TO INTRODUCE RESULTS OR CONCLUSIONS

as a result	therefore
consequently	thus
hence	to sum up
in conclusion	in consequence
it follows that...	so, and so

As a result, hence

Both of these are used to show that the idea being talked about in one sentence follows from, or is the result of, what was spoken of in the previous sentence.

e.g.	His car ran out of gas. As a result, he was late for his appointment.
or	His car ran out of gas. Hence, he was late for his appointment.

Notice the difference between these two and words such as *because* and *since*; we would say "Because [or since] his car ran out of gas, he was late for the appointment."

---

466. *Hence* should not be used to join two clauses into one sentence.

wrong	Her phone is out of order hence it will be impossible to contact her.
right	Her phone is out of order. Hence, it will be impossible to contact her.

Common Errors in English # 466.

| *wrong* | It is not the film but the advertising that is exploitative, hence pornographic. |
| *right* | It is not the film but the advertising that is exploitative, and hence pornographic. |

So

This word may be used to introduce results when one wants to mention both cause and result in the same sentence (e.g., "Her phone is out of order, so it will be impossible to contact her"). It is usually best not to use *so* to begin a sentence, in order to avoid writing sentence fragments.

---

467. If *so* is used, *because* is not needed, and vice versa. One of the two is enough.

wrong	Because he was tired, so he went to bed early.
right	Because he was tired, he went to bed early.
or	He was tired, so he went to bed early.

---

468. **therefore:** *Therefore* should not be used to join two clauses into one sentence.

| *wrong* | Training is perceived as good, therefore the payment of a $30 million subsidy to Chrysler can be made to look like a benign act. (*Wall Street Journal,* March 17, 1993) |
| *right* | Training is perceived as good; therefore the payment of a $30 million subsidy to Chrysler can be made to look like a benign act. |

WORDS USED TO EXPRESS PURPOSE

| in order to | so that |
| in such a way as to | so as to |

So that

---

469. **so that:** When used beside each other (see also *so . . . that* below) these two words show purpose; they indicate that we will be told <u>why</u> an action was taken. Examples:

He sent the parcel early so that it would arrive before Christmas.

She wants to see you so that she can ask you a question.

The words *such that* should never be used in this way to indicate purpose.

wrong	The doctor will give you some medicine such that you will be cured.
right	The doctor will give you some medicine so that you will be cured.
wrong	Fold the paper such that it forms a triangle.
right	Fold the paper so that it forms a triangle.
or	Fold the paper in such a way that it forms a triangle.

WORDS USED TO INTRODUCE EXAMPLES

for example   such as
for instance   : [colon]
in that

For example, for instance, such as

The three expressions are used differently, even though they all introduce examples. *Such as* is used to introduce a single word or short phrase. It always relates to a plural noun that has appeared just before it.

Crops such as tea and rice require a great deal of water.
(Here *such as* relates to the noun crops.)

Several African tribes, such as the Yoruba of Nigeria and the Makonde of Tanzania, attach a special ceremonial importance to masks.
(*Such as* relates to tribes.)

For example and *for instance*, on the other hand, are complete phrases in themselves, and are normally set off by commas. Each is used to show that the entire sentence in which it appears gives an example of a statement made in the previous sentence. Examples:

Some crops require a great deal of water. Tea, for example, requires an annual rainfall of at least 1500 mm.

Several African peoples attach a special ceremonial importance to masks. The Yoruba and the Makonde, for example, both believe that spirits enter the bodies of those who wear certain masks.

Tornadoes are not only a Deep South phenomenon. In 1987, for instance, over 20 people were killed by a tornado in Edmonton, Alberta.

Common Errors in English # 469.

470. *For example* and *for instance* should not be used to introduce phrases that give examples. In such situations use *such as* instead.

wrong	In certain months of the year, for example July and August, Penticton receives very little rainfall.
right	In certain months of the year, such as July and August, Penticton receives very little rainfall.
or	In certain months of the year Penticton receives very little rainfall. July and August, for example, are almost always extremely dry.

In that

471. **in that:** Do not confuse with *in the way that*.

wrong	He is cruel in the way that he treats his wife harshly.
right	He is cruel in that he treats his wife cruelly.
or	He is cruel in the way that he treats his wife.

Such as

472. **such as:** The addition of *and others* at the end of a phrase beginning with *such as* is redundant.

wrong	In contrast to this perspective, sociological studies of ethnicity written from the 'class' perspective (such as Bollaria and Li, Chan, Cormack, and others) have argued that ethnic inequality is only a special class of inequality in general.
right	In contrast to this perspective, sociological studies of ethnicity written from the 'class' perspective (such as Bollaria and Li; Chan; and Cormack) have argued that ethnic inequality is only a special class of inequality in general.

WORDS USED TO INDICATE ALTERNATIVES

either...or	otherwise
if only	rather than
instead, instead of	unless
in that case	whether...or
neither...nor	or

If only

This expression is normally used when we wish that something would happen, or were true, but it clearly will not happen, or is not true.

If only he were here, he would know what to do.
(This indicates that he is not here.)

Common Errors in English # 470.

"If only there were thirty hours in a day..." she kept saying.

In that case

This expression is used when we wish to explain what will happen if the thing spoken of in the previous sentence happens, or turns out to be true. Examples:

> He may arrive before six o'clock. In that case we can all go out to dinner.

> It is quite possible that many people will dislike the new law. In that case the government may decide to change it.

Do not confuse *in that case* with *otherwise*, which is used in the reverse situation (i.e., when one wishes to explain what will happen if the thing spoken of in the previous sentence does <u>not</u> happen, or turns out to be false.)

Otherwise

This word has two meanings. The first is *in other ways* (e.g. "I have a slight toothache. Otherwise I am healthy"). The second meaning can sometimes cause confusion: *otherwise* used to mean *if not*. Here the word is used when we want to talk about what will or may happen if the thing spoken of in the previous sentence does not happen. Examples:

> I will have to start immediately. Otherwise I will not finish in time.
>
> (This is the same as saying, "If I do not start now, I will not finish in time.")
>
> The general decided to retreat. Otherwise, he believed, all his troops would be killed.
>
> (This is the same as saying, "The general believed that if he decided not to retreat, all his troops would be killed.")
>
> You must pay me for the car before Friday. Otherwise I will offer it to someone else.
>
> (i.e., "If you do not pay me for the car before Friday, I will offer it to someone else.")

---

473. When used to mean *if not*, *otherwise* should normally be used to start a new sentence. It should not be used in the middle of a sentence to join two clauses.

Common Errors in English # 473.

wrong	I may meet you at the party tonight, otherwise I will see you tomorrow.
right	I may see you at the party tonight. Otherwise I will see you tomorrow.

WORDS USED TO SHOW DEGREE OR EXTENT

for the most part	to some extent
so...that	too...for...to
such...that	to some degree
to a certain extent	

So . . . that

474. so . . . that: When separated from each other by an adjective or adverb, these two words express degree or extent, answering questions such as "How far . . . ?", "How big . . . ?", "How much. . . ?". Examples:

How fat is he? He is so fat that he cannot see his feet.

How large is Canada? It is so large that you need about six days to drive across it.

So...that is the only combination of words that can be used in this way; it is wrong to say "very fat that..." or "too large that," just as it is wrong to leave out the word *so* and simply use *that* in such sentences.

wrong	She was very late for dinner that there was no food left for her.
right	She was so late for dinner that there was no food left for her.
wrong	Dominic speaks quickly that it is often difficult to understand him.
right	Dominic speaks so quickly that it is often difficult to understand him.

Such . . . that

475. such . . . that: Like *so . . . that*, the expression *such . . . that* is used to express degree or extent, answering questions such as, "How big . . . ?", "How long . . . ?", "How fast . . . ?". Notice the difference in the way the two are used.

right	How far is it? It is <u>such</u> a long way <u>that</u> you would never be able to get there walking.

Common Errors in English # 474.

or	It is <u>so</u> far <u>that</u> you would never be able to reach there walking.
right	How fat is he? He is <u>such</u> a fat man <u>that</u> his trousers need to be made specially for him.
or	He is <u>so</u> fat <u>that</u> his trousers need to be made specially for him.

The difference between the two is of course that only <u>one</u> word is normally used between *so* and *that*, whereas two or three words (usually an article, an adjective, and a noun) are used between *such* and *that*. Be careful not to confuse the two, or to leave out *such*.

| *wrong* | It was a hot day that nobody could stay outside for long. |
| *right* | It was such a hot day that nobody could stay outside for long. |

That and which

To understand when to use *that* and when to use *which* one must understand the difference between a restrictive and a non-restrictive clause. A restrictive clause restricts the application of the noun it modifies. Here is an example:

> The horse that was injured yesterday should recover.

Here the clause *that was injured yesterday* restricts the meaning of the subject of the sentence — *horse* — to a particular horse. The clause helps to define the subject. A non-restrictive clause does not restrict the application of the noun it modifies.

> The injured horse, which was the favorite to win the race, should recover in time for the Derby.

Here the clause *which was the favorite to win the race* tells us more about the horse but is not necessary to its definition. Notice that the non-restrictive clause is set off by commas. Restrictive clauses, on the other hand, follow directly on after the noun they describe. As you can see, *that* is used with restrictive clauses, and *which* with non-restrictive ones.

Common Errors in English # 475.

476. **which:** The use of the word *which* provokes a violent reaction among many English instructors. They are frequently irritated by the number of times *which* is used incorrectly in restrictive clauses:

wrong	The only store which sells this brand is now closed.
right	The only store that sells this brand is now closed.
wrong	The position which Marx adopted owed much to the philosophy of Hegel.
right	The position that Marx adopted owed much to the philosophy of Hegel.

There are some instances, however, in which one is quite justified in using *which* in a restrictive clause. Such is the case when the writer is already using at least one *that* in the sentence:

wrong	He told me that the radio that he bought was defective.
right	He told me that the radio which he had bought was defective.

Better yet is to avoid the use of a second relative pronoun by rephrasing:

right	He told me that the radio he had bought was defective.

Indeed, instructors who object to *which* point out that often rephrasing can make the sentence shorter and crisper:

fair	The ending, which comes as a surprise to most readers, is profoundly unsettling.
better	The ending is both surprising and unsettling.
fair	The 1999 campaign, which had been carefully planned, was an enormous success.
better	The carefully-planned 1999 campaign was an enormous success.

But *which* is not a special case in this regard. *That, who* and *whose* can often be fruitfully removed in the same way:

fair	The surplus that we now project for 2002 will probably be exceeded in 2003.
better	The projected 2002 surplus will probably be exceeded in 2003.
fair	Eisenhower hired as his personal driver a woman who turned into a long-term friend.
better	Eisenhower and his driver became close friends.

Common Errors in English # 476.

The vice, then, is not *which* per se, but wordiness in general. Those who focus their attention on the one word and rail that "witches ride on broomsticks" might do better to treat the excessive use of *which* as a symptom of a much broader disease.

WORDS USED TO MAKE COMPARISONS

by comparison	on the one hand...
in contrast	...on the other hand

OTHER JOINING WORDS AND EXPRESSIONS

as illustrated above/below	in other words
as mentioned above/below	in the event of
as we can see/we can see that	in the light of
assuming that	in this respect/in some respects
as shown in the diagram	above/below
in that	firstly/in the first place
these findings indicate that	secondly/in the second place
to begin with	for one thing
whereby	

Common Errors in English # 476.

PUNCTUATION

The Period

■ The most important mark of punctuation is the full stop (or period), which is used to separate one sentence from another, and the most common punctuation mistakes involve the use of the full stop. The first of these is the run-on sentence: a sentence that continues running on and on instead of being broken up into two or more sentences. (Where a comma has been used instead of a period, the term *comma splice* is often used to denote a run-on sentence.) The second is the incomplete sentence (or *sentence fragment*): a group of words that has been written as if it were a full sentence, but that needs something else to make it complete.

477. **run-on sentence/comma splice:** The basic idea of a sentence is that it expresses one complete idea. Often, remembering this simple fact will be enough to keep run-on sentences at bay, particularly if one reads work over to oneself (aloud, if it's not too embarrassing) and notices where one pauses naturally.

wrong	Early last Thursday we were walking in the woods it was a bright and clear morning.
right	Early last Thursday we were walking in the woods. It was a bright and clear morning.

In the above example it should be quite clear that there are two separate ideas, and that these should be put into two separate sentences. Sometimes, though, it is not so simple. In particular, certain words may be used to join two clauses into one sentence, while other words should not be used in this way. We have already seen (in our survey of joining words) some examples of words that cause problems of this sort. Here is a review:

Common Errors in English # 477.

and: The appearance of more than one *and* in a sentence is often a sign that the ideas would be better rephrased.

wrong	Beaverbrook effectively mobilized the resources of the country to serve the war effort overseas and he later was knighted and he is also well-known for creating a media empire.
right	Beaverbrook effectively mobilized the resources of the country to serve the war effort — an accomplishment for which he later was knighted. He is also well-known for creating a media empire.
or	Beaverbrook, who had created a vast media empire before the war, then distinguished himself by effectively mobilizing the resources of the country to serve the war effort. It was in recognition of this service that he was knighted.
or	Beaverbrook, who had created a vast media empire before the war, then distinguished himself by effectively mobilizing the resources of the country to serve the war effort; it was in recognition of this service that he was knighted.

hence:

wrong	With the exception of identical twins no two people have exactly the same genetic makeup hence it is impossible for two people to look exactly the same.
right	With the exception of identical twins no two people have exactly the same genetic makeup. Hence, it is impossible for two people to look exactly the same.

however:

wrong	During the rainy season more water flows over Victoria Falls than over any other falls in the world however several other falls are higher than Victoria.
right	During the rainy season more water flows over Victoria Falls than over any other falls in the world. However, several other falls are higher than Victoria.
or	During the rainy season more water flows over Victoria Falls than over any other falls in the world; several other falls, however, are higher than Victoria.

otherwise:

wrong	You had better leave now otherwise we will call the police.
right	You had better leave now. Otherwise, we will call the police.
or	You had better leave now; otherwise, we will call the police.

Common Errors in English # 477.

therefore:

wrong	Training is perceived as good, therefore the payment of a $30 million subsidy to Chrysler can be made to look like a benign act.
	(*Wall Street Journal*, March 17, 1993)
right	Training is perceived as good; therefore the payment of a $30 million subsidy to Chrysler can be made to look like a benign act.

Notice in the above cases that one way to correct a comma splice is often to use a semi-colon. Unlike a comma, a semi-colon may be used as a connector between clauses. (The exercise on page 270 may be helpful in this connection.)

An even more common cause of run-on sentences than any of the above is the word *then*.

---

478. **then:** Unlike *when*, *then* should not be used to join two clauses together into one sentence. *And then* may be used, or a semi-colon, or a new sentence may be begun.

wrong	We applied the solution to the surface of the leaves then we made observations at half-hour intervals over the next twelve hours.
right	We applied the solution to the surface of the leaves. Then we made observations at half-hour intervals over the next twelve hours.
or	We applied the solution to the surface of the leaves; then we made observations at half-hour intervals over the next twelve hours.
or	We applied the solution to the surface of the leaves and then we made observations at half-hour intervals over the next twelve hours.
wrong	On June 10, 1999 Yugoslav troops began withdrawing, then the NATO bombing was suspended and the war in Kosovo ended.
right	On June 10, 1999 Yugoslav troops began withdrawing. Then the NATO bombing was suspended and the war in Kosovo ended.
wrong	The Montreal Canadiens produced vital late-period goals then they wrapped their iron defense around the Calgary Flames to take an upper hand in the game.
right	The Montreal Canadiens produced vital late-period goals and then wrapped their iron defense around the Calgary Flames to take an upper hand in the game.

---

479. **abbreviations:** The period is also used to form abbreviations. If in any doubt about whether or not to use a period in an abbreviation,

or where to put it, think of (or look up) the full form of what is being
abbreviated.

wrong	Jones, Smithers et. al. will be there in person.
	(et al. is short for the Latin et alia, "and others".
right	Jones, Smithers et al. will be there in person.

---

480. **incomplete sentences:** A good writer always asks herself as she
checks her work if each sentence is complete in itself; in this way the
more obvious errors will almost always be caught. For example, if
"When the meeting ends tomorrow" is in the rough draft as a
complete sentence, re-reading will probably lead to the realization
that the idea is not complete; the group of words needs another
group of words to finish it (e.g., "When the meeting ends tomorrow
we should have a comprehensive agreement.") Be particularly
careful with longer sentences to make sure they are complete. For
example, the group of words "Marina walked to the sea" is a
complete sentence, but the following sentence is incomplete, even
though it is much longer; it doesn't tell us what happened when she
was walking.

wrong	While Marina was walking to the sea and thinking of her father and the sound of a woodthrush.
right	While Marina was walking to the sea she heard the sound of a woodthrush and thought of her father.
wrong	Unemployment was a serious problem in Britain in the early 1990s. In fact, throughout the world.
right	Unemployment was a serious serious problem in the early 1990s, both in Britain and abroad.
wrong	So long as you have a place to live and enough to eat.
right	So long as you have a place to live and enough to eat, you have some reason to be thankful.

The three words which most frequently lead students to write
incomplete sentences are *and*, *because* and *so*.

---

481. **and:** Although there are certain cases in which it is possible to
begin a sentence with *and*, these are extremely difficult to sense. It
is usually better for all except professional writers not to begin
sentences with *and* if they wish to avoid incomplete sentences.

worth checking	To make this crop grow well you should add Compound 'D' fertilizer to the soil. And you should

	add top dressing a few months later.
right	To make this crop grow well you should add Compound 'D' fertilizer to the soil, and top dressing a few months later.

482. **because:** In order to prevent young children who have difficulty in writing long sentences from writing incomplete sentences, many primary school teachers wisely tell their pupils not to begin sentences with *because*. In fact it is not incorrect to begin with *because*, so long as the sentence is complete. The rule to remember is that any sentence with *because* in it must mention <u>both</u> the cause <u>and</u> the result. Whether the word *because* comes at the beginning or in the middle of the sentence does not matter; what is important is that the sentence has two parts.

wrong	In the early 1980s Sandinista leaders told their people to be ready for war. Because the United States had been trying to destabilize Nicaragua.
right	In the early 1980s Sandinista leaders told their people to be ready for war, because the United States had been trying to destabilize Nicaragua.
wrong	Because of the cold and wet weather which affected the whole area. Many people were desperately trying to find more firewood.
right	Because of the cold and wet weather which affected the whole area many people were desperately trying to find more firewood.

483. **so:** This word is probably the biggest single cause of incomplete sentences. As is the case with *and*, there are certain situations in which professional writers manage to get away with beginning sentences with *so*, but normally this should not be attempted. *So* should be used to join ideas together into one sentence, not to separate them by starting a new sentence.

wrong	I did not know what was happening. So my friends explained the procedure to me.
right	I did not know what was happening, so my friends explained the procedure to me.
wrong	The meat was too heavily spiced. So most of it had to be thrown away.
right	The meat was too heavily spiced, so most of it had to be thrown away.

Ellipses

Three dots are used to indicate the omission of one or more words needed to complete a sentence or other grammatical construction.

---

484. Note that when used in quotation ellipses come *inside* the quotation marks, and that when ellipses precede a period the sentence should end with *four* dots.

wrong	Harris shows more than a trace of paranoia in her book; she speaks, for example, of "the elements trying to subvert the essence of liberal society, of tolerance, of goodwill... They are all around us."
right	Harris shows more than a trace of paranoia in her book; she speaks, for example, of "the elements trying to subvert the essence of liberal society, of tolerance, of goodwill.... They are all around us."

The Comma

Although the omission or wrong use of a comma sounds like a small mistake, it can be very important. The following group of words, for example, forms a sentence only if a comma is included.

wrong	Because of the work that we had done before we were ready to hand in the assignment.
right	Because of the work that we had done before, we were ready to hand in the assignment.

The omission or addition of a comma can also completely alter the meaning of a sentence — as it did in the Queen's University Alumni letter that spoke of the warm emotions still felt by alumni for "our friends, who are dead," (rather than "our friends who are dead"). The second would have been merely a polite remembrance of those alumni who have died; the first suggests that *all* the friends of the reader are dead.

---

485. **omission of commas:** Commas very commonly come in pairs, and it is common to omit the second comma in a pair. Be particularly careful when putting commas around a name, or around an adjectival subordinate clause.

wrong	My sister Caroline, has done very well this year in her studies.
right	My sister, Caroline, has done very well this year in her

studies.

wrong	The snake which had been killed the day before, was already half-eaten by ants.
right	The snake, which had been killed the day before, was already half-eaten by ants.

486. **extra comma:** Writers often add a comma when they feel a sentence is getting long, regardless of whether one is needed or is appropriate.

wrong	The ever-increasing gravitational pull of the global economy, is drawing almost every area of the earth into its orbit.
right	The ever-increasing gravitational pull of the global economy is drawing almost every area of the earth into its orbit.

487. **terminal comma:** An important use of commas is to separate the entries in lists. Many authorities feel that a comma need not appear between the last and second-last entries in a list, since these are usually separated already by the word *and*. Omitting the terminal comma will occasionally lead to ambiguity, though; when in doubt, include the terminal comma. And when the list includes items that have commas within them, use a semi-colon to separate the items in the list.

wrong	This book is dedicated to my parents, Ayn Rand and God.
right	This book is dedicated to my parents, Ayn Rand, and God.

wrong	The three firms involved were McCarthy and Walters, Harris, Jones, and Engleby, and Cassells and Wirtz.
right	The three firms involved were McCarthy and Walters; Harris, Jones, and Engleby; and Cassells and Wirtz.

The Question Mark

488. All students know that a question should be followed by a question mark, but it is easy to forget, particularly if one is writing quickly or if the question mark should appear within other punctuation.

wrong	Would Britain benefit from closer ties with Europe. Almost 30 years after the UK joined the EC, the question continues to bedevil British political life.

Common Errors in English # 486.

right   Would Britain benefit from closer ties with Europe?
                 Almost 30 years after the UK joined the EC, the
                 question continues to bedevil British political life.

The Exclamation Mark

!

This mark is used to give extremely strong emphasis to a statement. It should be used very sparingly, if at all, in formal written work: most good writers avoid it completely, since they realize that it does not lend any additional impact to what they are saying.

The Semi-colon

;

This mark is used to separate ideas that are closely related to each other. In most cases a period could be used instead; the semi-colon simply signals to the reader the close relationship between the two ideas. In the following example the second sentence reinforces the statement of the first; a semi-colon is thus appropriate, although a period is also correct.

                 This book is both exciting and profound. It is one of
                 the best books I have read.
or   This book is both exciting and profound; it is one of
                 the best books I have read.

Similarly in the following example the second sentence gives evidence supporting the statement made in the first sentence. Again, a semi-colon is appropriate.

                 The team is not as good as it used to be. It has lost
                 four of its past five games.
or   The team is not as good as it used to be; it has lost
                 four of its last five games.

The semi-colon is also used occasionally to divide items in a series that includes other punctuation:

                 The following were told to report to the coach after
                 practice: Jackson, Form 2B; Marshall, Form 3A;
                 Gladys, Form 1B.

Common Errors in English # 488.

The Colon

: This mark is often believed to be virtually the same as the semi-colon in the way it is used. In fact, there are some important differences. The most common uses of the colon are as follows:

- in headings, to announce that more is to follow, or that the writer is about to list a series of things
- introducing a quotation
- between two clauses, indicating that the second one provides an explanation of what was stated in the first

This last use is very similar to the main use of the semi-colon. The subtle differences are that the semi-colon can be used in such situations when the ideas are not quite so closely related, and the colon asks the reader to pause for a slightly longer period. Note that a colon must be preceded by an independent clause; what comes before it, in other words, could be a full sentence on its own. Here are some examples:

UNQUIET UNION: A Study of the Federation of Rhodesia and Nyasaland.

In the last four weeks he has visited five different countries: Mexico, Venezuela, Panama, Haiti, and Belize.

The theory of the Communists may be summed up in the single phrase: abolition of private property.

---

489. Be sure to use a colon to introduce a list.

wrong	The operation in Toronto has supplied Mr. Bomersbach with four luxury cars, two Cadillacs, a Mercedes, and a Jaguar.
	(The Globe and Mail)
right	The operation in Toronto has supplied Mr. Bomersbach with four luxury cars: two Cadillacs, a Mercedes, and a Jaguar.

The Hyphen

- This mark may be used to separate two parts of a compound word (e.g., tax-free, hand-operated). Notice that many such word

Common Errors in English # 489.

combinations are only hyphenated if the combination acts as an adjective:

> No change is planned for the short term.
> (*Term* acts here as a noun, with the adjective *short* modifying it.)
> This is only a short-term plan.
> (Here the compound acts as a single adjective, modifying the noun *plan*.)

Hyphens are also used to break a word at the end of a line if there is not enough space.

---

490. A hyphen should never be used to break up proper nouns, and should only be used to break up other words when it is placed between syllables. Any noun beginning with a capital letter (e.g., Halifax, Mulroney, January, Harriet) is a proper noun.

wrong	Thomas Huxley coined the word "agnostic" to refer to someone who does not believ-e in the existence of God, but is not prepared to rule out the possibility either.
right	Thomas Huxley coined the word "agnostic" to refer to someone who does not believe in the existence of God, but is not prepared to rule out the possibility either.

Whenever one is uncertain about whether or not to use a hyphen, the easy solution is to put the entire word on the next line.

The Dash

Dashes are often used in much the same way as parentheses, to set off an idea within a sentence. Dashes, however, call attention to the set-off idea in a way that parentheses do not:

> Peterborough, Ontario (home of Broadview Press) is a pleasant city of 70,000.

> Peterborough, Ontario — home of Broadview Press — is a pleasant city of 70,000.

A dash may also be used in place of a colon to set off a word or phrase at the end of a sentence:

> He fainted when he heard how much he had won: one million dollars.

Common Errors in English # 490.

> He fainted when he heard how much he had won — one million dollars.

491. Most typewriters and word processors do not have a dash on the keyboard; in such circumstances use — (instead of -) to distinguish a dash from a hyphen.

wrong	Malaysia's Petronas Towers-the tallest buildings in the world-were completed in 1997. A tower in Shanghai is expected to surpass the record early in the new century.
right	Malaysia's Petronas Towers—the tallest buildings in the world—were completed in 1997. A tower in Shanghai is expected to surpass the record early in the new century.

Parentheses

( )

Parentheses are used to set off an interruption in the middle of a sentence, or to make a point which is not part of the main flow of the sentence. They are frequently used to give examples, or to express something in other words using the abbreviation *i.e.*. Example:

> Several world leaders of the 1980s (Deng in China, Reagan in the US, etc.) were very old men.

Square brackets

[ ]

Square brackets are used for parentheses within parentheses, or to show that the words within the parentheses are added by another person.

> Lentricchia claims that "in reading James' Preface [to *What Maisie Knew*] one is struck as much by what is omitted as by what is revealed."

Apostrophe

,

The two main uses of the apostrophe are to show possession (e.g., "Peter's book") and to shorten certain common word combinations

Common Errors in English # 491.

(e.g., *can't, shouldn't, he's*).

---

492. Misuse of the apostrophe:. This error may occur either through the use of a contraction in an inappropriate context, or through a failure to understand or to remember the function of the apostrophe in showing possession.

Contractions are used frequently in this book, which is relatively informal in its style. Abbreviations or contractions, however, should not be used in more formal written work. Use *cannot*, not *can't; did not*, not *don't*; and so on.

informal	The experiment wasn't a success, because we'd heated the solution to too high a temperature.
more formal	The experiment was not a success, because we had heated the solution to too high a temperature.

The correct placing of the apostrophe to show possession can be a tricky matter. When the noun is singular, the apostrophe must come before the *s* (e.g., *Peter's, George's, Canada's*), whereas when the noun is plural and ends in an *s* already, add the apostrophe after the *s*.

wrong	We have been asked to dinner by Harriets mother.
right	We have been asked to dinner by Harriet's mother.
worth checking	His parent's house is filled with antiques.
right	His parents' house is filled with antiques.
wrong	All three groups of parents attended their infant's one month pediatric checkup, and observations were made of father's interactions with their infants.
right	All three groups of parents attended their infants' one month pediatric checkup, and observations were made of fathers' interactions with their infants.

When a singular noun already ends in *s*, authorities differ as to whether or not a second *s* should be added after the apostrophe:

correct	Ray Charles' music has been very influential.
correct	Ray Charles's music has been very influential.

Whichever convention a writer chooses, he should be consistent. And be sure in such cases not to put the apostrophe before the first *s*.

wrong	Shield's novel is finely, yet delicately constructed.
	(concerning novelist Carol Shields)
right	Shields' novel is finely, yet delicately constructed.
	[or "Shields's novel")

Quotation Marks

" "

The main use of quotation marks is to show that the exact words spoken or written are being repeated, For a discussion of difficulties associated with this use see the chapter on direct and indirect speech immediately following.

According to different coventions, words that are being mentioned rather than used may be set off by quotation marks, single quotation marks, or italics:

The words "except" and "accept" are sometimes confused.

The words 'except' and 'accept' are sometimes confused.

The words *except* and *accept* are sometimes confused.

Quotation marks (or single quotation marks) are sometimes used to indicate that the writer does not endorse the quoted statement, claim, or description. Quotation marks are usually used in this way only with a word or a brief phrase. When they are so used they have the connotation of *supposed* or *so-called*; they suggest that the quoted word or phrase is either euphemistic or downright false:

After a violent workout the weightlifters would each a "snack" of a steak sandwich, a half-dozen eggs, several pieces of bread and butter, and a quart of tomato juice.

In the following two versions of the same report the more sparing use of quotation marks in the second version signals clearly to the reader the writer's scepticism as to the honesty of the quoted claim.

President Yeltsin appeared to stagger as he left the plane. "The President is feeling tired and emotional," his Press Secretary later reported.

Common Errors in English # 492.

A "tired and emotional" President Yeltsin appeared to stagger as he left the plane.

---

493. **misuse of quotation marks to indicate emphasis** Quotation marks (unlike italics, bold letters, capital letters or underlining) should never be used to try to lend emphasis to a particular word or phrase. Because quotation marks may be used to convey the sense *supposed* or *so-called* (see above), the common misuse of quotation marks to try to lend emphasis often creates ludicrous effects.

> *wrong*   All our bagels are served "fresh" daily.
>   (The unintended suggestion here is that the claim of freshness is a dubious one.)
> *right*   All our bagels are served fresh daily.
> *or*   All our bagels are served **fresh** daily.
>   (if emphasis is required in an advertisement)
> *wrong*   Dogs must be "leashed". (BC ferries sign, January 1998)
> *right*   Dogs must be leashed.

Single Quotation Marks

' '

In North America the main use of single quotation marks is to mark quotations within quotations:

> According to the Press Secretary, "When the President said, 'I never inhaled,' he meant it."

Depending on convention, single quotation marks may also be used to show that a word or phrase is being mentioned rather than used (see above, p. 164).

In the United Kingdom and some other countries, quotation marks and single quotation marks are used for direct speech in precisely the opposite way that North Americans use them; single quotation marks (or inverted commas, as they are sometimes called) are used for direct speech, and double marks are used for quotations within quotations. Here is the correct British version of the above sentence:

> According to the Press Secretary, 'When the President said, "I never inhaled", he meant it.'

Note here that UK usage also places the comma outside the quotation mark.

DIRECT AND INDIRECT SPEECH

Direct Speech

Direct speech is a written record of the exact words used by the person speaking. The main rules for writing direct speech in English are as follows:

- The exact words spoken — and no other words — must be surrounded by quotation marks (inverted commas).

- A comma should precede a quotation, but according to American convention other punctuation should be placed inside the quotation marks. Examples:
  He said, "I think I can help you."
  (The period after *you* comes before the quotation marks.)
  "Drive slowly," she said, "and be very careful."
  (The comma after *slowly* and period after *careful* both come inside the quotation marks.)

- With each change in speaker a new paragraph should be begun. Example:
  "Let's go fishing this weekend," Mary suggested. "It should be nice and cool by the water."
  "Good idea," agreed Faith. "I'll meet you by the store early Saturday morning."

British convention, however, places the punctuation *outside* the quotation marks:

'An iron curtain is descending across Europe', declared Winston Churchill in 1946.

Canadian usage allows writers either to follow the American convention *or* to make an exception when the punctuation clearly pertains only to the structure of the surrounding sentence and not to the quoted word or phrase:

"An iron curtain is descending across Europe," declared

Common Errors in English # 493.

Winston Churchill in 1946.

Churchill described the post-war division between newly Communist Eastern Europe and the West as "an iron curtain".

The most common difficulties experienced when recording direct speech are as follows:

---

494. omission of quotation marks: This happens particularly frequently at the end of a quotation.

wrong	She said, "I will try to come to see you tomorrow. Then she left.
right	She said, "I will try to come to see you tomorrow." Then she left.

---

495. placing punctuation outside the quotation marks:

wrong	He shouted, "The house is on fire"!
right	He shouted, "The house is on fire!"

---

496. including the word "that" before direct speech: *That* is used before passages of indirect speech, <u>not</u> before passages of direct speech.

wrong	My brother said that, "I think I have acted stupidly."
right	My brother said, "I think I have acted stupidly."
or	My brother said that he thought he had acted stupidly.
wrong	The official indicated that, "we are not prepared to allow galloping inflation."
right	The official said, "We are not prepared to allow galloping inflation."
or	The official indicated that his government was not prepared to allow galloping inflation.

---

497. In a formal essay, any quotation longer than three lines should normally be single-spaced and indented to set it off from the body of the text. Any quotation of more than a single line from a poem should also be single-spaced and indented. Quotations set off from the body of the text in this way should not be preceded or followed by quotation marks.

wrong

> Larkin's last great poem, 'Aubade', is haunted by the fear of death: "Not to be here, Not to be anywhere, And

Common Errors in English # 494.

soon; nothing more terrible, nothing more true." Some have called the vision of the poem unremittingly grim, but it is filled with subtle shadings.

right

Larkin's last great poem, 'Aubade', is haunted by the fear of death:

> Not to be here,
> Not to be anywhere,
> And soon; nothing more terrible, nothing more true.

Some have called the vision of the poem unremittingly grim, but it is filled with subtle shadings.

See under **Sequence of Tenses** (p. 19) and **Writing About Literature** (pp. 214-16) for discussions of other difficulties in using quotation.

Indirect Speech

Indirect speech reports what was said without using the same words that were used by the speaker. The rules for writing indirect speech are as follows:

- Do not use quotation marks.

- Introduce statements with the word *that*, and do not put a comma after *that*. Questions should be introduced with the appropriate question word (*what, why, whether, if, how, when,* etc.)

- Change first person pronouns and adjectives (e.g., *I, me, we, us, my, our*) to third person ones (*he, she, they, him, her, them, his, hers,* etc.).

"I am not happy with our team's performance," said Paul.

Paul said that he was not happy with his team's performance.

- Second person pronouns must also sometimes be changed.
- Change the tenses of the verbs to agree with the main verb of the sentence. Usually this involves moving the verbs one step back into the past from the tenses that were used by the speaker in direct speech. Notice in the above example, for instance, that the present tense *am* has been changed to the past tense *was* in indirect speech. Here are other examples:

Common Errors in English # 497.

"We will do everything we can," he assured me.

He assured me that they would do everything they could.

(*Will* and *can* change to *would* and *could*.)

"You went to school near Brandon, didn't you?" he asked me.

He asked me if I had gone to school near Brandon.

(*Went* changes to *had gone*.)

● Change expressions having to do with time. This is made necessary by the changes in verbs discussed above. For example, *today* in direct speech normally becomes *on that day* in indirect speech, *yesterday* becomes *on the day before*, *tomorrow* becomes *the next day,* and so on.

The most common problems made when indirect speech is being used are as follows:

---

498. **confusion of pronouns:** Many writers do not remember to change all the necessary pronouns when shifting from direct to indirect speech.

When I met him he said, "You have cheated me."

(direct speech)

wrong	When I met him he said that you had cheated me.
right	When I met him he said that I had cheated him.

He will probably say to you, "I am poor. I need money."

wrong	He will probably tell you that he is poor and that I need money.
right	He will probably tell you that he is poor and that he needs money.

---

499. **verb tenses:** Remember to shift the tenses of the verbs one step back into the past when changing something into indirect speech.

She said, "I will check my tires tomorrow."

wrong	She said that she will check her tires the next day.
right	She said that she would check her tires the next day.

"Can I go with you later this afternoon?" he asked.

wrong	He asked if he can go with us later that afternoon.
right	He asked if he could go with us later that afternoon.

Common Errors in English # 498.

PARAGRAPHING

499. error in paragraphing: There is a degree of flexibility when it comes to the matter of where and how often to start new paragraphs. Sometimes a subtle point in an argument will require a paragraph of almost an entire page to elaborate; occasionally a single sentence can form an effective paragraph. Yet separating ideas into paragraphs remains an important aid to the processes of both reading and writing. Here are some guidelines as to when it is appropriate to begin a new paragraph:

a) in narration :

- whenever the story changes direction ("This was the moment Preston Manning had been waiting for...", "When Napoleon left Elba he...")

- when there is a gap in time in the story ("Two weeks later the issue was raised again in cabinet...")

b) in description:

- whenever you switch from describing one place, person or thing to describing another ("Even such a brief description as this has been is enough to give some sense of the city and its pretensions. Much more interesting in many ways are some of British Columbia's smaller cities and towns... ")

c) in persuasion or argument:

- when a new topic is introduced ("There can be little doubt that Austen's asides on the literary conventions of her time provide an amusing counterpoint to her story. But does this running commentary detract from the primary imaginative experience of *Northanger Abbey*?")

- when there is a change in direction of the argument ("To this point we have been looking only at the advantages of a guaranteed annual income. We should also ask, however, whether or not it would be practical to implement.")

d) when changing from one mode to another:

- Description, narration and argument are commonly blended together in writing. If, for example, a text moves from describing an experiment to analysing its significance, it's a good time to start a new paragraph. If it moves from telling where Napoleon went and what he did to discussing why events unravelled in this way, the same holds true.

Common Errors in English # 499.

GENERALIZATION, ABSTRACTION, JARGON, AND DOUBLESPEAK

Generalization is the process of moving from an observation or conclusion about a single thing or a small number of things to a conclusion about all or most of that group. Abstraction, on the other hand, is at its most basic level the isolation of some particular quality of a thing from the rest of its properties — the consideration of the colour of a particular object, for example.

Many people are a bit hazy on the difference between abstraction and generalization — not surprisingly, since the two are related activities that we often perform simultaneously. Perhaps the best way of keeping them straight is to remember that (as Christopher Hallpike puts it) while the opposite of 'general' is 'particular', the opposite of 'abstract' is 'concrete':

> *Emotions* is a broad general category; *love* and *hate* are particular emotions. (Neither is a concrete thing.)

> The greenness of the Brazilian flag is an abstraction; the flag itself is a concrete thing.

> (We may also, of course, speak of one particular Brazilian flag or of the Brazilian flag in general, or of all flags in general; there can be numerous levels of both abstraction and generalization.)

A great deal of writing involves shifts not only from the general to the particular and back again but also from one level of generalization to another:

- An article on Chippendale chairs would probably refer to particular examples from the eighteenth century studio of Thomas Chippendale himself, generalize about all chairs of that type, generalize further about the furniture of the period, and perhaps generalize at one higher level about how and why such designs suited the overall sensibilities of eighteenth century England.

Common Errors in English # 499.

● An English literature essay might make a general claim about Jane Austen's use of irony. It might then descend one level of generality to discuss the differences in the degree to which the generalization applies in the various novels. It might then move to a lower level of generality, distinguishing between the scenes in *Northanger Abbey* that are suffused with the characteristic Austen sense of irony and those (apparently remaining from the first draft of the novel) that are almost pure melodrama with no irony to them whatsoever. Finally, the essay would doubtless give particular examples — quote sentences or paragraphs that exemplify an ironic tone and a melodramatic one.

Both abstraction and generalization are important mental processes for any writer; they help us, as Janet Giltrow puts it, to "name and manage otherwise unruly details." But writers have to learn to use them with care. As a rule, generalizations must be supported by evidence. (Generalizations that are commonplaces may be made without support; one does not need to provide evidence in support of the generalization that dogs have four legs or that war is a terrible thing.) And they should be precise. "Most Canadians voted against the Free Trade Agreement in the 1988 election" is an imprecise generalization. "In the 1988 election most Canadians voted for parties that opposed the Free Trade Agreement" is more accurate. Such concern for precision may seem like pedantry; is there any difference between the two? Yes, there is. In that election, many Canadians who opposed Free Trade nevertheless voted for the Conservatives, just as many Canadians who supported Free Trade voted for the Liberals or the NDP. Free Trade was the most contentious issue in the campaign, but not the only one; it *was* an election, not a referendum. Being careful about such distinctions is an important element of good writing.

---

500. **Mixed levels of abstraction or generalization:** When a comparison is being drawn or an extended argument is being shaped, the levels of abstraction or generalization should be kept consistent.

wrong   Ethnicity, like the aged, women, and others, is believed by some scholars to be best understood within a broad context of inequality, and outside of any specific 'cultural' argument.

Common Errors in English # 500.

right   Ethnicity, like age, gender and other categories on the basis of which discrimination may occur, is believed by some scholars to be best understood within a broad context of inequality, and outside of any specific 'cultural' argument.

---

501. Excessive abstraction: Almost any combination of abstract words can create fuzziness of meaning unless the writer exercises extreme care. Look at the following passage, for example:

> There are two features of Nyerere's view in 1968 of the transition to socialism which distinguish it from his earlier view. First, the trends in Tanzanian society which he felt would soon greatly increase the strength of the opposition to socialism led him to a greater sense of urgency about the need seriously to set in train the transition to socialism. Second, in 1967 he had a much clearer perception of the initiatives the government should take to achieve an effective transition to socialism.
>
> This new perception of the transition to socialism owed much, of course, to the character of the socialist society which Nyerere finally hoped to achieve. It was however very much shaped as well by his understanding of the political realities of Tanzania in 1967.
>
> It was Nyerere's ideas on the transition to socialism rather than his vision of a transformed Tanzania which had a direct and major impact upon policy and politics in the years after 1967. (Cranford Pratt, *The Critical Phase in Tanzania*)

This is the sort of thing English instructors have in mind when they tell their students to use concrete words rather than abstractions. By itself there is nothing wrong with any of the words *features, transition, socialism, distinguish, trends, opposition, perception, initiatives, perception, transition, socialism, character, socialist society, understanding, political realities, ideas, transition, socialism, vision, transformed, impact* or *policy*. But put them together in a string like this — unbroken by any words like *dog*, or *box*, or *tree*, or *paper* — and you have writing that puts even the most determined reader to sleep. Moreover, the writer who consistently uses such words is likely to find herself circling round and round in a fog. (It should not be inferred that Cranford Pratt is such a writer;

the point of including a passage from a book by this distinguished professor is rather that even the best writers must be wary of such problems.) Let's try the first paragraph again:

> By 1968 Nyerere had realised how deeply and strongly the currents of opposition to socialism flowed; he would have to move fast. But he had also realised much more clearly by this time what the government could do to speed up the process.

Some academics might complain that this version is too journalistic, but at least it has the virtue of clarity. What about the rest? Pratt seems to be saying something like this:

> How much did Nyerere's vision of socialism itself have to do with the change in his view of how it should be achieved? Some, of course, but not much. It was his concept of how the vision should be achieved rather than the vision itself that shaped Tanzanian politics after 1967.

Does this in fact say anything of importance? Not really, so it would be better to cut the entire paragraph. But until one trims some of the verbal foliage away, it is difficult to see how little is being said.

---

502. **Jargon:** Every academic discipline and indeed every area of human life has its own jargon; it is no fault in English to use jargon appropriate to one's subject matter and audience. But it is easy to overdo the use of jargon, and all too easy to write in ways that may only be appreciated by a small number when one's subject justifies aiming for a larger audience.

The excessive use of jargon may be as much a problem of psychology as it is of English grammar and usage. It often comes from people being more concerned with making themselves sound knowledgeable and intellectual than with acquiring knowledge or developing their intelligence; more concerned with making their ideas sound important than with thinking them through and expressing them clearly. The best way to guard against excessive jargon is always to ask yourself if you are saying what you mean in the simplest possible way. Let us look at some examples:

> The very fact that these articles criticising the Soviet

Common Errors in English # 502.

> government had been published in *Pravda* told the reader something of consequence. It indicated that these were the parameters within which debate had been sanctioned by the Central Committee of the Communist party. (*The Guardian*)

The jargon word here is of course *parameters*. This word has a very specific technical meaning in mathematics, and should not be used in other contexts. It gained currency out of a confusion with *perimeter* (the boundary of a closed area), and out of people's desire to use words that sound impressive but are clearly understood by neither writer nor reader. *Sanction* is another troublesome word in the passage — it would be a perfectly good word if it had not come to take on two diametrically opposed meanings. Here one presumes it means to *approve of*, but it is possible that it means to *restrict* instead. Because of such ambiguity the word is best avoided. The more general question is whether this writer has expressed his or her meaning in the clearest and most concise way possible. Let's try again:

> The very fact that these articles criticising the Soviet government had been published in *Pravda* told the reader that the Central Committee of the Communist party had allowed debate in these areas.

Notice the other changes we have made: cutting the wordy "told the reader something of consequence," and changing from a passive verb (*had been sanctioned*) to an active one (*had allowed*). This change puts the subject (*the Central Committee*) at the beginning of the second clause, and allows us to cut "It indicated."

The final result is a sentence that is a good deal simpler and shorter. One cannot be fooled into thinking it says anything particularly profound, but nor does one have to waste any time in puzzling out what the writer means.

jargon	The plan is more philosophical than operational in terms of framework. (Alexander Haig)
clear	The plan is still only an idea; it hasn't yet been tried, and it may not work.
jargon	This paper argues that by interrogating the author's constructions of difference we may more nearly approach the critical taxonomy by which she de-centers and indeed subverts the tropes of race and

Common Errors in English # 502.

	of gender.
clear	How does the author construct difference? What categories does she see things falling into? This paper argues that she de-centers and indeed subverts the tropes through which race and gender have traditionally been presented.

(Note that the clearer version here is created more by re-phrasing than by removing jargon.)

jargon	The great interfaces across the entire spectrum of Canadian-American relations are in order.
clear	Canada and the United States are on good terms.

Here is a list of commonly used jargon words and expressions; if you find yourself using them a good deal, think about whether you might better re-phrase.

access	commence
enhance	impact on
implement	interface
optimal	opt for
parameter	point in time
previous to	prior to
prioritize	specificity
structure	totality
utilize	viable

-wise (money-wise, sales-wise, weather-wise etc.)

---

503. **Doublespeak:** George Orwell coined the word *doublespeak* in *1984* to describe the use of language to disguise one's true meaning. This is a variant of jargon that one should try particularly hard to avoid. Here are a few humorous but saddening examples:

poor	The government must deal with the issue of revenue enhancement.
better	The government will have to raise taxes.
poor	Our guest rooms feature the most prestigious body cleaning systems.
better	We have good bathtubs.
poor	We provide outplacement consulting to companies involved in downsizing their operations.
better	We advise companies on how best to fire people.

These examples are taken from the *Quarterly Review of Doublespeak*, which is published by the National Council of Teachers of English, 1111 Kenyon Rd., Urbana. Ill. 61801.

Common Errors in English # 503.

BIAS-FREE LANGUAGE

504. Biased language: The healthy revolution in attitudes towards gender roles in the last generation has created some awkwardness in English usage—though not nearly so much as some have claimed. *Chair* is a simple non-sexist replacement for *chairman*, as is *business people* for *businessmen*. Nor is one forced into *garbageperson* or *policeperson*; *police officer* and *garbage collector* are entirely unobjectionable even to the linguistic purist. *Fisher* is a quite delightful replacement for *fisherman*; here again, there is no need for the *-person* suffix.

The use of *mankind* to mean *humanity*, and of *man* to mean *human being*, have for some years been rightly frowned upon. (Ironically enough, *man* originally had *human being* as its **only** meaning; in Old English a *werman* was a male adult human being, a *wifman* a female.) A remarkable number of adults still cling to sexist usages, however, and even still try to convince themselves that it is possible to use *man* in a gender-neutral fashion. Among them are the editors of *The Economist*, who posed the question, "What is Man?" in the lead article of their September 14, 1996 issue. "To what extent are men's actions determined by their genes?" the article asked, and clearly did not intend the answer to apply to only one-half the human race.

Well, why **can't** *man* be gender neutral? To start with, because of the historical baggage such usage carries with it. Here, for example, is what the best-selling novelist Grant Allen had to say on the topic in a magazine called *Forum* in 1889:

> In man, I would confidently assert, as biological fact, the males are the race; the females are merely the sex told off to recruit and reproduce it. All that is distinctly human is man—the field, the ship, the mine, the workshop; all that is truly woman is merely reproductive—the home, the nursery, the schoolroom.

But the baggage is not merely historical; much of the problem remains embedded in the language today. As it happens, a useful litmus test appeared in the same issue of *The Economist*. Further on in the magazine this sentence appears:

> One of the most basic distinctions in human experience—that between men and women—is getting blurrier and blurrier.

Now let's try the same sentence using *man's* instead of *human*:

> One of the most basic distinctions in man's experience—that between men and women—is getting blurrier and blurrier.

In this sort of context we are all forced to sense that something is amiss. We have to realise when we see such examples that *man* and *he* and even *mankind* inevitably carry with them some whiff of maleness; they can never fully and fairly represent all of humanity. (If they didn't carry with them some scent of maleness it wouldn't be possible to make a joke about the difficulty of turning *men* into *human beings*.) Most contexts are of course more subtle than this, and it is thus often easy for humans—but especially for men—not to notice that the male terms always carry with them connotations that are not gender-neutral. *Humanity, humans, people*—these words are not in any way awkward or jargon-ridden; let's use them.

To replace *man* with *humanity* is not inherently awkward to even a slight degree. But the pronouns are more difficult. Clearly the consistent use of *he* to represent both sexes is unacceptable. Yet *he/she, s/he*, or *he or she* are undeniably awkward. *S/he* is quite functional on the printed page, but defies translation into oral English. Another solution is to avoid the singular pronoun as much as possible either by repeating nouns ("An architect should be aware of the architect's clients' budgets as well as the architect's grand schemes") or by switching to the plural ("Architects should be aware of their clients' budgets as well as of their own grand schemes"). Of these two the second is obviously preferable. In longer works some prefer a third strategy that eliminates awkwardness entirely: to alternate between the masculine pronoun "he" and the feminine pronoun "she" when referring to a single, generic member of a group. Using *she* to refer to, say, an architect, or a professor, or a sports star, or a prime minister can have the salutary effect of reminding readers or listeners that there is nothing inherently male in these occupations. In a short piece of writing, however, it can be distracting to the reader if there are several bounces back and forth between female and male in the same paragraph. And a cautionary

Common Errors in English # 504.

note should accompany this strategy even when it may conveniently be employed; be **very** careful not to assign *he* to all the professors, executives, or doctors; and *she* to all the students, secretaries, or nurses.

Undoubtedly the most troublesome questions for those who are concerned both about gender equality and about good English arise over situations involving singular pronouns such as *everyone, anyone, anybody, somebody, someone, no one, each, either, neither.* It can be difficult enough to re-cast sentences involving such words so that everything agrees even before the issue of gender enters the picture.

> Everybody felt that the film was better than any other they had seen that year.

According to the rules most of us have been taught, that sentence is wrong; *everybody* is singular, and *they* must therefore be changed:

> Everybody felt that the film was better than any other she had seen that year.

> Everybody felt that the film was better than any other he had seen that year.

> Everybody felt that the film was better than any other she or he had seen that year.

But, as Robertson Cochrane has pointed out ('Sex and the Single Pronoun,' *The Globe and Mail*, May 1992), the insistence on the singularity of such pronouns is a relatively recent phenomenon, dating from the codification of English grammar that took root in the eighteenth century. Before that time Chaucer, Shakespeare, Swift, and the rest had no qualms about using *they* or *their* to refer to *anyone* and *everyone*. Cochrane persuasively argues that returning to the ways of Chaucer and Shakespeare in this respect is better than constantly trying "to write around the pronoun problem, and [it is] certainly less offensive than arrogantly and 'properly' applying masculine labels to all of humankind."

inappropriate	Mankind cannot bear too much reality.
gender neutral	Human kind cannot bear too much reality.
inappropriate (though 'correct')	Everyone will have a chance to express his views before the meeting is over.

Common Errors in English # 504.

gender neutral
(though 'incorrect')   Everyone will have a chance to express their views....

Before leaving the issue of gender and language, let me raise the issue of the attitude we bring with us when we read or write. The reason that it must continually be emphasised that bias-free coinages are in almost all cases simple to adopt is that some writers seem to *prefer* to think of gender-neutral language as inherently awkward or absurd. Here's an example of what I mean, taken from a recent and widely-adopted textbook:

> Maintaining Objectivity
> Avoiding discriminating language is important. Just as important, however, is avoiding a witch hunt. Taken to extremes, "political correctness" will weaken your writing. *Middleman*, for example, is a perfectly legitimate term, widely understood. There is no point in confusing readers by substituting *distributional intermediary* merely to avoid the suffix *-man*. Little is gained by referring to a stripper as an ecdysiast when most readers will not recognise the euphemism. And no one is going to take seriously a writer who calls short people vertically challenged. Remember, the point of considerate language is to be fair and polite, not to be obscure or silly. (Bonnie Carter & Craig Skates, *The Rinehart Guide to Grammar and Style*. Fort Worth: Rinehart, 4/e 1996)

Think about this for only a moment, and it may seem quite unexceptionable — entirely reasonable, even. Think again. The tip-off here is the way that the question of the word *middleman* has been approached. Not as the occasion for an interesting, if possibly difficult search for ways of expressing ourselves that will avoid both awkwardness *and* bias, but rather as a matter that will inevitably involve a choice between the two. The authors here seem more interested in finding reasons to ridicule the struggle for fairness than in joining in the effort to improve things.

Let's approach the word in a different frame of mind. To start with, the fair comparison is not between *distributional intermediary* and *middleman* but between *intermediary* and *middleman*. Perhaps the former is more awkward, but it is not obviously so:

> One of the reasons for high prices in this industry is that there are too many middlemen.
> One of the reasons for high prices in this industry is that there are too many intermediaries.

Alternatives in different circumstances may include *wholesalers, distributors, go-betweens* — none of them obscure, confusing, or laughable. *Ecdysiast* is indeed a laughable euphemism, but not one

Common Errors in English # 504.

that is needed to circumvent biased usages. (*He's a male stripper* suffers from the same defect as *He's a male nurse*, but *stripper* in itself is gender-neutral.) And, though there is indeed a societal bias against short people, no one seriously suggests euphemism as a solution.

For many years now "politically correct" has been used with quotation marks around it to mean "aesthetically distasteful and ethically wrong-headed"—and we are often meant to be left with the suggestion that those who criticise the "politically correct" do not themselves have a political agenda; they are "maintaining objectivity." It is telling in this connection that the authors of *The Rinehart Guide* couch the matter as an issue of etiquette rather than one of equity: "the point of considerate language is to be fair and polite." To be sure, it is a virtue to be polite and considerate. But unquestioning politeness to those in positions of power and privilege may sometimes entail an acceptance of terms of reference that are anything but fair. Sometimes one may have to choose beween being fair and being polite. And the point of searching for bias-free ways of expressing oneself is in fact not to be polite, but to be fair. Sometimes it comes to a choice; language can be an instrument of positive change, or an instrument of repression. In that context we can probably never avoid being biased in one direction or the other, and we are wise to remember that complete objectivity is impossible.

None of this should be taken to suggest that there are not awkwardnesses to struggle with in the search for bias-free coinages. (*Statesman* and *manned spaceflight*, for example, resist easy substitutions.) But these are surprisingly few. In most cases one need not resort to the oft-lampooned *-person* suffix. *Chair* and *flight attendant* felt a little odd at first (in language as in the rest of life it may take a while to get used to new things), but no one is bothered by them now. *First-year student* still feels odd to many Americans, but not in Canada, where it has always been used. And the process continues. *Snowbody* is a wonderful word that my daughter and a friend of hers helped me make up, but I suspect it will be years before *snowman* begins to sound as clunky as *stewardess*. Try it, though—and try to smile in fun rather than in derision. Put the accent on the first syllable. And remember, there are few things more gender-neutral than a body made up of three spheres of snow.

Although gender is the most contentious issue in the struggle for

Common Errors in English # 504.

bias-free language, it is not the only one. Almost everyone is aware of the terms for particular racial and cultural groups that one should avoid on these grounds (see the list below). A few such terms are so deeply encoded in the language that people may use them without being aware of their underlying meaning.

offensive   I'm convinced that the shopkeeper tried to gyp me.
      (*Gyp* originated in the prejudice that gypsies were congenital cheats.)
bias-free   I'm convinced that the shopkeeper tried to cheat me.

(Given the generally high level of awareness in Western society of the evils of anti-semitism it is extraordinary that *jew* is still sometimes used in casual conversation as a verb in the same way that *gyp* is used. It is a use that should never be allowed to go unchallenged—and when such usages are cha;llenged speakers will often realise they have been unthinkingly using a coinage learnt in childhood—and will change.)

We think of bias-free language as referring to matters of gender, race, culture and religion. But class is also relevant. Look at this example:

When it appears in July, the Fusca will cost $6,850. According to a recent study, only 1 per cent of Brazilians can afford to buy a new car. Thus, Mr. Franco's 'car of the people' will inevitably become the car of the middle class. (*Globe and Mail*, March 8, 1995)

Notoriously, many developing countries are polarized between rich and poor; effectively they lack a middle class. But to deal with that situation by defining the top one per cent as the 'middle' is to subtly distort both the nature and the extent of the economic disparity.

In one important respect the issue of bias-free usage differs from every other issue discussed in this book. Throughout, our focus has been on formal writing, and it has frequently been emphasized that many informal and colloquial usages that are inappropriate to formal writing may be quite unexceptionable in other forms of writing, or in speech. The same cannot be said of the difference between biased and bias-free language. It is no less damaging to use sexist, racist or homophobic language in speech than it is in writing; indeed, it may be even more so. The cumulative repetition in speech of colloquial expressions—including such 'innocent' expressions as the contemptuous use of "that's so gay"—probably does considerably more to reinforce human prejudice than does the written word.

Common Errors in English # 504.

Bias-free Vocabulary: A Short List

actress	actor
alderman	councillor
bad guy	villain
bellboy	bellhop
bogeyman	bogey monster
businessman	businessperson, entrepreneur
caveman	cave-dweller
chairman	chair
clergyman	minister, member of the clergy
congressman	representative
con-man	con-artist
draftsman	drafter
Eskimo	Inuit

N.B. Some Alaskan groups still prefer *Eskimo*.

fireman	fire fighter
fisherman	fisher
foreman	manager, supervisor
freshman	first-year student
garbageman	garbage collector
gunman	shooter
gyp	cheat, con
henchmen	thugs, lackeys, hangers-on
Indian	Native, First Nations

N.B. As with *Eskimo/Inuit* and *African American / black*, the key consideration is sensitivity to audience. If you do not belong to the group but you know the people you are writing about prefer a particular designation, that is the one to use.

infantryman	footsoldier
layman	layperson
longshoreman	shiploader, stevedore
mailman	letter carrier, mail carrier
male nurse	nurse
man	humanity
man [an exhibit]	staff
man [a barricade]	fortify, occupy
man [a ship]	crew
manhandle	rough-up, maul
manhole	sewer hole, access hole, street hole
manhole cover	sewer cover, street hole cover
mankind	human kind, people, humanity, humans
manly	self-confident, courageous, straightforward
manmade	handmade, human-made, constructed
middleman	intermediary
negro	black, African American
policeman	police officer
postman	letter carrier, mail carrier
salesman	salesperson
snowman	snowbody (rhymes with *nobody*)
sportsman	sportsperson
stewardess	flight attendant
unsportsmanlike	unsporting
weatherman	weather forecaster
womanly	warm, tender, nurturing, sympathetic
workman	worker, laborer

N.B. A much more complete guide is Rosalie Maggio's *The Bias-Free Word Finder* (Boston: Beacon Press, 1991).

Common Errors in English # 504.

METAPHOR AND MEANING

Metaphors may either enliven prose or deaden it; it is all in how you use them. In that sentence there are two metaphors; the verbs *enliven* and *deaden* both implicitly compare writing to a living thing. As this suggests, a metaphor is a comparison of one thing to another made through the use of a word or words that do not apply literally. "My love is a red, red rose" is a metaphor. "My love is <u>like</u> a red, red rose" is a simile — a type of metaphor that uses the word *like*.

We do not often use poetic metaphors like this in prose, but nevertheless our writing is likely to be strongly laced with metaphorical language. Phrases such as the following are all too familiar to us:

That will be the acid test.

The United States has always been a melting pot.

He is barking up the wrong tree.

I threw caution to the winds.

This reorganization lays the foundation for future change.

We were told that we would have to bite the bullet.

The government's move has paved the way for a resumption of talks.

We are opening up new horizons.

The university was then a hotbed of unrest.

For the most part these are what are known as dead metaphors — metaphors that have been used so frequently that they no longer conjure up any physical image in the minds of those who hear or read them. When we hear the phrase "miss the boat" we do not think of a boat, any more than we think of pavement when we hear the expression "paved the way for." It is a moot point whether a dead metaphor is better than no metaphor at all, but certainly a fresh metaphor is far better than either. Instead of "paved the way," for

Common Errors in English # 504.

example, what about "blazed a path?" Instead of a *hotbed* try a *cauldron*. Instead of "nipping something in the bud," try "digging up the seedlings." It may take a little longer, but the improvement in one's writing is worth it.

So many people have been using metaphors for so long that it is extremely difficult to find fresh ones for every idea you wish to express. One useful compromise is to try to bring dead metaphors to life by using them in new ways. For example, no one thinks of a wave if you say "The Mayor has been riding a wave of popular support since his election." Mention the wave again in a slightly different way, however, and it becomes water again to the reader:

> The Mayor has been riding a wave of popular support since the election. The question now is when that wave will crest.

> The company wanted to nip in the bud the spreading unrest among its employees before it became a tangled, snake-infested jungle.

505. **Mixed metaphors:** A dead metaphor all too often becomes a mixed metaphor as well. Mixed metaphors occur when we are not really thinking of the meaning of the words we use. "If we bite the bullet we have to be careful not to throw the baby out with the bathwater"; "We will leave no stone unturned as we search for an avenue through which the issue may be resolved." As soon as one really thinks about such sentences one realises that the bullet is really better off out of the baby's bathwater, and that the best way to search for an avenue is not to turn stones over.

wrong	Now Chrétien is out on a limb because his colleagues pulled the rug out from under him.
right	Now Chrétien is out on a limb and some of his colleagues are preparing to saw it off.
wrong	The man in the street has trouble keeping his head above water.
right	The average person today has trouble keeping his head above water.

Common Errors in English # 505.

SLANG AND INFORMAL ENGLISH

506. Slang / informal English: The following words and expressions are often used in conversation, but not in formal English. The more formal word is listed afterwards. The most frequently troublesome entries are given a separate number.

anyways	anyway
anywheres, anyplace	anywhere
awful	poor, miserable, sick
awfully	very, extremely

Some authorities continue to hold that *awful* should retain its original meaning of "filled with or inspiring awe". In any case, a better replacement can always be found. The same is even more true of the use of the adverb *awfully* as an intensifier to mean *very* ("awfully good," "awfully small," etc.).

boss	manager, supervisor
bunch (except for grapes, bananas, etc.)	group
buy (as a noun — "a good buy", etc.)	bargain
kid	child, girl, boy
kind of, sort of	rather, in some respects
let's us	let us
lots of	a great deal of
mad (unless the meaning is "insane")	angry

---

507. **could care less**   couldn't care less

Several years ago people started to say sarcastically "I could care less" to mean the opposite—that they could*n't* care less. Now "I could care less" is taking over, regardless of the tone of voice used, and the meaning of the words themselves is in danger of being lost.

---

508. get : should not be used to mean *come, go, be,* or *become*

wrong   Henry and Jane Seymour got married in 1536, only ten days after the death of Anne Boleyn.

right   Henry and Jane Seymour were married in 1536, only ten days after the death of Anne Boleyn.

Common Errors in English # 508.

509. go (to mean *say*)

| *wrong* | He goes, "What do you mean?" |
| *right* | He said, "What do you mean?" |

510. have got (to mean *have*)

| *iess formal* | He has got two houses and three cars. |
| *more formal* | He has two houses and three cars. |

In conversational English *got* has become widely used as an auxilliary verb, probably because of the awkwardness of pronouncing certain combinations involving common contractions. Thus we would never shorten "I have you covered" to "I've you covered;" instead we would say, "I've got you covered." *Have got* is also an informal synonym for *have* in the sense of *possess*. Both these uses of *got* are usually to be avoided in formal writing.

511. let's say: This expression should be omitted entirely from writing.

| *wrong* | Let's say for example a relative dies, a poor family will have to deal with financial worries as well as with grief. |
| *right* | If a relative dies a poor family will have to deal with financial worries as well as with grief. |

512 like (to mean *say* or *indicate through gesture*: An expressive idiom, but one to be avoided in formal writing.

| *conversation* | She's like, "Why do we have to be here?" and I'm like, "Duh! |
| *formal* | She wondered why we had to be there; to me it was obvious. |

513. off (to mean *from*)

| *wrong* | I got it off him for two dollars. |
| *right* | I bought it from him for two dollars. |

514. put across, get across (one's point), express, convince

| *wrong* | He could not get his point across. |
| *right* | He could not persuade us he was right. |

515. well: In conversation *well* is often added to sentences while you are thinking of what to say. Do not do this in writing.

| *wrong* | Well, at the end of the war there was some doubt within the Cabinet as to which course to take. |
| *right* | At the end of the war there was some doubt within the Cabinet as to which course to take. |

516. when you get right down to it: usually best omitted; use *otherwise*, *indeed*, or *in fact*.

Common Errors in English # 509.

Form

THE WRITING PROCESS

What are the most important things to think of when writing? First, that you have something to say. And second, that you keep in mind who you are writing for.

Though some of the finest essays are narrative or descriptive, most of the extended writing that most of us will be expected to do—whether as students, business people, bureaucrats or academics—is structured in order to persuade. This is true even of most writing that is not 'argumentative' in any narrow sense. It may through analysis try to persuade the reader of the validity or usefulness of a particular approach; it may employ description or narration in the service of persuasion. But normally it will have as a central purpose a desire to persude the reader of something. To persuade us through description that St. John's, Newfoundland, is the most entertaining town in North America. To persuade us through selective narration that the Americans were or were not justified in dropping the atomic bomb on Japan in 1945. To persuade us through analysis of the narrative structure of *The Remains of the Day* that Ishiguro's novel leads the reader to invest emotional energy in the character of Stevens. To persuade us through argument that high housing densities are necessary to vibrant urban life, or that wind-power is the most cost-effective method of generating electricity over the long term.

Almost every book about writing will tell you of the importance of the thesis, and of the thesis statement. And there is no doubt that it is as helpful to the writer to try to ensure that the main idea of an essay or report can be expressed concisely and directly as it is helpful to the reader to have it so expressed (see adjacent box). Often, though, what one begins with as the main thing one wants to say will be modifed or qualified during the research and writing process—and

Common Errors in English # 516.

occasionally it may be entirely reversed; one may become convinced that the precise opposite of what one began by trying to demonstrate is in fact the case. Writing an essay or a report is in this respect not unlike conducting an experiment. One begins with a hypothesis. The hypothesis is tested during the process of research, writing and revision. Refined into the thesis, it is the central thread of the essay or report.

---

517. poor thesis or thesis statement:

poor Art is important to society in many ways, and I will talk about them in this essay. One of the artists I will focus on is Robert Mapplethorpe, the subject of much recent controversy.

Yawn. The statement is too general and too vague to have significance.

better The art of Robert Mapplethorpe deserves to be exhibited — and at public expense — even if most people find it abhorrent.

This statement is more precise, more limited, more interesting.

poor In this paper I will examine various reasons for launching the war in Kosovo in 1999.

This is a statement of topic rather than of thesis. It's also wordy.

better The moral case for the US and its allies to wage a bombing-only war against Yugoslavia in 1999 was stronger than the strategic one; air attacks alone had never before been enough to win a war.

Suddenly there is an argument being made.

poor The purpose of this essay is to explore the interplay between poetry and the novel. I will prove that good poets don't usually write good novels and vice versa.

Full points for ambition, but it's the subject for a book, not a term paper. At most, a short paper might justifiably speculate about such a large question in its conclusion; the main focus should be much narrower. Also, the statement is far too bold in its generalization. ("What about Thomas Hardy?" the professor will ask. "What about Boris Pasternak?").

better Ondaatje's characters seem thin and unreal to the reader — alternately brittle and transparent. Paradoxically, however, it may be precisely these qualities that allow the poetic power of his prose — at once brutal and fragile — to strike the reader with full force.

A much narrower but still controversial thesis exploring the connections between poetry and prose.

Books about writing also often emphasise the importance of having a plan for any essay or report. And rightly so; it is very useful to draw up a point-form summary of the idea, laid out so as to show the flow of ideas, and the way in which they should flow together as paragraphs. Any such plan should usually include headings grouping the ideas:

- three reasons why Alberta has in the past chosen coal rather than wind for generating electricity
- two false assumptions on which many of the arguments in favour of dropping the bomb are based
- examples of the ways in which Ishiguro's syntactical structures support his narrative techniquese
- examples of the ways in which the spareness of his descriptions does the same

And so on. But if it is important to have a plan, it is equally important to be willing to change it. To be able to recognise halfway through the writing process that in fact the whole section on the general historical context in which something happened would better go before the direct presentation of the arguments as to why it happened, and that the rebuttal of the arguments of Jones should not be introduced until after Smith's contentions have been thoroughly discussed. To be able to cut large chunks, no matter how interesting, if they turn out not to be relevant to the main point. To be able to add sections that will provide necessary qualification for one's thesis. And to pay attention to the ideas that one is likely to have *while one is writing*; interesting and original ideas are as likely to surface during the process of writing as during the process of reading and researching.

Last but far from least, it is important to let the writing process have several stages. The first of these (and for many people the most difficult) is simply to get words onto paper, or onto a screen and into a computer memory. At this stage it may be fruitful to remember that nothing is at stake where a first draft is concerned; no one but yourself need see it or see the flaws that will be an inevitable part of it. Get something on paper first — and then worry about improving it.

Part of overcoming writers' block, then, is often an acceptance by the writer that the writing process will have several stages — and that at least two of these will be stages not of planning or of writing but of revising. That too may end up requiring a good deal of often unexpected writing. And at a minimum it should involve not only a willingness but a determination to improve the writing throughout rather than merely to correct obvious errors. Too many students — not to mention people in business and bureaucrats — feel that they have essentially finished the job when they have completed a first draft. The checklist below is intended largely to help writers think through the revising process. But the essential first stage is psychological—the recognition of the value of taking the time to do two, three, or more drafts. As Ian Cameron of Carleton University recommends in *For All Practical Purposes*:

> A few students feel that they are as likely to make more mistakes in checking and correcting their work as they are to correct the mistakes they have already made, but in fact almost every student is able to improve his or her work at least fifteen per cent by checking it slowly and carefully. Remember, you are not checking simply for details such as spelling; you should be trying to replace words, to re-arrange paragraphs, to cut entire sections, to alter almost every sentence.

By its very nature, revising is likely to lead to more cuts than additions. Might this not cause damage? "Aren't I more likely to do well," some may ask themselves, "if I've written more than has been asked for?" If the instructor has asked for 1,000 words, they feel they should write 1,500; if 2,500 words are requested, they are sure to top 3,000. Experienced writers have learnt that quantity matters much less than quality; unless an essay or report is well below the requested number of words the only thing that matters is what it says, and how well it says it.

* * *

Advice on the writing process may also be found elsewhere in these pages. In particular, it may be helpful to consult the chapters on Putting Ideas Together, Paragraphing, and Writing With Computers.

Essay Checklist

___ Does this piece of writing have a clear purpose? Have I made that purpose clear to the reader?

___ What audience is this written for? Is the tone suited to the intended audience throughout?

___ Of what am I trying to persuade my audience? Is this made completely clear near the beginning (whether in a formal thesis statement or otherwise)? Is it again made clear near the conclusion?

___ Does the essay follow a clear path? Are there too many digressions? Is there any extraneous material that should be cut, or transferred out of the body of the text and into a note?

___ Is the structure of the argument signalled by the paragraphing? Does the paragraph remain the unit of composition throughout?

___ Does the point I am making remain clear in every paragraph? In every sentence?

___ Is there some variety in sentence structure? Have I avoided awkward sentence constructions? And run-on sentences?

___ Are most verbs in the active voice?

___ Do the verbs always agree with the subjects?

___ Do I use concrete and specific language wherever possible? Do I avoid excessive use of jargon or unnecessarily obscure language?

___ Am I careful in my use of qualifiers, avoiding statements that are too bald or extreme, but not qualifying all the strength or interest out of my argument?

___ Is my writing ever wordy? Where could I still trim?

___ Did I revise (from hard copy) and rewrite the essay thoroughly? Did I proofread after I had revised?

___ Have I checked the punctuation carefully throughout?

___ Have I proofread as well as used a computer spell-check?

___ Have I used the correct system of documentation? Do the references follow this system consistently throughout?

___ Have I given appropriate acowledgement to all the sources I used? Is there any point at which I might have been guilty of plagiarism by paraphrasing without acknowledgement?

___ Does the format (spacing, margins etc.) follow specifications?

___ Have I answered all the above questions honestly?

Common Errors in English

Examinations

Even those who realize the value of taking the time to revise an essay or report have a natural — and understandable — tendency to assume that entirely different principles apply to examinations. There are differences, of course, but the basic similarities should also be kept in mind. Time allocation involves greater pressure in this context, but planning and revision are just as important; again, quantity matters less than quality. If at all possible, then, avoid writing madly to the last moment of the exam. A well-written short answer is almost invariably better received than a sloppy, long-winded one, and even a few moments spent on checking and revising will almost always be of enormous value. Here are two additional pointers:

- Take your time in reading the examination questions; many a student has done a marvellous job answering a question that wasn't asked, where a few extra moments of calm reflection while reading the examination would have made all the difference.
- For long essay questions take the time to make even the roughest of plans for your answer. Not only will this help you to remember the points you wish to make; it will also lead to a better-structured answer.

Note: An excellent guide to the peculiarities of exam-writing is *Making Your Mark* by Catherine Taylor et al., published by the Academic Skills Centre at Trent University.

WRITING BY COMPUTER

Computers and the Writing Process

No one born later than, say, 1950, needs to be convinced of the advantages of computers for writing. But many of us need to remind ourselves periodically of some of the pitfalls of word-processed writing. Some problems are readily avoided if one retains the habit of careful proofreading: the perils of spell-check, for example (see below) or the dangers of search and replace. It is all too easy to come to rely on the computer a little too heavily in such contexts—as I found myself doing recently when I instructed my computer to do a search and replace on a contract, replacing all occurrences of "author" in the contract with the words "senior editor." What need could there be to confirm? The contract was almost in the mail before "senior editorization" and "senior editority" caught my eye. I certainly had not *senior editor*ized the change, but my computer had no way of stopping once I had unleashed its search and replace engine.

Proofreading may be enough to check some of the bad cognitive habits that computers breed in many writers who work only on screen; it certainly will not eliminate them all. For some of us computers can be wonderful facilitators of flow; many people find it easier to get a lot of ideas out of their heads and 'on paper' by using a computer than by using a pen and paper. But the same habits of scrolling that can facilitate flow in writing and in reading can distort our ability to arrange ideas in an ordered fashion so as to best present an argument. Though researchers are far from understanding why, they have now assembled a considerable body of evidence suggesting that seeing a succession of printed pages enables one to combine and connect ideas in ways that are not always evident if one restricts oneself to scrolling text on the screen. This is why it is vitally important to work with paper as well as on screen. It is ironic that the very means by which the re-ordering of blocks of text has become a matter of effortlessly keyboarding (rather than of laboriously cutting, pasting, and retyping) also acts to dull the cognitive processes that are required for humans to re-order those blocks most effectively. But that is the reality all writers must come to terms with.

If computer technology may facilitate the sort of writing flow that is the best tonic for writers' block, the speed with which that technology changes may also sometimes give us an excuse not to write. It is all too easy to decide that it will be impossible to finish a thesis or complete a report unless and until one upgrades software, replaces that old hard drive, or acquires a faster machine. In almost all cases this is really just a way of trying to avoid the hard job of getting down to writing. We should all make it a firm rule not to let our fascination with technology get in the way of our writing.

A note on spell-check

Commonly used words are also commonly misspelled words — and not only because they occur frequently. Most of us have the sense when we use a word such as *surreptitiously* to check the spelling in a dictionary, or with the spell-check mechanism on our computer. But words such as *its* and *it's*, or *than* and *then*, or *compliment* and *complement* we tend to use without thinking — and no computer spell-check will tell us if we have had a mental lapse and used the wrong one. (It would be difficult for me to count the times as a publisher that I have received manuscripts that began with a *Forward* rather than a *Foreword*.) It is worth remembering that no computer can be a substitute for careful proofreading.

Common Errors in English

The Internet

In 1992 the media was full of references to the need to create an "electronic highway." But within a year almost everyone had realised that one had already been created. The Internet had originally been the product of the American Defence Department's desire to build diffuse lines of communication as a defense against attacks on the country's infrastructure. Made available for use by academics in the 1980s, it had quietly developed by the early 1990s into an extraordinarily efficient and inexpensive means of communication. And as Web technology has developed, its potential has continued to grow.

Technology that can be used in so many ways can of course also be misused in many ways. Given the pace of change — and the complexity of the topic — it would be unwise in a book of this size to attempt any comprehensive treatment of how to use the Internet as a resource tool for writing. But some general guidelines may be useful.

The Internet may seem like a goldmine when it comes to research. But if so, the likeness is to a vein of ore that is not always sufficiently concentrated as to make the mining of it economic. Sometimes the most difficult thing is to decide when it is worth one's while to commit one's resources to the mining operation. Search engines are likely to turn up vast amounts of material on almost any topic. But often much of it will be unreliable — and it is extraordinarily difficult for the novice to tell what is likely to be reliable and what isn't.

At one end of the spectrum, many refereed scholarly journals are available on-line — and some are available *only* on the Internet. The best way to consult reference works that are constantly updated (such as the *Oxford English Dictionary*) is through the Internet. And some academic disciplines are now turning to publication via the Internet for scholarly monographs. (The historian Robert Darnton, for example, has led an initiative by the American Historical Association and Columbia University Press to publish through the Internet monographs which are of real importance but of very specialized academic interest.)

At the other end of the spectrum are countless materials that have not been reviewed either by academic authorities or by publishers.

How is one to gauge the reliability of such material? Should one just stick to established sources in the library? How is it possible to avoid spending a large amount of time merely to amass a large quantity of unreliable source material?

There are no easy answers to these questions, and the best strategies are likely to vary depending on the sort of research one is doing. The most important thing for the novice may be simply to consult one's instructor on the issue of what sources — whether in the library or on the Internet — may be most appropriate to use for a given assignment.

Many of the principles of library research apply to research on the Web too. Perhaps above all, it is important to note each source you consult in writing an essay, report, or thesis. (Be sure as well to mark clearly any passages or phrases that are a direct quote rather than a summary or your own commentary on what you have read, so as not to confuse your own ideas or phrasings with those of the authors you have consulted.) In the case of an Internet reference it may be more convenient to store the information on your hard drive or on a disc rather than on a card or piece of paper — but the principle of noting sources carefully remains the same.

If many of the principles are the same, the mechanisms of Web research are very different from the mechanisms of using the library, and are constantly changing. A number of good guidebooks devoted entirely to using Internet sources are now available,* and are updated regularly. Referencing styles also change frequently. Some of the essential points of referencing Internet sources appear below in the chapter on referencing. The fullest and most up-to-date treatments of referencing according to particular styles, however, are to be found through the websites of the relevant organizations: the MLA, APA and so on.

---

* See for example Andrew Harnack and Eugene Kleppinger's *Online: A Reference Guide to Using Internet Sources* (New York: St. Martin's, 1st edition 1998).

Observing Netiquette

"Netiquette" is a clever little pun that seems to have stuck. It neatly encapsulates the notion that standards of courtesy and consideration are as important in cyberspace as they are in other areas of human existence — and that the Internet is sufficiently different from other forms of communication as to make some new guidelines advisable.

Anyone who has used email has probably sensed that the medium lends itself to a higher degree of informality (for both sender and recipient) than does the sending of a letter printed on corporate or departmental letterhead. The combination of distance, informality and invisibility that electronic communication embodies seems to encourage the spontaneous expression of emotion in ways that might otherwise not feel appropriate. It often seems to foster a breeziness that is as friendly as it is efficient. But it also seems to lend itself to the venting of certain sorts of anger, in ways that other mediums of communication do not. And sometimes it leads people to divulge personal information that on reflection they might rather have kept to themselves. These tendencies of email — to foster sometimes unexpected degrees of intimacy, and to facilitate the unbridled expression of anger — argue for the wisdom of taking the time to edit and proof any electronic message, checking its tone quite as much as its grammar.

The increasing use of electronic communication in a wide variety of contexts continues to raise issues of appropriate tone and of level of formality. For the most part, no one expects emails to conform to all the conventions of more formal communications; it would be foolish to worry about a typo or two in an email dashed off to a friend. But any email should be clear, unambiguous, and written in an appropriate tone; again, it is wise to edit and proofread carefully any message you send. And, if you are using email as a convenient way to convey a more formal document, that document should indeed conform to the conventions of standard usage. A proposal submitted electronically or a memo circulated electronically should be phrased, proofed and presented as carefully as you would the same document in hard copy form. As with writing, faxing or phoning, then, the context and the expectations of your audience are always important.

Privacy issues are at least as important with electronic communications as they are with other forms of communication. As a recipient, consider the feelings of the sender; unless it is obviously appropriate to forward a message, for example, ask the permission of the sender before you pass it on. And as a sender, it is worth remembering that electronic communication can often end up being less private than regular mail. Since recipients are not always as considerate as one might wish (and since errors in filing and forwarding can occur) it is wise to consider whether the potential recipients of a message may be a much larger group than intended — and word the message accordingly.

Plagiarism and Copyright

Keeping careful track of your sources — and clearly indicating for your own reference what is a quotation and what is your own comment on a work you have consulted — not only saves time; it also prevents unintentional plagiarism.

Although the possibilities both for unintended and for intentional plagiarism are vastly greater with the Web than they were when hard copy materials were the only resources, the mechanisms for detection have expanded as well; search engines can often confirm for an instructor in seconds that a particular string of words in a student essay has been lifted unacknowledged from another source.

Copyright rules for written materials apply to the Internet just as they do to books or articles; written work is under copyright protection for many years after it is published.* Except for quoting brief passages (with the proper acknowledgement), you may not reproduce material from the Web without the permission of the copyright holder. Nor may you post copyrighted materials on the Web without permission from the copyright holders.

*In the United States the 1998 Sonny Bono Copyright Amendment Act significantly extended copyright protection; most written material published in 1924 or later will remain in copyright for many years to come; in the UK and other European countries work is in copyright for 70 years after the death of the author (or translator); in Canada work is in copyright for 50 years after the death of the author or translator.

Common Errors in English

Point-form Netiquette

- keep messages clear and brief.

- edit/proof all messages before sending—for tone as well as form.

- use clear subject headings.

- make the text as easy to read as possible; leave a line between paragraphs (rather than indenting); for italics place an underscore mark before and after the relevant word(s); use only well-known abbreviations.

- when quoting from a previous message, quote only the necessary passage(s).

- address the message carefully.

- attachments: if you want to send an attachment to a message, check first with the recipient if it will be possible to download. The alternative (provided the material is no more than a few pages long) is to embed material from another document into your message .

- visuals: remember that (s)he may not have the same technology you do. Think twice, for example, before sending a large file of graphic information that may take the recipient an inordinate amount of time to download—if indeed (s)he has the capacity to do so.

- listservs/chatgroups/newsgroups/ bulletin boards: There are a variety of Internet mechanisms for sharing information among many individuals with a common interest. Conventions may vary with each group; it makes sense to pay attention to the procedures followed and the tone adopted by established users before you start to play an active role yourself. And if in any doubt as to appropriate procedures, ask the listowner / bulletin board organizer.

- post only information that is likely to be of interest to others—and as with email, be as clear and as brief as possible.

- be particularly sensitive to the demands you may be making on the time of others. If, for example, you are sending an 'information-only' email to a department head who may deal with a hundred emails a day, make it clear in the heading or at the beginning of the message that this is for information only, and that no reply is required.

- the overriding principle: always show consideration for your reader(s).

SPELLING

The wittiest example of the illogicalitites of English spelling remains Bernard Shaw's famous spelling of *fish* as *ghoti*. The *gh* sounds like the *gh* in *enough*; the *o* sounds like the *o* in *women* (once spelled *wimmen*, incidentally); and the *ti* sounds like the *ti* in *nation* or *station*. Shaw passionately advocated a rationalization of English spelling; it still has not happened, and probably never will.

Perhaps the best way to learn correct spelling is to be tested by someone else, or to test yourself every week or so on a different group of words. For example, you might learn the words from the list below beginning with *a* and *b* one week, the words beginning with *c* and *d* the next week, and so on.

A note on spell check

As discussed above (p. 198), it is important to remember that no computer can be a substitute for careful proofreading. Spell-check is wonderful, but it cannot tell if it is your friend or your fiend.

Spelling and Sound

518. Many spelling mistakes result from similarities in the pronunciation of words with very different meanings. These are covered in the list below. Other words that cause spelling difficulties are listed separately.

absent (adjective)	absence (noun)
absorb	absorption
accept	except
access (entry)	excess (too much)
advice (noun)	advise (verb)
affect (to influence)	effect (result)
allowed (permitted)	aloud
alter (change)	altar (in a church)
appraise (value)	apprise (inform)
bitten	beaten
base (foundation)	bass (in music)
bath (noun)	bathe (verb)
believe (verb)	belief (noun)
berry (fruit)	bury (the dead)
beside (by the side of)	besides (as well as)
birth	berth (bed)
bizarre (strange)	bazaar (market)
bloc (political grouping)	block
breath (noun)	breathe (verb)
buoy (in the water)	boy
buy (purchase)	by
cash	cache (hiding place)
casual (informal)	causal (to do with causes)
cause	case
ceased (stopped)	seized (grabbed)
ceiling (above you)	sealing
chick	cheek
chose (past tense)	choose (present tense)
cite (make reference to)	sight site
climatic	climactic
cloths (fabrics)	clothes
coma (unconscious)	comma (punctuation)
compliment (praise)	complement (make complete)
conscious (aware)	conscience (sense of right)
contract	construct
conventional (usual)	convectional
conversation	conservation concentration
cord (rope)	chord (music)
convinced	convicted (of a crime)
council (group)	counsel (advice)

course	coarse (rough)	
credible (believable)	creditable (deserving credit)	
critic (one who criticises)	critique (piece of criticism)	
defer (show respect)	differ	
deference (respect)	difference	
deprecate (criticise)	depreciate (reduce in value)	
desert (dry place)	dessert (sweet)	
device (thing)	devise (to plan)	
died/had died	dead/was dead	
dissent (protest)	descent (downward motion)	
distant (adjective)	distance (noun)	
edition (of a book etc.)	addition (something added)	
emigrant	immigrant	
envelop (verb)	envelope (noun)	
except	expect	
fear	fair	fare (payment)
feeling	filling	
fell	feel	fill
flaunt (display)	flout	
formally	formerly (previously)	
forth (forward)	fourth (after third)	
forward	foreword (in a book)	
foul	fowl (birds)	
future	feature	
genus (biological type)	genius (creative intelligence)	
greet	great	grate (scrape)
guerillas	gorillas	
guided (led)	guarded (protected)	
had	heard	head
heat	heart	hate
heir (inheritor)	air	
human	humane (kind)	
illicit (not permitted)	elicit (bring forth)	
illusion (unreal image)	allusion (reference)	
immigrate	emigrate	
independent (adjective)	independence (noun)	
inhabit (live in)	inhibit (retard)	
instance (occurrence)	instants (moments)	
intense (concentrating)	intents	
isle (island)	aisle (to walk in)	
know	no	now
kernel	colonel	
lack	lake	
later	latter	letter
lath (piece of wood)	lathe (machine)	
lead	led	
leave	leaf	
leave	live	
leaving	living	

Common Errors in English # 518.

lessen (reduce)	lesson	
let	late	
liable (responsible)	libel (legal action)	
lightning (from clouds)	lightening (becoming lighter)	
lose (be unable to find)	loose (not tight)	
mad (insane)	made	maid (servant)
man	men	
martial (to do with fighting)	marshal	
mental	metal	
merry	marry	
met	meet	mate
minor (underage)	miner (underground)	
mist (light fog)	missed	
moral (ethical)	morale (spirit)	
mourning (after death)	morning	
new	knew	
of	off	
on	own	
ones	once	
pain	pane (of glass)	
patients (sick people)	patience (ability to wait)	
peer (look closely)	pier (wharf)	
perpetrate (be guilty of)	perpetuate (cause to continue)	
perquisite (privilege)	prerequisite (requirement)	
personal (private)	personnel (employees)	
perspective (vision)	prospective (anticipated)	
poor	pour (liquid)	pore
precede (go before)	proceed (continue)	
precedent	president	
presents (gifts)	presence (being there)	
price (cost)	prize (reward)	
principle	principal (of a school)	
prostate	prostrate	
quay (wharf - pronounced key)	key	
quite	quiet (not noisy)	
rein (to control animals)	rain	reign
release (let go)	realize (discover)	
relieve (verb)	relief (noun)	
response (noun)	responds (verb)	
rid	ride	
ridden	written	
rise	rice	
rite (ritual)	right	write
rod	rode	reared
rote (repetition)	wrote	
saved	served	
scene (location)	seen	
saw	so	sew
seam (in clothes etc.)	seem (appear)	

Common Errors in English # 518.

secret	sacred (holy)	
sell (verb)	sale (noun)	sail (boat)
senses	census (population count)	
shed	shade	
shone	shown	
shot	short	
sit	sat	set
smell	smile	
snake	snack (small meal)	
soar	sore (hurt)	
sole (single)	soul (spirit)	
sort (type or kind)	sought (looked for)	
stationery (paper)	stationary (not moving)	
steal (present tense)	stole (past tense)	
straight (not crooked)	strait (of water)	
striped (e.g., a zebra)	stripped (uncovered)	
suite (rooms or music)	suit	sweet
super	supper (meal)	
suppose	supposed to	
sympathies (noun)	sympathize (verb)	
tale (story)	tail	
talk	took	
tap	tape	
than	then	
they	there	their
thing	think	
this	these	
throw	threw (past tense)	
through	thorough	
tied	tired	
urban (in cities)	urbane (sophisticated)	
vanish (disappear)	varnish	
vein (to carry blood)	vain	
vision (sight)	version	
waist (your middle)	waste	
wait	weight (heaviness)	
waive (give up)	wave	
wants	once	
weak (not strong)	week	
weather (sunny, wet, etc.)	whether (or not)	
wedding	weeding	
were	where	
wholly (completely)	holy (sacred)	holly
woman	women	
won	worn	
yoke (for animals)	yolk (of an egg)	

519. **a, an:** Authorities agree that an 'n' should be added to the indefinite article when the following word begins with a vowel or an

'h' that is not sounded. Some go a step further to ridicule the common habit of saying "an hysterical grandmother" or "an historical introduction."

We sound the 'h' in such words, goes the argument, and therefore we should use *a* rather than *an*. But what is the rationale for this 'rule' in the first place? Simply that it is awkward for most of us to say "*a egg*" or "*a hour*;" we find that it sounds better to add an 'n'. And the fact is that many people find it easier to say "an historical introduction" than "a historical introduction." (Interestingly, the same does not apply to *an history*; the shift in stress in the adjective to the second syllable seems to weaken the force of the *h*.) So why the fuss? We may reasonably disagree over which sounds better, but there is surely no justification for referring to usages such as *an historical introduction* as barbarisms. Such phrases are quite correct whether or not one chooses to end the indefinite article with an *n*.

---

520. **British spelling, American spelling, Canadian spelling** A number of words that cause spelling difficulties are spelled differently in different countries. In the following list the British spelling is on the right, the American on the left. Either is correct in Canada, so long as one is consistent.

behavior	behaviour
center	centre
cigaret	cigarette
favor	favour
favorite	favourite
fulfill	fulfil
humor	humour
likable	likeable
maneuver	manoeuvre
marvelous	marvellous
neighbor	neighbour
omelet	omelette
program	programme
Shakespearian	Shakespearean
skillful	skilful
skeptical	sceptical
theater	theatre
traveling	travelling

Other Commonly Misspelled Words

521. Here is a list of other commonly misspelled words.

abbreviation
absence
accelerator
accident
accidentally
accommodation
achieve
acknowledge
acquire
acquisition
acquit
acre
across
address
adjacent
advertisement
affidavit
ambulance
amoeba
among
ammonia
amortize
amount
anachronism
analogous
analysis
anchor
androgenous
annihilate
antecedent
anti-Semitic
anxious
apocalypse
apparatus
apparently
appreciate
approach
architect
arguable
argument
arsonist

arteriosclerosis
artillery
asinine
author
auxiliary
bacteria
basically
battery
beautiful
beginning
believe
boast
boastful
breakfast
bulletin
burglar
burial
buried
business
candidate
capillary
cappuccino
Caribbean
carpentry
cautious
ceiling
changeable
character
chlorophyll
choir
cholesterol
chrome
chromosome
chronological
chrysalis
chrysanthemum
coincidence
colleague
colonel
colossal
column
commitment

Common Errors in English # 521.

committee
comparative
competition
competitor
complexion
conceive
condemn
conjunction
connoisseur
consensus
consistent
controller
convenience
cooperation
cooperative
courteous
courtesy
creator
creature
criticism
cyst
decisive
definite
delicious
description
desirable
despair
despise
destroy
develop
diesel
different
dilemma
dining
disappear
disappoint
disastrous
discrimination
disease
disintegrate
dissatisfied
dominate
dormitory
double
doubtful
drunkard
drunkenness
duchess
due
dying

eclipse
effective
efficient
eighth
embarrass
employee
encourage
enemy
enmity
enormous
entertain
enthusiasm
entitle
entrepreneur
environment
enzyme
epidermis
epididymis
erroneous
esophagus
especially
espresso
essential
exaggerate
excessive
excite
exercise
exhilaration
existence
existent
experience
extraordinary
Fahrenheit
faithful
faithfully
farinaceous
fault
financial
foreigner
foretell
forty
fourth
gauge
gamete
germination
government
grammar
grateful
gruesome
guarantee

Common Errors in English # 521.

guerrillas
guilty
happened
happiest
hatred
hectare
helpful
hyena
hypothesis
ichthyology
idiosyncratic
imaginary
imagine
immigration
immersible
impeccable
importance
impresario
inchoate
incomprehensible
indigenous
independent
indestructible
indispensable
ineffable
infinitesimal
inoculate
insufferable
intention, intentional
interrupt
irrelevant
irresponsible
isosceles
isthmus
itinerary
jealous
jeopardy
journalist
jump
junction
kneel
knowledge
knowledgeable
laboratories
laboratory
language
lazy, laziness
ledger
leisure
liaise

liberation
library
licence
lieutenant
liquid, liquefy
literature
lying
medicine
medieval
membrane
merciful
mermaid
millenia
millennium
millionaire
mischief
mischievous
modern
naked
naughty
necessary
necessity
noticeable
nuclear
nucleus
obscene
obsolescent
obsolete
occasion
occasional
occupy
occur
occurred
occurrence
omit
ourselves
paid
parallel
parliament
parliamentary
party
permissible
permission
perpendicular
perseverance
photosynthesis
playful
possess
possession
poultry

Common Errors in English # 521.

predictable
pregnancy
pregnant
prerogative
prescription
privilege
properly
psychiatric
psychological
punctuation
pursue
questionnaire
really
receipt
recommend
referee
reference
regret
repeat
repetition
replies
reply
residence (place)
residents (people)
restaurant
revolutionary
rheumatism
rhododendron
rhombus
rhubarb
rhyme
rhythm
saddest
sandals
scene
schedule
schizophrenic
science
scintillate
scissors
scream
scrumptious
search
seize
sense
separate
shining
shotgun
sigh
significant

simultaneous
sincerely
slippery
slogan
smart
solemn
spaghetti
speech
spongy
sponsor
stale
stingy
stomach
stubborn
studious
studying
stupefy
stupid
subordinate
subpoena
substitute
subtle, subtlety
suburbs
succeed
success, successful
sue, suing
summary
surprised
surreptitious
surrounded
survive
symbol
talkative
tarred
television
temperature
tendency
theoretical
theory
title
tough
tragedy
trophy
truly
unique
until
vacancy
vacillate
valuable
vegetable

Common Errors in English # 521.

vehicle
vicious
visitor
volume
voluntary
Wednesday

welcome
whisper
writer
writing
written
yield

VOCABULARY: SOME NATIONAL VARIATIONS

The following list of variants from some nations in which English is a primary first language does not include slang or idioms.

Australia	Canada
announcer/host/presenter	announcer/host
attic/loft	attic
autumn	fall/autumn
award rate	minimum wage
baby carriage/pram	baby carriage
back yard	back yard/garden
back bacon	back bacon
baked potato/jacket potato	baked potato
bangs [hair]	bangs
bathers/cozzy	bathing suit/swimsuit
beanie	toque
billion	billion
biscuit	cookie
bitumen road	paved road
block of land	plot of land
bowser	gas pump
brew [tea]	steep
by bus/coach (inter-city)	by bus
cake (layer)	cake (layer)
can of/tin of [food]	can of/tin of
car(rail passenger)	car
chemist	drugstore/pharmacy
chips [potato]/crisps	chips
Cludo	Clue [board game]
coloured pencil	coloured/colored pencil
concrete block	concrete block
constituency	riding/constituency
[House of Representatives]	[House of Commons]
contraceptive	condom/safe
corn starch/flour	corn starch
dam	pond/lake
[human-made]	
dessert/pudding	dessert
diaper/nappy	diaper
different from/to	different from
drapes	curtains/drapes

How many railway sleepers are there in the pile?

Put on your toque; it's cold.

Pull over on the verge, please.

She never drinks soda; it's too sweet for her.

Do you sell university calendars here?

England	United States
presenter/host	host/announcer
loft	attic
autumn	fall/autumn
minimum wage	minimum wage
pram	baby carriage
back garden	back yard
back bacon	Canadian bacon
jacket potato	baked potato
fringe	bangs
swimming costume	swimsuit
woolly hat	wool hat
thousand million	billion
biscuit	cookie
metalled road	paved road
plot of land	plot of land
petrol pump	gas pump
brew	steep
by coach	by bus
gateau	cake (layer)
tin of	can of
carriage	car
chemist	drugstore
crisps	chips
Cludo	Clue
pencil crayon	colored pencil
breeze block/concrete block	concrete block
constituency	district
[House of Commons]	[House of Representatives]
condom/rubber	condom/safe
corn flour	corn starch
pond/lake	pond/lake
a sweet/pudding	dessert
nappy	diaper
different from/to	different from/than
curtains	drapes/curtains

Common Errors in English

Australia	Canada
dumpster	dumpster
editorial/leader	editorial
eggplant/aubergine	eggplant
electrical cord/flex	electrical cord
elevator/lift	elevator
engaged (phone)	busy
eraser	rubber/eraser
escalator/moving staircase	escalator
extension cord/lead	extension cord
fire plug	fire hydrant
fire station/fire hall	fire station
fire engine	fire engine
first-year student	first-year student
fish fingers	fish sticks
fizzy drink	soft drink
flashlight/torch	flashlight
fly [trousers]	fly
frankfurts	hotdogs/weiners
freeway/motorway	expressway/freeway
gas/petrol [for a car]	gas
general store	grocery store
generator/dynamo	generator
get a rise [in pay]	get a raise
give [someone] a bell	a call/ring
globe [light]	bulb
grazier	farmer
green beans	green beans
grumble	grumble
gum boots	rubber boots
hamburger[prepared]/mince	hamburger
half-mast (flag)	half-mast
hang up/ring off	hang up
hood/bonnet (of a car)	hood
hot water bag	hot water bottle
hot-water service	hot water heater
house for sale	house for sale
house for let	house for rent
icing [cake]	icing
in the post	in the mail/by post
intersection	intersection
invigilate [exam]	invigilate
kerosene/parafin	kerosene
latex paint/emulsion paint	latex paint
lima beans/broad beans	lima beans
locked/shut tight	locked/shut tight
lollies	candies
match/game	game
Mothers' Day	Mothers' Day

[Fathers' Day is the same in all cases]

moving companies	van lines
muffler/silencer (of a car)	muffler
nature strip	shoulder

England	United States
rubbish skip	dumpster
leader	editorial
aubergine	eggplant
flex	electrical cord
lift	elevator
engaged	busy
eraser	rubber
moving staircase	escalator
lead	extension cord
fire hydrant	fire hydrant
fire hall	fire station
fire truck	fire engine
first-year student	freshman
fish fingers	fish sticks
fizzy drink	soda
torch	flashlight
flies	fly
frankfurters	franks/weiners/hotdogs
dual carriageway/motorway	freeway/thruway
petrol	gas
grocer	grocery store
dynamo	generator
get a rise	get a raise
a ring	a call
bulb	bulb
farmer	farmer
runner beans	green beans
grouse/grumble	grumble
wellingtons	rubber boots / rainboots
beefburger/mince	hamburger
half-mast	half-staff
ring off	hang up
bonnet	hood
hot water bottle	hot water bottle
immersion heater	hot water heater
house under offer	house for sale
house for let	house for rent
frosting	icing
in the post/by the post	in the mail/by mail
junction	intersection
proctor	invigilate
paraffin	kerosene
emulsion paint	latex paint
broad beans	lima beans
made fast/locked	locked/shut tight
sweets	candies
fixture/match	game
Mothering Sunday	Mothers' Day
removals	van lines
silencer	muffler
verge	shoulder

Australia	Canada
odometer/milometer	odometer
outbuildings [at a farm]	outbuiildings
outside toilet	outhouse
oval/sports field	sports field
pacifier	pacifier/soother
paddock	field
parka	windbreaker/raincoat
	rain jacket/jacket
phone cord	phone cord
pie/flan	pie
post box	post box/mail box
prawns	shrimps
prospectus [university]	calendar
public holiday	public holiday
railway/railroad	railway/railroad
car hire/rental	car rental
ring off (phone)	hang up
row boat	row boat
rubbish tin	wastebasket
rubbish tip/tip	garbage dump
run [for election]	run
runners	track shoes
sailboat/sailing boat	sailboat
sand shoes	running shoes
scrap yard/car breaker	scrap yard [car]
second floor	second floor
semi- [trailer]	semi- /transport trailer
(road train = more than one trailer]	
shallots	green onions
skirting board	baseboard
skivvy	turtle neck shirt
sleepers	ties [railway]
soft drink/fizzy drink	soft drink
standings [sports]	standings
station[sheep or cattle]	ranch/farm
sticky tape	scotch tape
stockyard	stockyard
stretcher	cot
stroller	stroller
study/revise [for a test]	study
subway/underground	subway
sunbake	sunbathe
surgery	doctor's office
sweater/jumper	sweater
take away [food]	take-out
taxi-truck	rent-a-truck
thongs [footwear]	flip-flops
traffic circle	traffic circle
trailer/caravan	trailer/camper
trousers	pants/trousers/slacks
truck/lorry	truck
ute (utility vehicle)	pick-up truck

England	United States
milometer/trip meter	odometer
outhouses	outbuildings
outdoor privy	outhouse
pitch/sports field	sports field
dummy	pacifier/soother
field	field
anorak/mac	windbreaker/ rainjacket
phone lead	phone cord
flan	pie
pillar box	mail box
prawns	shrimps
prospectus	catalog
bank holiday	public holiday
railway	railroad
car hire	car rental
ring off	hang up
rowing boat	rowboat
waste paper basket	wastebasket
rubbish tip/refuse tip/tip	garbage dump
stand	run
trainers	track shoes
sailing boat	sailboat
plimsoles	sneakers
car breaker	scrap yard
third floor	second floor
articulated lorry	eighteen wheeler
spring onions	green onions
skirting board	baseboard
polo-neck top	turtleneck shirt
sleepers	ties
fizzy drink	soda
tables	standings
farm	ranch
sellotape	scotch tape
cattle pen	stockyard
camp bed	cot
pushchair/pusher	stroller
revise [for a test]	study
underground/tube	subway
sunbathe	sunbathe
surgery	doctor's office
jumper	sweater
take away	take out
van hire service	rent-a truck
thongs	thongs
roundabout	traffic circle
caravan	trailer
trousers	slacks/pants
lorry	truck
	pick-up truck

Australia	Canada
trucks [railway]	freight cars [railway]
trunk/boot (of a car)	trunk
turf/sods	turf
underground walkway	underground walkway
vacuum/hoover	vacuum
vest	vest/waistcoat
wait on	wait for
wake [someone else] up	wake up
washcloth/flannel	washcloth
washing-up liquid	dish detergent
winery	vineyard
woolgrower	sheepfarmer
zillion	zillion

England	United States
trucks	freight cars
boot	trunk
sods	turf
subway/underpass	underground walkway
hoover	vacuum
waistcoat	vest
wait for	wait for
knock up/wake up	wake up
flannel	washcloth
washing-up liquid	dish detergent
vineyard	vineyard
sheepfarmer	sheepfarmer
billion	zillion

WRITING ABOUT LITERATURE

All subject areas have their own conventions and specialized vocabulary, and readers are well advised to consult guidebooks dealing with the practices of any subject they are specializing in — recommended research techniques as well as style guidelines and so on. Writing about literature is singled out here for very brief special treatment not because its practices are inherently more important than those of other subjects but because its conventions present fundamental problems at the level of sentence structure to those new to the discipline.

522. **Tense errors when writing about literature:** The simple past tense is of course normally used to name actions which happened in the past. But when writing about what happens in a work of literature, convention decrees that we use the simple present tense. This should be done regardless of whether we are speaking about the way the book is written or recounting the events in the story, and regardless of whether the story takes place in 1987 or in 1543.

wrong	Romeo fell in love with Juliet as soon as he saw her.
right	Romeo falls in love with Juliet as soon as he sees her.
wrong	In her short stories Alice Munro explored both the outer and the inner worlds of small town life with a deceptively simple style.
right	In her short stories Alice Munro explores both the outer and the inner worlds of small town life with a deceptively simple style.

If literature in its historical context is being discussed, however, the simple past tense is often more appropriate.

Common Errors in English # 522.

wrong	Marlowe writes *Doctor Faustus* when he is only twenty-nine.
right	Marlowe wrote *Doctor Faustus* when he was only twenty-nine.

Often the context may require shifting back and forth between the past and present tenses in an essay about literature. In such cases one is very likely to make mistakes during the writing of the first draft; even experienced writers have to think carefully during the revision process about the tense of each verb.

wrong	In *The Two Gentlemen of Verona*, then, Shakespeare exhibited a degree and a variety of technical accomplishment unprecedented in the English drama. He still of course had much to learn as a dramatist and as a poet; in its wit or its power to move us emotionally *The Two Gentleman* was at an enormous remove from the great works of a few years later. But already, in 1592, Shakespeare had mastered all the basic techniques of plot construction that were to sustain the structures of the great plays.
right	In *The Two Gentlemen of Verona*, then, Shakespeare exhibits a degree and a variety of technical accomplishment unprecedented in the English drama. He still of course had much to learn as a dramatist and as a poet; in its wit or its power to move us emotionally *The Two Gentleman* is at an enormous remove from the great works of a few years later. But already, in 1592, Shakespeare had mastered all the basic techniques of plot construction that were to sustain the structures of the great plays.

523. **Writing about literature — quotations:** When writing about history or politics — in the <u>past</u> tense — one is likely to find difficulty with quotations in the <u>present</u> or <u>future</u> tenses. When writing about literature the problem is the reverse; one is writing in the <u>present</u> tense, but many of the quotations one usually wishes to use are in the <u>past</u> tense.

wrong	Emma Bovary lives largely through memory and fantasy. She daydreams frequently, and as she reads, "the memory of the Vicomte kept her happy."
right	Emma Bovary lives largely through memory and fantasy. She daydreams frequently, and as she reads "the memory of the Vicomte" keeps her happy.

Common Errors in English # 523.

or

Emma Bovary lives largely through memory and fantasy. She daydreams frequently, and blends fiction and memory in her imaginings: "Always, as she read, the memory of the Vicomte kept her happy. She established a connection between him and the characters of her favorite fiction."

wrong

In *The Mayor of Casterbridge* the strength of Henchard's personality is felt even after his death. The extraordinary series of requests he writes as he is dying, "was respected as far as practicable by Elizabeth-Jane...from her independent knowledge that the man who wrote them meant what he said."

right

In *The Mayor of Casterbridge* the strength of Henchard's personality is felt even after his death. The extraordinary series of requests he writes as he is dying is "respected as far as practicable" by Elizabeth-Jane, who realizes that Henchard means what he has said.

or

In *The Mayor of Casterbridge* the strength of Henchard's personality is felt even after his death: "What Henchard had written in the anguish of his dying was respected as far as practicable by Elizabeth-Jane, though less from a sense of the sacredness of last words, as such, than from her independent knowledge that the man who wrote them meant what he said."

Common Errors in English # 523.

MLA STYLE

524. Wrong or inconsistent referencing: Three styles of documentation dominate in the Humanities and the Social Sciences—that of the Modern Language Association (MLA), that of the American Psychological Association (APA), and that of *The Chicago Manual of Style*. The former is commonly used in the Humanities, the latter two in the Social Sciences.

The preface to this book provides an extended sample of the MLA referencing style. Under this system a quotation or specific reference to another work is followed by a parenthetical page reference:

> Bonnycastle refers to "the true and lively spirit of opposition" with which Marxist literary criticism invigorates the discipline (204).

The book is then listed under 'Works Cited' at the end of the essay:

> Bonnycastle, Stephen. In Search of Authority: An Introductory Guide to Literary Theory. 2nd ed. Peterborough: Broadview, 1996.

If the context does not make it clear who the author is, that must be added to the parenthetical reference:

> Even in the 1990s some have continued to believe that Marxist literary criticism invigorates the discipline with a "true and lively spirit of opposition" (Bonnycastle 204).

The basic principles of the parenthetical reference system are the same regardless of whether one is citing a book, an article in a journal or a magazine, a newspaper, a multi-volume work, a book review, or a literary work. For poems one cites line numbers rather than page numbers, however, and for any novel available in more than one edition or format it is advisable to include chapter number as well as page number:

Common Errors in English # 524.

Urban renewal is as much a matter of psychology as it is of bricks and mortar. As Paul Goldberger has described, there have been many plans to revitalize Havana (50-61). But both that city and the community of Cuban exiles in Florida remain haunted by a sense of absence and separation. As Lourdes Casal reminds us,

> Exile
>
> is living where there is no house whatever
>
> in which we were ever children;   (1-3)

The psychology of outsiders also makes a difference. Part of the reason Americans have not much noticed the dire plight of their fifth-largest city is that it does not "stir the national imagination" (Rybczynski 12). Conversely, there has been far more concern over the state of cities such as New Orleans and Quebec, whose history and architecture excite the romantic imagination. As Nora Phelps has discussed, the past is in itself a key trigger for romantic notions, and it is no doubt inevitable that cities whose history is particularly visible will engender passionate attachments. And as Stephanie Wright and Carole King have detailed in an important case study, almost all French-speaking Quebecers feel their heritage to be bound up with that of Quebec city (2: 171-74). (Richard Ford's character Frank Bascombe has suggested that "New Orleans defeats itself" by longing "for a mystery it doesn't have and never will, if it ever did" [48; ch. 3] but this remains a minority view.)

Georgiana Gibson is also among those who have investigated the interplay between urban psychology and urban reality (Cities 64-89). Gibson's personal Web site now includes the first of a set of working models she is developing in an attempt to represent the effects of various psychological schema on the landscape.

The above references would connect to Works Cited as follows:

Casal, Lourdes. "Definition." Trans. Elizabeth Macklin. New Yorker 26 Jan. 1998: 79.

Ford, Richard. The Sportswriter. 1986. New York, Random House, 2nd Vintage Edition, 1995.

Gibson, Georgiana. Cities in the Twentieth Century. Boston: Beacon, 1997.

Common Errors in English # 524.

- - - . Home page. 10 June 1999. 30 July 1999 <http:www.geography.byu.edu/gibson/personal.htm>.

- - - . "The Mind and the City." Urban Myths: A History. Ed. Brian Earn and Shelagh Towson. San Francisco: Harbor, 1993. 176-84.

Goldberger, Paul. "Annals of Preservation: Bringing Back Havana." New Yorker 26 Jan. 1998: 50-62.

Phelps, Nora. "Pastness and the foundations of romanticism." Romanticism On the Net 11. Aug. 1998. 6 July 1999 <http://users.ox.ac.uk/~scat0385/phelpsmws.html>.

Rybczynski, Witold. "The Fifth City." Rev. of A Prayer for the City, by Buzz Bissinger. New York Review of Books 5 Feb. 1998: 12-14.

Wright, Stephanie, and Carole King. Quebec: A History. Montreal: McGill-Queen's UP, 1998. 2 vols.

Among the details to notice in this reference system:

- Where two or more works by the same author are included in Works Cited, the reference must make clear which work is being referred to. Second and subsequent entries substitute three hyphens and a period for the author name.
- All important words in titles are capitalized.
- The date appears in Works Cited only.
- The parenthetical reference comes before the period or comma in the surrounding sentence. (If the quotation ends with punctuation other than a period or comma, then this should precede the end of the quotation, and a period or comma should still follow the parenthetical reference.)
- If a parenthetical reference occurs within text in parentheses, square brackets are used for the reference.
- When a work has appeared in an edited collection information on the editors must be included in the reference.
- Only the first author's first and last names are reversed.
- If a book or film review has a title, that should appear under Works Cited, which should also indicate the title of the book or film being reviewed.
- Translators should be included under Works Cited.
- Publisher as well as city of publication should be given.
- UP is the abbreviation used for University Press.
- Online citations include the date of publication or of last revision followed by the date of access.

Common Errors in English # 524.

The Bible and works of drama available in many editions should also be cited in a way that enables the reader to check the reference in any edition. Here are parenthetical references for Shakespeare's *The Merchant of Venice*, Act 2, Scene 3, lines 8-13; and for *Genesis*, Chapter 2, verse 14::

(MV 2.3 8-13)   (Gen. 2.14)

For scholarly journals the Works Cited listing should include issue number and page numbers:

> Raedts, Peter. "The Children's Crusade of 1212." <u>Journal of Medieval History</u> 3.4 (1977): 279-325.
>
> Hurka, T.M. "Improving on Perfectionism." <u>Philosophical Review</u> 99 (1996): 462-73.

Unsigned articles in newspapers and magazines are listed by title:

> "Clash over Nobel Cash." <u>Washington Post</u> 11 Feb. 1998: A14.

Similarly, books with no author should be alphabetized by title, except where you have referred to only one entry in an encyclopedia or dictionary:

> "Artificial." <u>Oxford English Dictionary</u> 2nd edition. Oxford: Oxford UP: 1989.

If the Works Cited list includes two or more authors with the same last name, the parenthetical reference should supply both first and last names:

> One of the leading economists of the time advocated wage and price controls (Harry Johnston 197).

If you refer to something from a Preface, Introduction or Foreword, the reference under Works Cited should begin with the name of the author of that Preface, Introduction or Foreword:

> Warkentin, Germaine. Introduction. <u>Set in Authority</u>. By Sara Jeannette Duncan. Peterborough: Broadview, 1996. 9-51.

Films, radio or television programs, interviews, dramatic performances, musical recordings, and paintings should be listed as follows:

Wag the Dog. Dir. Barry Levinson. With Robert DeNiro, Dustin Hoffman. Alliance, 1997.

Twitch City. With Don MacIvor. CBC TV, 13 Jan. 1998.

Bellow, Saul. Interview. Books in Canada. Sept. 1996: 2-6.

Counts, Dorothy Ayers, and David R. Counts. Interview. Pamela Wallin Live. CBC Newsworld. 26 Nov. 1997.

Rosengarten, Herbert. Personal interview. 21 Jan. 1998.

A Doll's House. By Henrik Ibsen. Dir. Anthony Page. With Janet McTeer and Owen Teale. Belasco, New York. 22 May, 1997.

Dylan, Bob. "Out of Love." Time Out of Mind. Columbia, 1997.

Housser, Yvonne McKague. Cobalt. 1931. National Gallery of Canada, Ottawa.

APA Style

524. Wrong or inconsistent referencing: Three styles of documentation dominate in the Humanities and the Social Sciences – that of the Modern Language Association (MLA), that of the American Psychological Association (APA), and that of *The Chicago Manual of Style*. The former is commonly used in the Humanities, the latter two in the Social Sciences.

The APA system emphasises the date of publication, which must appear within an in-text citation:

> Bonnycastle (1996) refers to "the true and lively spirit of opposition" (p. 204) with which Marxist literary criticism invigorates the discipline.

If the reference does not involve a quotation (as it commonly does not in social science papers) only the date need be given as an in-text citation, providing the author's name appears in the signal phrase:

> Bonnycastle (1996) argues that the oppositional tone of Marxist literary criticism invigorates the discipline.

The reference under 'References' at the end of the paper would in either of the above cases be as follows:

> Bonnycastle, Stephen (1996). <u>In search of authority: An introductory guide to literary theory</u> (2nd ed.). Peterborough: Broadview Press.

If the context does not make it clear who the author is, that must be added to the in-text citation.

> Even in the 1990s some have continued to believe that Marxist literary criticism invigorates the discipline with a "true and lively spirit of opposition" (Bonnycastle, 1996, p. 204).

The basic principles of the in-text citation and reference system are the same regardless of whether one is citing a book, an article in a journal or a magazine, a newspaper, a multi-volume work, a book review, or a literary work (though literary works are rarely cited in papers that follow APA style):

> Urban renewal is as much a matter of psychology as it is of bricks and mortar. As Goldberger (1998) has described, there have been many plans to revitalize Havana. But both that city and the community of Cuban exiles in Florida remain haunted by a sense of absence and separation. As Lourdes Casal (1998) reminds us,
>
> > Exile
> >
> > is living where there is no house whatever
> >
> > in which we were ever children;   (l. 1-3)
>
> The psychology of outsiders also makes a difference. Part of the reason Americans have not much noticed the dire plight of their fifth-largest city is that it does not "stir the national imagination" (Rybczynski, 1998, p. 12). Conversely, there has been far more concern over the state of cities such as New Orleans and Quebec, whose history and architecture excite the romantic imagination. As Nora Phelps (1998) has discussed, the past is in itself a key trigger for romantic notions, and it is no doubt inevitable that cities whose history is particularly visible will engender passionate attachments. And as Stephanie Wright and Carole King (1998) have detailed in an important case study, almost all French-speaking Quebecers feel their heritage to be bound up with that of Quebec city. (Richard Ford's character Frank Bascombe has suggested that "New Orleans defeats itself" by longing "for a mystery it doesn't have and never will, if it ever did" [Ford, 1986, 48] but this remains a minority view.)
>
> Georgiana Gibson (1997) is also among those who have investigated the interplay between urban psychology and urban reality. Gibson's personal Web site (1999) now includes the first of a set of working models she is developing in an attempt to represent the effects of various psychological schema on the landscape.

The in-text citations above would connect to References as follows:

> Casal, L. (1998, January 26). Definition. (Elizabeth Macklin, Trans.) New Yorker, 79.

Ford, R. The sportswriter. (1986, 2nd Vintage ed. 1995). New York, Random House.

Gibson, G. (1993). The mind and the city. In B. Earn & S. Towson (Eds.), Urban myths: A history (pp. 176-84). San Francisco: Harbor.

Gibson, G. (1997). Cities in the twentieth century. Boston: Beacon.

Gibson, G. (1999, June 10). Homepage. <http:www.geography. byu.edu/GIBSON/personal.htm> (1999, July 30).

Goldberger, P. (1998, January 26). Annals of preservation: Bringing back Havana. New Yorker 50-62.

Phelps, N. (1998). Pastness and the foundations of romanticism. Romanticism On the Net, 11. <http://users.ox.ac.uk/~scat0385/phelpsmws.html> (1999, July 6).

Rybczynski, W. (1998, February 5). The fifth city. [Review of the book A prayer for the city]. New York Review of Books, 12-14.

Wright, S. & King, C. (1998). Quebec: A history (Vols. 1-2). Montreal: McGill-Queen's University Press.

Among the details to notice in this reference system:

- Where two or more works by the same author are included in References, they are ordered by date of publication.
- APA style prefers author initials rather than first names
- Only the first words of titles and subtitles are capitalized, except for proper nouns.
- The date appears in brackets at the beginning of each entry in References.
- The in-text citation comes before the period or comma in the surrounding sentence.
- If an in-text citation occurs within text in parentheses, square brackets are used for the reference.
- When a work has appeared in an edited collection information on the editors must be included in the reference.
- Authors' first and last names are reversed; note the use of the ampersand [&] between author names.
- Translators should be included under Works Cited.
- Publisher as well as city of publication should be given.
- Months and publisher names are not abbreviated; the day of the month follows the name of the month.
- Online references include the date of publication or of last revision in parentheses immediately after the aurthor's name, and date of access, also in parentheses, at the end of the entry.

Common Errors in English # 524.

For scholarly journals the References listing should include volume number, issue number and page numbers:

> Raedts, Peter (1977). The children's crusade of 1212. <u>Journal of Medieval History 3</u> (4), 279-325.

> Hurka, T.M. (1996). Improving on perfectionism. <u>Philosophical Review 99</u>, 462-73.

Unsigned articles in newspapers and magazines are listed by title:

> Clash over Nobel cash. (1998, February 11). <u>Washington Post</u>, A14.

Books with an unknown author should be alphabetized in the References list by title or publisher name:

> <u>Oxford English Dictionary</u> (2nd ed.). (1989). Oxford: Oxford University Press.

If the References list includes two or more authors with the same last name, the signal phrase before the in-text citation should supply first name (or initials):

> One of the leading economists of the time, H. Johnston (1977) advocated wage and price controls.

For works with three to five authors, identify all authors in the signal phrase or the parentheses the first time the source is cited, but thereafter use only the first author's name followed by "et al.".

Chicago Style

524. Wrong or inconsistent referencing: Three styles of documentation dominate in the Humanities and the Social Sciences — that of the Modern Language Association (MLA), that of the American Psychological Association (APA), and that of *The Chicago Manual of Style*.

The Chicago Manual of Style is commonly used as a guide to documentation by several disciplines. The *Manual* lists an 'A' style and a 'B' style, the latter of which is commonly used in social sciences such as Political Science. As with the APA system, this style requires that the date of publication appear within an in-text citation:

> Bonnycastle refers to "the true and lively spirit of opposition" with which Marxist literary criticism invigorates the discipline (Bonnycastle 1996, 204).

If the reference does not involve a quotation (as it commonly does not in social science research papers) only the date need be given as an in-text citation, providing the author's name appears in the signal phrase:

> Bonnycastle (1996) argues that the oppositional tone of Marxist literary criticism invigorates the discipline.

The reference under 'Bibliography' at the end of the paper would in either of the above cases be as follows:

> Bonnycastle, S. 1996. In search of authority: An introductory guide to literary theory 2d ed. Peterborough: Broadview Press.

The basic principles of the in-text citation and reference system are the same regardless of whether one is citing a book, an article in a journal or a magazine, a newspaper, a multi-volume work, a book review, or a literary work (though literary works are rarely cited in papers that follow Chicago B style):

Urban renewal is as much a matter of psychology as it is of bricks and mortar. As Goldberger (1998) has described, there have been many plans to revitalize Havana. But both that city and the community of Cuban exiles in Florida remain haunted by a sense of absence and separation. As Lourdes Casal (1998) reminds us,

> Exile
>
> is living where there is no house whatever
>
> in which we were ever children;   (lines 1-3)

The psychology of outsiders also makes a difference. Part of the reason Americans have not much noticed the dire plight of their fifth-largest city is that it does not "stir the national imagination" (Rybczynski 1998, 12). Conversely, there has been far more concern over the state of cities such as New Orleans and Quebec, whose history and architecture excite the romantic imagination. As Nora Phelps (1998) has discussed, the past is in itself a key trigger for romantic notions, and it is no doubt inevitable that cities whose history is particularly visible will engender passionate attachments. And as Stephanie Wright and Carole King (1998) have detailed in an important case study, almost all French-speaking Quebecers feel their heritage to be bound up with that of Quebec city. (Richard Ford's character Frank Bascombe has suggested that "New Orleans defeats itself" by longing "for a mystery it doesn't have and never will, if it ever did" [Ford 1986, 48] but this remains a minority view.)

Georgiana Gibson (1997) is also among those who have investigated the interplay between unban psychology and urban reality. Gibson's personal Web site (1999) now includes the first of a set of working models she is developing in an attempt to represent the effects of various psychological schema on the landscape.

The in-text citations above would connect to the Bibliography as follows:

Casal, Lourdes. 1998. Definition. (trans. E. Macklin) New Yorker, 26 January, 79.

Ford, Richard. 1986. The sportswriter. 2d Vintage ed. 1995. New York: Random House.

Gibson, Georgiana. 1993. The mind and the city. In Urban myths: A history, edited by Brian Earn & Shelagh Towson. San Francisco: Harbor, 1993.

Gibson, Georgiana. 1997. Cities in the twentieth century. Boston: Beacon.

Gibson, Georgiana. 1999. Homepage, 10 June, 1999. <http:www.geography.byu.edu/Gibson/personal.htm>   (30 July 1999).

Goldberger, Paul. 1998. Annals of preservation: Bringing back Havana. New Yorker, 26 January, 50-62.

Phelps, Nora. 1998. Pastness and the foundations of romanticism. Romanticism On the Net 11, (August 1999) <http://users.ox.ac.uk/~scat0385/phelpsmws.html> (6 July 1999),

Rybczynski, Witold. 1998. Review of A prayer for the city by D.B. Smith. New York Review of Books, 5 February, 12-14.

Wright, Stephanie and Carole King. 1998. Quebec: A history. Vols. 1-2. Montreal: McGill-Queen's University Press.

Among the details to notice in this reference system:
- Where two or more works by the same author are included in the Bibliography, they are ordered by date of publication.
- Only the first words of titles and subtitles are capitalized, except for proper nouns.
- The date appears at the beginning of each entry in the Bibliography.
- There is no punctuation between author and date in the in-text citation.
- When a work has appeared in an edited collection information on the editors must be included in the reference.
- Authors' first and last names are reversed except for second authors.
- Translators should be included in the bibliographic reference.
- Publisher as well as city of publication should be given.
- Months and publisher names are not abbreviated.
- The day of the month precedes the name of the month.
- Online references include the year of publication after the author's name, and the date of access in parentheses at the end of the entry.

Common Errors in English # 524.

For scholarly journals the Bibliography should include volume number, issue number and page numbers:

Raedts, Peter. 1977. The children's crusade of 1212. Journal of Medieval History 3 (4): 279-325.

Hurka, T.M. 1996. Improving on perfectionism. Philosophical Review 99: 462-73.

Newspaper items are rarely listed separately. Instead, the name of the paper and the relevant run of dates may be given.

Books with no specific or known author should be alphabetized in the Bibliography by title:

Oxford English Dictionary. 1989. 2d ed. Oxford: Oxford University Press.

If the Bibliography includes two or more authors with the same last name, the signal phrase before the in-text citation should supply first name (or initials):

One of the leading economists of the time, H. Johnston (1977) advocated wage and price controls.

Unpublished material is treated much as are journal articles:

Perkins, B. 1998. An investigation of voting patterns in the 1993 Canadian election. Ph.D. diss., university of Alberta, Edmonton.

Canada. House of Commons. Debates, 17 March 1997.

Canada. Senate. Special Committee on Election Spending. Interim report. 1988.

U.S. Congress. House. Committee on Ways and Means. Hearings on Extension of North American Free Trade Agreement. 99th Cong., 1st sess., 1997. Vol. 1.

US Congress. House. Committee on Ways and Means. Subcommittee on Trade. Hearing #105-32 on Free Trade Area of the Americas. 105th Congress. 10 August 1997. <http://frwebgate.access.gpo.gov/cgi-bin/getdoc.cgi?dbname =_house_hearings&docid=f:50672.wais> (22 July 1999).

APPENDIX 1: A Reference Guide to Basic Grammar

PARTS OF SPEECH

NOUNS

Nouns are words that name people, things, places or qualities. Some examples follow:

boy John parent	names of people
hat spaghetti fish	names of things
Saskatoon Zambia New York	names of places
silence intelligence anger	names of qualities

Nouns can be used to fill the gaps in sentences like these:

I saw_____at the market yesterday.

He dropped the _____into the gutter.

Has she lost a lot of _____?

Hamilton is a _____with several hundred thousand _____living in it.

Some nouns (e.g. *sugar, milk, confusion*) are uncountable — that is, we cannot say "a sugar, two sugars, three sugars".

PRONOUNS

Pronouns replace or stand for nouns. For example, instead of saying, "The man slipped on a banana peel" or "George slipped on a banana peel," we can replace the noun *man* (or the noun *George*) with the pronoun *he* and say "He slipped on a banana peel."

Definite and Indefinite Pronouns: Whereas a pronoun such as "he" refers to a definite person, the words *each, every, either, neither, one, another,* and *much* are indefinite. They may be used as pronouns or as adjectives; in either case, a *singular* verb is needed.

> Each player wants to do his best.
> (Here the word *each* is an adjective, describing the noun *player*.)

> Each wants to do his best.
> (Here the word *each* is a pronoun, acting as the subject of the sentence.)

> Each of the players wants to do his best.
> (The word *each* is still a pronoun, this time followed by the phrase *of the players*. But it is the pronoun *each* that is the subject of the sentence; the verb must be the singular *wants*.)

Possessive Pronouns and Adjectives: See under *Adjectives* below.

Relative Pronouns: These pronouns relate back to a noun that has been used earlier in the same sentence. Look at how repetitious these sentences sound:
> I talked to the man. The man wore a red hat.

We could of course replace the second *man* with *he*. Even better, though, is to relate or connect the second idea to the first by using a relative pronoun:
> I talked to the man who wore a red hat.

> I found the pencil. I had lost the pencil.

> I found the pencil that I had lost.

The following are all relative pronouns:

who	whose (has other uses too)
which	that (has other uses too)
whom	

Try replacing the second noun in these pairs of sentences with a relative pronoun, so as to make only one sentence out of each pair:

1) I polished the table. I had built the table.

2) Premier Romanow is vacationing this week in Quebec's

Common Errors in English

Eastern Townships. The Premier cancelled a planned holiday last fall.

3) The word "other" has developed a special cachet among literary theorists. "Other," incidentally, is usually put in quotation marks when so used.

Pronouns Acting as Subject and as Object

We use different personal pronouns depending on whether we are using them as the subject or the object.

Subject Pronouns

I	we
you	you
he/she/it	they
who, what, which	who, what, which (interrogative)

Object Pronouns

me	us
you	you
him/her/it	them
whom, what, which	who, what, which (interrogative)

He shot the sherrif.
(Here the pronoun *he* is the subject of the sentence.)

The sherrif shot him.
(Here the word *him* is the object; *the sherrif* is the subject.)

That's the man who shot the sherrif.
(Here the pronoun *who* is the subject of the clause *who shot the sherrif.*)

That's the man whom the sherrif shot.
(Here the pronoun *whom* is the object; *the sherrif* is the subject.)

The distinctions between *I* and *me* and between *who* and *whom* are treated more fully under **Pronoun Problems**.

ARTICLES

These are words used to introduce nouns. There are only three of them — *a*, *an* and *the*. Articles show whether or not one is drawing attention to a <u>particular</u> person or thing.

For example, we would say "I stood beside a house" if we did not want to draw attention to that particular house, but "I stood beside the house that the Taylors used to live in" if we did want to draw attention to the particular house. *A* (or *an* if the noun following begins with a vowel) is an <u>indefinite</u> article – used when you do not wish to be definite or specific about which thing or person you are referring to. *The* is a <u>definite</u> article, used when you do wish to call attention to the particular thing or person. Remember that if you use *the*, you are suggesting that there can only be <u>one</u> of what you are referring to.

Choose the appropriate article ("a", "an" or "the"):

1) _____moon shone brightly last night.

2) She had _____long conversation with _____friend of hers.

3) Have you ever driven _____car?

4) Have you driven _____car that your wife bought on Monday?

ADJECTIVES

Adjectives are words used to tell us more about (*describe* or *modify*) nouns or pronouns. Here are some examples of adjectives:

big	good	heavy
small	bad	expensive
pretty	careful	fat
quick	slow	thin

e.g.   The fat man lifted the heavy table.
(Here the adjective *fat* describes or tells us more about the noun *man*,
and the adjective *heavy* describes the noun *table*.)

e.g.   The fast runner finished ahead of the slow one.
(*Fast* describes *runner* and *slow* describes *one*.)

Notice that adjectives usually come before the nouns that they describe. This is not always the case, however; when the verb *to be* is used, adjectives often come after the noun or pronoun, and after the verb:

e.g.   That woman is particularly careful about her finances.
(*Careful* describes *woman*.)

e.g.   It is too difficult for me to do.
                          (*Difficult* describes *it.*)

Adjectives can be used to fill the gaps in sentences like these:

1) This _____ sweater was knitted by hand.
2) As soon as we entered the _____ house we heard a _____ clap of thunder.
3) Those shoes are very _____.
4) Derrida's argument at this point could fairly be described as _____.

Some words can be either adjectives or pronouns, depending on how they are used. That is the case with the indefinite pronouns (see above), and also with certain possessives (words that show possession):

Possessive Adjectives

my	our
your	your
his/her	their
whose	whose

Possessive Pronouns

mine	ours
yours	yours
his/hers	theirs
whose	whose

e.g.   I have my cup, and he has his.
              (Here the word *his* is a pronoun, used in place of the noun *cup*.)
e.g.   He has his cup.
              (Here the word *his* is an adjective, describing the noun *cup*.)

Whose book is this?
(Here the word *whose* is a possessive adjective, describing the *book*.)
Whose is this?
(Here the word *whose* is a possessive pronoun, acting as the subject of
the sentence.)

Common Errors in English

VERBS

Verbs are words that express actions or states of affairs. Most verbs can be conveniently thought of as *doing* words (e.g. *open, feel, do, carry, see, think, combine, send*), but a few verbs do not fit into this category. Indeed, the most common verb of all — *be* — expresses a state of affairs, not a particular action that is done.

Verbs are used to fill gaps in sentences like these:

1) I _____very quickly, but I _____not _____up with my brother.

2) She usually _____to sleep at 9:30.

3) Stephen _____ his breakfast very quickly.

4) They _____a large farm near Newcastle.

5) There _____many different languages that people in India _____.

One thing that makes verbs different from other parts of speech is that verbs have <u>tenses</u>; in other words, they change their form depending on the time you are talking about. For example, the present tense of the verb *to be* is *I am, you are, he is*, etc., while the past tense is *I was, you were, he was*, etc. If unsure whether or not a particular word is a verb, one way to check is to ask if it has different tenses. For example, if one thought that perhaps the word *football* might be a verb, one need only ask oneself if it would be correct to say, *I footballed, I am footballing, I will football* and so on. Obviously it would not be, so one knows that *football* is the noun that names the game, not a verb that expresses an action. See the first chapter in this book for a discussion of verb tenses.

ADVERBS

These words are usually used to tell us more about (*describe* or *modify*) verbs, although they can also be used to tell us more about adjectives or about other adverbs. They answer questions like "How...?", "When...?", and "To what extent...?", and often they end with the letters *ly*. Here are a few examples, with the adjectives also listed for comparison.

ADJECTIVE	ADVERB
careful	carefully
beautiful	beautifully
thorough	thoroughly
sudden	suddenly
slow	slowly
easy	easily
good	well
	today
	often
	very

He walked carefully.

> (The adverb *carefully* tells us <u>how</u> he walked; it describes the verb, *walked*.)

He is a careful boy.

> (The adjective *careful* describes the noun *boy*.)

My grandfather died suddenly last week.

> (The adverb *suddenly* tells <u>how</u> he died; it describes the verb *died*.)

We were upset by the sudden death of my grandfather.

> (The adjective *sudden* describes the noun *death*.)

She plays the game very well.

> (The adverb *well* tells us <u>how</u> she plays; it describes the verb *plays*. The adverb *very* describes the adverb *well*.)

She played a good game this afternoon.

> (The adjective *good* describes the noun *game*.)

She played a very good game.

> (The adverb *very* describes the adjective *good*, telling us <u>how</u> good it was.)

According to his Press Secretary, Bush will meet Gorbachev soon.

> (The adverb *soon* describes the verb *will meet*, telling <u>when</u> the action will happen.)

Choose adverbs to fill the gaps in these sentences:

1) Ralph writes very _____.

2) The Judge spoke _____ to Milken after he had been convicted on six counts of stock manipulation and fraud.

3) They were _____ late for the meeting this morning.

PREPOSITIONS

Prepositions are joining words, normally used before **nouns** or **pronouns**. Some of the most common prepositions are as follows:

after	from	off
across	in	over
at	into	to
before	of	until
for	on	with

Choose prepositions to fill the gaps in these sentences:

1) I will tell you _____it _____the morning.

2) Please try to arrive _____eight o'clock.

3) He did not come back _____Toronto _____yesterday.

4) I received a letter _____my sister.

CONJUNCTIONS

Conjunctions are normally used to join groups of words together, and in particular join clauses together. Some examples:

because	unless	after
although	until	if
and	since	or
as	before	that

They stopped playing because they were tired.

(The conjunction *because* joins the group of words "because they were tired" to the group of words, "They stopped playing")

I will give her your message if I see her.

(The conjunction *if* introduces the second group of words and joins it to the first.)

Many conjunctions can also act as other parts of speech, depending on how they are used. Notice the difference in each of these pairs of sentences:

He will not do anything about it until the morning.

(Here *until* is a preposition joining the noun *morning* to the rest of the sentence.)

Common Errors in English

He will not do anything about it until he has discussed it with his wife.

> (Here *until* is a conjunction introducing the clause "until he has discussed it with his wife.")

I slept for half an hour after dinner.

> (Here *after* is a preposition joining the noun *dinner* to the rest of the sentence.)

I slept for half an hour after they had gone home.

> (Here *after* is a conjunction introducing the clause "after they had gone home.")

She wants to buy that dress.

> (Here *that* is an adjective describing the noun *dress*: "Which dress?", "That dress!")

George said that he was unhappy.

> (Here *that* is a conjunction introducing the clause, "that he was unhappy.")

Choose conjunctions to fill the gaps in the following sentences:

1) We believed _____ we would win.

2) They sat down in the shade _____ it was hot.

3) My father did not speak to me _____ he left.

PARTS OF SENTENCES

SUBJECT

The subject is the thing, person, or quality about which something is said in a clause. The subject is usually a noun or pronoun.

The man went to town.

> (The sentence is about the man, not about the town; thus the noun *man* is the subject.)

Groundnuts are an important crop in Nigeria.

> (The sentence is about groundnuts, not about crops or about Nigeria; thus the noun *groundnuts* is the subject.)

Common Errors in English

Nigeria is the most populous country in Africa.

> (The sentence is about Nigeria, not about countries or about Africa; thus the noun *Nigeria* is the subject.)

He followed me wherever I went.

> (The pronoun *He* is the subject.)

Core Subject: The core subject is the single noun or pronoun that forms the subject.

Complete Subject: The complete subject is the subject together with any adjectives or adjectival phrases modifying it.

e.g.   The lady in the huge hat went to the market to buy groceries.

> The core subject is *the lady* and the complete subject is *the lady in the huge hat.*

OBJECT

An object is something or someone towards which an action or feeling is directed. In grammar an object is the thing, person or quality affected by the action of the verb. (To put it another way, it receives the action of the verb.) Like a subject, an object normally is made up of a noun or pronoun.

Direct object: The direct object is the thing, person, or quality directly affected by the action of the verb. A direct object usually answers the question, "What...?" or "Who...?". Notice that direct objects are not introduced by prepositions.

Indirect object: The indirect object is the thing, person, or quality that is indirectly affected by the action of the verb. All indirect objects *could be* expressed differently by making them the objects of the prepositions *to* or *for*. Instead, the prepositions have been omitted. Indirect objects answer the questions, "To whom?" and "For whom?".

McGriff hit the ball a long way.

> (What did he hit? The ball. *The ball* is the direct object of the verb *hit*)

She threw me her hat.

> (What did she throw? Her hat. *Her hat* is the direct object. To whom did she throw it? To me. *Me* is the indirect object. Note that the

Common Errors in English

sentence could be rephrased, "She threw her hat to me.")

They gave a watch to their father for Christmas.

(direct object is *watch*; indirect object *father*)

Predicate

The predicate is everything that is said about the subject. In the above example, "went to the market to buy groceries" is the predicate. A predicate <u>always</u> includes a verb.

CLAUSE

A distinct group of words that includes both a subject and a predicate. Thus a clause always includes a verb.

PHRASE

A distinct group of words that does <u>not</u> include both a subject and a verb. Examples:

CLAUSES	PHRASES
because he is strong	because of his strength (no verb)
before she comes home	before the meeting (no verb)
the professor likes me	from Halifax
a tree fell down	at lunch
who came to dinner	in the evening

TYPES OF CLAUSES

Main clause

A main clause is a group of words which is, <u>or could be</u>, a sentence on its own.

Subordinate clause

A subordinate clause is a clause which could <u>not</u> form a complete sentence on its own.

Except for *and, but,* and *or,* conjunctions do not introduce main clauses, so if a clause begins with a word such as *because, although, after* or *if,* you can be confident it is a subordinate clause. Similarly, relative pronouns introduce subordinate clauses — never main clauses.

She lives near Pittsburgh.

(One main clause forming a complete sentence. The pronoun *She* is the subject, *lives* is the verb, and the preposition *near* and the noun *Pittsburgh* together form a phrase.)

He danced in the street because he was feeling happy.

main clause: He danced in the street

subject:_____

verb:_____

subordinate clause: because he was feeling happy

subject:_____

verb:_____

Mavis has married a man who is older than her father.

main clause: Mavis has married a man

subject:_____

verb:_____

subordinate clause: who is older than her father

subject: who

verb: _____

TYPES OF SUBORDINATE CLAUSES

Adjectival subordinate clause: a subordinate clause that tells us more about a noun or pronoun. Adjectival clauses begin with relative pronouns such as *who*, *whom*, *whose*, *which*, and *that*.

Adverbial subordinate clause: a subordinate clause that tells us more about the action of the verb—telling how, when, why or where the action occurred.

Noun subordinate clause: a clause that acts like a noun to form the subject or object of a sentence.

Examples:

He talked at length to his cousin, who quickly became bored.

("Who quickly became bored" is an adjectival subordinate clause, telling us more about the noun *cousin*.)

subject of subordinate clause: the pronoun *who*

verb in subordinate clause:_____

subject of main clause: the pronoun *He*

verb of main clause:_____

My husband did not like the gift that I gave him.

("That I gave him" is an adjectival subordinate clause telling us more about the noun *gift*.)

subject of subordinate clause: the pronoun *I*

verb in subordinate clause:_____

subject of main clause:_____

verb in main clause:_____

The boy whom she wants to marry is very poor.

("Whom she wants to marry" is an adjectival subordinate clause telling us more about the noun *boy*. Notice that here the subordinate clause appears <u>in the middle of</u> the main clause, "The boy is very poor".)

subject of subordinate clause:_____

verb in subordinate clause:_____

subject of main clause:_____

verb of main clause:_____

I felt worse after I had been to the doctor.

("After I had been to the doctor" is an adverbial subordinate clause telling you <u>when</u> I felt worse.)

He could not attend because he had broken his leg.

("Because he had broken his leg" is an adverbial subordinate clause telling you <u>why</u> he could not attend.)

She looked as if she had seen a ghost.

("As if she had seen a ghost" is an adverbial subordinate clause telling you <u>how</u> she looked.)

What he said was very interesting.

("What he said" is a noun clause acting as the subject of the sentence, in the same way that the noun *conversation* acts as the subject in "The conversation was very interesting.")

Sue-Ellen told me that she wanted to become a lawyer.

("That she wanted to become a lawyer" is a noun clause acting as the

object, in the same way that the noun *plans* acts as the object in
"Sue-Ellen told me her plans.")

Types of Phrases

Adjectival phrase: a phrase that tells us more about a noun or pronoun.

Adverbial phrase: a phrase that tells us more about the action of a verb, answering questions such as "When...?", "Where...?", "How...?" and "Why...?".

> The boy in the new jacket got into the car.
>
> ("In the new jacket" is an adjectival phrase telling us more about the noun *boy*.)
>
> I drank from the cup with a broken handle.
>
> ("With a broken handle" is a phrase telling us more about the noun *cup*.)
>
> We went to the park.
>
> ("To the park" is an adverbial phrase telling <u>where</u> we went.)
>
> They arrived after breakfast.
>
> ("After breakfast" is an adverbial phrase telling <u>when</u> they arrived.)

Phrases and Clauses

> They were late because of the weather.
>
> ("Because of the weather" is an adverbial _____ telling us <u>why</u> they were late. It has no verb.)
>
> They were late because the weather was bad.
>
> ("Because the weather was bad" is an adverbial _____ telling us why they were late.)
>
> Subject:_____
>
> Verb:_____)
>
> The man at the corner appeared to be drunk.
>
> ("At the corner" is an adjectival _____ telling us more about the noun _____.)
>
> The man who stood at the corner appeared to be drunk.
>
> ("Who stood at the corner" is an _____, telling us more

Common Errors in English

about the noun _____.)

Subject:_____

Verb:_____

Parts of Speech and Parts of the Sentence

Example: After the generous man with the big ears has bought presents, he will quickly give them to his friends.

Parts of speech:

after: conjunction

generous:_____

with: _____

big: _____

has bought:_____

he:_____

quickly:_____

to:_____

friends:_____

the: article

man:_____

the:_____

ears: _____

presents:_____

will give:_____

them:_____

his:_____

Parts of the sentence:

Main clause: He will quickly give them to his friends.

subject:_____

predicate:_____

verb:_____

direct object:_____

indirect object:_____

Subordinate clause: After the generous man with the big ears has bought presents

Is this an adjectival or an adverbial subordinate clause?

Core subject: the noun _____

Complete subject:_____

Adjectival phrase: with the big ears

This phrase tells us more about the noun: _____

predicate:_____

direct object:_____

Common Errors in English

APPENDIX 2: Correction Key

Ab	Faulty abbreviation
Adj	Improper use of adjective
Adv	Improper use of adverb
Agr	Faulty agreement
Amb	Ambiguous
Awk	Awkward expression or construction
Cap	Faulty capitalization
D	Faulty diction
Dgl	Dangling construction
Frag	Fragment
lc	Use lowercase
Num	Error in use of numbers
‖	Lack of parallelism
P	Faulty punctuation
Ref	Unclear pronoun reference
Rep	Unnecessary repetition
R-O	Run-on
Sp	Error in spelling
SS	Faulty sentence structure
T	Wrong tense of verb
tr ⌒⌣	Transpose elements (e.g., to quickly go, recieve)
∨	Wrong verb form
Wdy	Wordy
⌄	Add apostrophe or single quotation mark
⌣	Close up
⋏	Add comma
ℓ	Delete
⋀	Insert
¶	Begin a new paragraph
No ¶	Do not begin a new paragraph
⊙	Add a Period
⌵ ⌵	Double quotation marks
#	Add space

EXERCISES

The numbers in the brackets that accompany most exercises correspond to the numbers assigned to errors throughout the body of the book. This is intended to make many of the exercises 'self-correcting'; by referring to the relevant number in the body of the book and reading the entry, you can see if your answer is correct.

EXERCISE   General Diagnostic or Review Exercise 1

Choose the correct alternatives:

1) Yesterday afternoon when he _____[ate/had eaten] his meal, he rushed outside. (8)

2) Not long ago much of the world was ruled by a few colonial powers. Most of Africa, indeed, was under colonial rule _____ (until/untill) the 1960s. Now,_____ (therefore/however), only a few countries,_____ (for example/such as) French Guiana and the Falkland Islands, are under colonial rule. (518, 470)

3) How did his criticism (affect/effect) you? (211)

4) He ran quickly _____(inorder/in order) to reach the bank before it closed. (390)

5) He is an intolerant person _____(in that/in the way that) he _____(believes/is believing) all Jews to be greedy. (471, 4)

6) The traffic is very heavy _____ [everyday/every day] at this time. (390)

7) Max invited me to his cottage, where he said we _____[can/could] go fishing. (499)

8) My cousin _____[may be/maybe] coming tonight, but I _____[can not/cannot] be there. (389, 390)

9) _____[May be/ Maybe] my friend will be _____ [arriving to/arriving at/arriving] Mirabel airport soon. (389, 74)

10) _____[They/There] are a number of stores _____ [near by/nearby]. (335, 389)

11) She _____[insisted/persisted]_____in/on finishing her work before watching television. (289)

12) Mrs. Murphy told me that she preferred _____ [living/leaving] in

Myrtle _____ [than/to] _____ [living/leaving] in a large city like Toronto. (518, 127, 518)

13) He was _____[quite/quiet] eager to _____ [avenge/revenge] the terrible things that had been done _____ [to/for] him. (518, 206, 101)

14) One of the boys _____[is/are] responsible _____ for keeping/to keep this _____ [domitory/dormitory] tidy. (2, 63, 521)

15) If he _____[shoots/shot] an innocent man, a policeman would be dismissed. (10)

16) It was _____ [wet that/so wet that/too wet that/ very wet that] _____ [they/there] was mud everywhere. (474, 335)

EXERCISE   General Diagnostic or Review Exercise 2

Correct the error(s) in each of the following.

1) They discussed about the bilateral agreement.(99)

2) All the people who was their they were happy.(2, 466, 174)

3) Businessmen create wealth just as surely as fishermen and farmers.(504, 215, 504)

4) The police arrived at their house quiet unexpectedly, than they arrested Mr. Svoboda.(518, 478, 518)

5) I can not meet you later today, I have a prior engagement.(277, 333)

6) In these circumtances morale and efficiency in the organization declines. (498, 2)

7) He had drank more than was good for him.(28)

8) He assured me that he was capable to do the work.(48)

9) Two other types of corporate concentration gives rise to concern. (2)

10) She accepted to organize the activities for Parents Day. (44, 492)

11) All of the students had good behaviors during the church service. (153)

12) The complaints against the law by the business community suggests that it must have had some affect. (2, 211)

13) Prof. Curtis unhappy with her work because he gave her an 'F'. (385, 461)

14) In addition to the gun which was used to commit the crime, the police is also in possesion of other evidence. (476, 172, 521)

15) The airlines carry children at lower fairs than adults, even though they take up seats and generally need more attention from airline staff. (518, 178)

16) She wanted some advise on how to invest her money. (182)

17) I had been told to try and not do any mistakes. (442, 423)

18) People living in the Kalahari dessert are few, and food is short. (346, 518, 432)

19) If one believes the rate of interest will rise, it would be wise to keep ones' asset's in cash untill the rise has taken place. (492, 518)

20) For years the USSR refused to allow its 'satelites' to be independent. (223)

21) Everything seem to be running satisfactory; let's let sleeping dogs lie rather than changing horses in mid-stream. (2, 181, 505)

22) She asked me if I can loan her fourty cents. (10, 206, 518)

23) Costa Rica is rather unique amoung Central American nations. (340, 521)

24) Rebecca always want to try and suceed. (2, 442)

25) Taking this into account, it becomes apparent that cost per square foot is neither the only nor the main factor that a firm such as this one should be considering. (13, 178)

26) In my opinion I think people with heavy jobs for example minors should be paid well. (371, 470, 518)

27) Instead of alternatively fighting inflation and unemployment, the goverment sometimes find that they have to fight both at the same time. (214, 2, 166)

28) On the eighteenth, too, the Canadians captured Trun, the village proposed by Montgomery for the meeting place with the Americans, who themselves were now nearing the village of Chambois just a few miles away, and yet on the night of August the nineteenth in a drizzly rain and early morning fog thousands of trapped German soldiers made their way stealthily through the narrow gap, and when the fog lifted on the morning of the twentieth the gap was still packed by the escaping army. (477)

29) To be sure, the American economy has continued to be the greatest engine for the creation of wealth and expansion of opportunity known to man, and Johnson's last vignette describes how women have conquered the professions and workplace and achieved equality. But is that all the American civic religion, the noble experiment, comes to in the end? Where does Paul Johnson come out on all this? [Walter A. McDougall, Book Review, *Times Literary Supplement*, November 21, 1997] (504)

EXERCISE   General Diagnostic or Review Exercise 3

Correct the error(s) in each of the following.

1) In Scott Fitzgeralds' story 'The Ice Palace' (which appear in the book, *Morden Short Stories*) Sally Carroll displays many sides to her character. (492, 2, 485, 521)

2) Susan has two brothers, one of them is looking forward to start university next year, and the other one is about to start high school. (477, 56)

3) He lied that his friend had been trying to kill him. (422)

4) It was there first time at the circus, and they were so excited. (335, 434)

5) Coffee may be short this year if demand remains at it's current high level. (432, 492)

6) ABC is not more superior than any of the other detergents. (424, 140)

7) All the students talked to each other. (163)

8) None of the wheels on my bicycle turn properly. (151)

9) The doctor told him not to drink and smoke for at least six months. (395)

10) Jackson was a member of the university's security force for close to four years at the time of his death. (8)

11) Neither of these books are very well-written. (164)

12) Humanists tends to downplay the usefulness of statitics. Whereas, all too often, social scientists ignore information which cannot be quantified. (2, 521, 480, 476)

13) Please remember all tools must be returned by 5 p.m. (385)

14) Perhaps the comparison between the moon landing and the discovery of the Titanic is valid, but for most of us the moon landing wins for sheer drama and technological ingenuity. But then it cost billions of dollars more, so it *should* have had a bigger impact. But in long-term benefits, the two achievments may not be so different. (449)

15) We have no plans to re-introduce the legislation, there's a lot more important things to do. (477, 2)

16) The proposed movie would include Nesmith, who choose to remain at home rather than join the current Monkees reunion tour. (25)

17) The American administration wanted a free trade agreement and so did the Canadian government, which would cover almost all goods and services. (178)

18) Its important to always be careful about punctuation. (193, 1)

19) When a corporation is expanding quickly, they often experience cash-flow problems. (2)

20) She visited a doctor with a bad case of the flu. (215)

21) Travelling 1,800 feet upwards in a matter of seconds, the CN Tower seems very impressive. (13)

22) Her sister, who lives in Buffalo has been visiting her this week. (485)

23) Man is an animal that breastfeeds its young. (504)

EXERCISE: Split Infinitives (1)

Change the following split infinitives:

1) They did not want to quickly decide the issue.

2) We were asked to patiently await the decision.

3) The contractor said that they would have to carefully restore the house.

4) Their policy was to perpetually maintain a state of economic equilibrium.

5) The choir began to loudly sing the anthem.

EXERCISE: Simple Present Tense (2)

Add an *s* where necessary to plural nouns, third person singular verbs, etc.

1) Train in Burma usually run on time, although it sometime take many hours to get from one place to another. The trip from Belowa to Rangoon, for example, last about eleven hour. The Railway Corporation use several different type of locomotive—steam, electric, and diesel. The newest are the electric locomotive that travel between Rangoon and Mutisa.

2) Most of the electricity that the State need come from the dam. When the water flow over the large turbine, it turn them and this produce large amount of electricity.

3) When a debate start, the Chair alway introduce the topic and then three speaker from each team argue for or against the resolution. Each speaker talk for several minute. At the end of the debate the Chair give all those in the crowd who wish to comment a chance to do so.

4) In politic as in everyday life the variation that interest us occur in two dimension. Sometime political scientist are curious about variation over time. For instance, they may ask why the number of vote received by the various parties fluctuate so much from one election to the next. At other time political scientist concentrate their attention on variation over space. They may be interested, for example, in why one nation government seem to enjoy more success than it neighbour in combatting inflation, or protecting human right.

EXERCISE: Subject-verb agreement (2)

Correct the subject-verb agreement error in each of the following:

1) Fowler (1962) pointed out that concern about the dangers of premature cognitive training and an overemphasis on personality development had delayed inordinately the recognition that the ability to talk, read and compute increase the child's self-respect and independent functioning.

2) Canada's chances of making it to the televised finals, where the big payoff to sponsors come, are not great.

(Financial Post, Nov. 23, 1987)

3) To make matters worse, none of the three in the Leaf's training camp have much playoff experience.

(*Toronto Star*, Sept. 20, 1991)

4) The technical aspect of the newspaper has also be re-evaluated. Typos, or mistakes in spelling and grammar, which makes comprehension difficult, has been made almost a thing of the past.

(Editorial in the student newspaper of the State University of New York at Stony Brook, as quoted in *The New Yorker*, Jan. 12, 1992.)

EXERCISE: Simple Present Tense

Fill in the correct tense of the verb:

1) Every day the sun _____ *[to rise]* in the east and _____ *[to set]* in the west. Because of this, some people _____ *[to think]* that the sun _____ *[to revolve]* around the earth. In fact, the opposite _____ *[to be]* true; the earth _____ *[to circle]* the sun once every day. While the sun _____ *[to shine]* on one side of the earth, it _____ *[to be]* night on the other side. (3)

2) This year she _____ *[to follow]* the same pattern of teaching in many lessons. As soon as she _____ *[to come]* into the class she _____ *[to ask]* several questions on the previous day's work. Then she usually _____ *[to introduce]* a new topic, and _____ *[to talk]* to us about it for several minutes. More often than not she then _____ *[to assign]* a written exercise to do in class. If the students _____ *[to finish]* the exercise before the end of the class, she _____ *[to correct]* it on the board. Sometimes if there _____ *[to be]* a few minutes remaining she _____ *[to tell]* a story or asks a student to tell a story. (3)

3) Shylock _____ *[to be]* the most important character in Shakespeare's *The Merchant of Venice*. We _____ *[to sympathize]* with him despite his streak of cruelty, because we _____ *[to be made]* to understand his resentment against the Christians. When Shylock _____ *[to accuse]* Antonio in Act One of having sworn at him and spat on him merely because of his religion, Antonio—far from denying the charges—_____ *[to say]* that he would do the same again. Moreover, Antonio's prejudice against Jews _____ *[to seem]* to be shared by all the Christian characters in the play. (522)

EXERCISE: Conditional Sentences (9, 10)

Complete the following sentences in any appropriate way.

1) If I wore no clothes at all...

2) If the government reduces taxes...

3) He would buy a truck if...

4) He will buy a truck if...

5) If an election is held next month...

6) She will win if...

7) She would win if...

8) If money were abolished...

9) Local farms would be more productive if...

10) If he sends me the money in time...

EXERCISE: The Conditional (9, 10)

Fill in either the conditional tense or the simple future tense in the main clause.

Example I [to help] him if I could.

I would help him if I could. (conditional)

1) If I found someone's wallet lying on the ground, I [to return] it.

2) If I find the wallet that you have lost, I [to return] it.

3) You [to find] the weather extremely cold if you lived at the North Pole.

4) You [to find] the weather extremely cold when you come to Canada this coming January.

5) If he gets here before three o'clock, I [to take] him to see the museum.

6) If you were the Prime Minister, what _____ you_____ [to do] about the situation?

7) I [to be] very happy if the company hires me as an apprentice.

8) If I were very rich, I [to buy] a house in West Vancouver.

Fill in either the simple past or the simple present tense in the subordinate clause:

9) I will ask him about it if I _____ [to see] him again later today.

10) If I _____ [to win] the lottery I will buy my parents a new car.

11) If I _____ [to win] the lottery I would buy my parents a new car.

12) He would do better if he _____ [to work] harder.

13) He will do better if he _____ [to work] harder next term.

14) If a burglar _____ [to come] into your room at night, what would you do?

15) I will lend you this CD if you _____ [to promise] to take good care of it.

16) He would look much better if he _____ [to arrange] his hair differently.

17) There can no longer be any doubt that people _____ [to live] longer if they _____ [to smoke] less.

EXERCISE: Conditional Sentences (9, 10)

Fill in the missing verbs.

1) He _____ *[to supply]* our company with what we need if we _____ *[to pay]* him $50,000. However, we only _____ *[to have]* $30,000 in liquid assets.

2) If he _____ *[to reply]* to me quickly, as I think he will, I _____ *[to be able]* to make reservations for our holiday.

3) If she _____ *[to believe]* in God she _____ *[to go]* to church. However, she _____ *[to be]* an atheist.

4) My friend and I are thinking of going to the game this afternoon. If we _____ *[to go]* we probably _____ *[to take]* our wives with us.

5) If we _____ *[to arrive]* sooner, we would have been able to help him.

6) If Montcalm's most important officer _____ not _____ *[to be hiding]* away with his mistress, the French troops _____ *[to be assembled]* earlier and the British _____ *[to lose]* the battle on the Plains of Abraham.

7) We would have been better off if we _____ *[to plant]* wheat instead of cotton.

8) If you had spoken to me about it, I _____ *[to do]* something sooner.

9) I would have told them the truth if they _____ *[to ask]* me.

10) The Titanic _____ probably not _____ *[to sink]* if it had struck the iceberg head on.

EXERCISE: Conditional and Past Conditional (11)

Correct the error in each of the following:

1) If we sent the cheque by special delivery now, it will reach her by Thursday.

2) If you would pay attention, you will understand a good deal more of what is said.

3) If they all won prizes, I'm sure some of them will still be sullen and unhappy.

4) If you would have eaten anything poisonous, there would have been some indication of trouble by now.

5) If they would have thought about it beforehand, they would not have acted so very foolishly.

6) And if second baseman Manny Lee made a play on a Scott Bradley grounder in the fourth, the Jays could have been out of the inning, trailing only 3-2.

(Toronto Star, July 10, 1988)

7) Had he been with the 1993 batch of Jays, his deficiencies may not have been all that conspicuous.

(The Globe and Mail, Aug 8, 1994)

8) If you would have come when I first called you, none of this would have happened.

EXERCISE: Active and Passive (12)

Improve each of the following sentences by changing the verb from the passive voice to the active. You may also be able to make other improvements.

1) Legislation has been passed by the government to ensure that the rights of individuals are protected.

2) After careful deliberation, it has been decided that the application for residential zoning of the building to be changed to commercial will be approved.

3) The economy was subjected to two serious oil price shocks in the 1970s; those with cars were forced to line-up for hours to obtain gasoline, and everyone was affected by inflation.

4) Research in this area was first carried out by Samuel Smith in the 1980s, and was completed after his death by a team directed by Marjorie Mullins.

EXERCISE: Verb Tenses: General Review

Fill in the correct tenses of the verbs.

1) This train always _____ *[to leave]* at exactly five o'clock. (3)

2) As he _____ *[to climb]* the mountain he _____ *[to lose]* his grip and _____ *[to plunge]* five hundred feet to his death.

3) After we _____ *[to make]* our way through the forest, we sat down to rest. (8)

4) This machinery _____ *[to be]* very reliable. It almost never _____ *[to break]* down and it _____ *[to need]* very little maintenance. (3)

5) He _____ *[to tell]* me before the meeting yesterday that they _____ *[to reach]* a decision already. (8)

6) The Cleveland Indians _____ *[to improve]* at the

moment, but I _____ [to not think] that they _____ [to be] as good as the Red Sox yet. (4)

7) The government _____ [to oppress] the people of East Timor for many years. I _____ [to hope] that it soon _____ [to be] forced to change its ways. (7)

8) _____ you ever _____ [to see] a flying saucer? (7)

9) I _____ [to tell] him what I knew if I _____ [to trust] him. Unfortunately, I don't trust him. (10)

10) If he _____ [to find out] about this he _____ [to be] very angry, but I am sure he will not find out. (10)

11) Greene's greatest novel _____ [to recount] the story of an alcoholic Mexican priest during a period in which the government _____ [to suppress] organized religion. (6)

EXERCISE: Dangling Constructions (13-16)

Correct the following sentences:

1) Riding the bus to work, his wife waved at him from the sidewalk.

2) When covered with aluminum siding, we will have a much more salable house.

3) Regarding the fiscal requirements of the government, an increase in taxes will be required if the deficit is to be reduced.

4) Looking for a moment at the implications of Smith's argument, he allows us to justify our selfish behavior.

5) Having covered the issue of stratification, the means of redistributing income will be dealt with next.

6) To obtain a sense of the density of structuralist prose, a few examples should suffice.

7) We have asked for a survey of the attitudes of consumers carried out randomly.

8) Considering all of this evidence, there is no doubt that an increased awareness of the usefulness of uniform and objectively-defined time led to the spread of clocks, and not the other way round.

9) Widely regarded as a failure by observers at the time, we can now see that Truman was a remarkably successful president.

10) To begin this essay, Faulkner's novel is written from several points of view.

11) To obtain a refund, any copies damaged in shipment must be returned promptly.

12) Having settled the issue of independence, questions of economic growth came to the fore in the public consciousness.

13) Smothered in mushrooms and lashed with HP sauce, I enjoyed the steak immensely.

14) Although redundant, the company president said the 250 workers

would be offered alternative jobs.

15) To help reduce the beaver colonies, the Department of Natural Resources has even begun allowing novice trappers to learn to trap in the comfort of their own living rooms.

(*The Globe and Mail*, August 12, 1991)

16) As reconstructed by police, Pfeiffer at first denied any knowledge of the Byrd murder.

(*The New York Times*, reprinted in Theodore Bernstein, *Watch Your Language*)

17) The woman had moved into an apartment where she was killed a few weeks before her death.

(quoted from a Montreal newspaper in *Word Watching*, a language newsletter)

18) Remy hit an RBI single off Hass' leg, which rolled into right field.

(*Webster's Dictionary of English Usage*)

19) When stewed, I like prunes.

[Note: Numbers 13-19 of the above exercise were quoted by Robertson Cochrane in a 1992 column in *The Globe and Mail*.]

EXERCISE: Dangling Constructions (13-16)

For each of the following write a complete sentence that incorporates the phrase given but does *not* allow it to dangle. Then re-write the sentence to remove the phrase.

1) Turning to Margaret Atwood's later novels...

2) Considering the developments of the past few years in Eastern Europe...

3) Looking at the connection between economic history and the history of ideas...

4) Regarding the claim that women and men are intrinsically different...

5) Having surveyed the four main theories of...

EXERCISE: Sequence of Tenses (17-19)

Correct the following sentences:

1) The Vice President said that "We will have to improve our productivity.

2) Tennyson's Ulysses says that "I have suffered greatly, both with those/That loved me, and alone."

3) Churchill claimed that "This is our finest hour."

4) Johnson at first believed that the Vietnam war will be over before the 1968 election.

5) For the most part the story of Chopin's *The Awakening* is narrated in a detached manner that leaves the reader to make her own inferences about the characters involved. Occasionally though, the narrative voice adopts a clear point of view. Such is the case, for example, when Mr. Pointellier "could see plainly that she was not herself. That is, he could not see that she was becoming herself and daily casting aside that fictitious self which we assume like a garment with which to appear before the world." Quite clearly, the aside concerning the "fictitious self" comes from the narrator, not from Mr. Pointellier.

EXERCISE: Irregular verbs (20-43)

Correct whichever of the following are incorrect:

1) She can do whatever she choses.

2) The book is well-written and beautifully layed out.

3) He says that he rung me over the phone.

4) They have stole everything I own.

5) This blouse shrunk when I washed it in hot water.

6) The ship sunk in a hundred metres of water.

Fill in the simple past tense of the verbs indicated:

1) She _____ (to choose) the material that _____ (to be) least expensive.

2) Samuel _____ (to drink) too much beer last night.

3) All the pipes _____ (to burst) and water covered the floor.

4) The little baby _____ (to fall) asleep as soon as he _____ (to lie) down.

5) The soldiers _____ (to flee) as soon as they _____ (to see) the size of the opposing force.

6) As soon as I apologised, my parents _____ (to forgive) me.

7) We _____ (to grind) the seeds into a fine powder.

8) He _____ (to lay) his book down for a moment, and then he _____ (to forget) where he had put it.

9) I _____ (to lend) him five dollars yesterday.

10) The letter carrier _____ (to ring) the bell four times.

11) His whole family _____ (to seek) refuge here after leaving Guatemala.

12) The moon _____ (to shine) very brightly last night.

13) The bandits _____(to shoot) the policeman in the back.

14) This sweater _____ (to shrink) when I washed it in hot water.

15) He _____ (to sing) at the top of his voice all afternoon.

16) When the *Titanic* _____ (to sink), over 1,500 lives _____ (to be) lost.

17) All my food _____ (to slide) off my plate onto the floor.

18) He _____ (to spend) his entire wages on beer and cigarettes.

19) The car _____ (to spin) out of control as it _____ (to go) around the corner.

20) He _____ (to spit) in disgust on the pavement.

21) She _____ (to split) the log into two easily.

22) The cougar _____ (to spring) out of the undergrowth at the deer.

23) We _____ (to swim) in the pool below the falls.

24) She _____ (to weep) for hours when she _____ (to hear) the sad news.

25) The python _____ (to wind) itself around his neck.

26) He _____ (to wring) out the wet clothing, and put it on the line.

EXERCISE: Infinitive or Gerund? (44-68)

Fill in the correct choice:

1) Mr. Carruthers accused me _____ *[to have laughed/of laughing]* at him behind his back.

2) He has a tendency _____ *[to speak/of speaking]* before he has thought about what effect his words may have.

3) Mary is certainly capable _____ *[to get/of getting]* an 'A' in this course.

4) He has often tried to discourage me _____ *[to try/from trying]* to get into Medical School.

5) They seemed _____ *[as if they were/to be]* about to attack us.

6) The Press suspected the senator *[to have been involved/of having been involved]* in a conflict of interest.

EXERCISE: Prepositions (69-148)

Fill in the correct preposition, or leave blank if no preposition is needed.

1) My father was very angry _____me when I did not do what he had asked me to.

2) We should arrive _____Denver in time for dinner.

3) The three of them were chased _____from school.

4) The group departed _____ Paris in the early morning.

5) We discussed _____ the problem with him for a whole afternoon.

6) We were told to continue _____ our work.

7) We must refer _____ to the first chapter to find the most important clue to the protagonist's identity.

8) The geopolitical situation in late 1938 was different _____ what it had been only a few months earlier.

9) He asked me what type _____ VCR we wanted.

10) She is convinced that this brand of detergent is superior _____ that one.

Which of the following sentences are incorrect? Correct whatever preposition mistakes you find.

1) By the time troops arrived the Russian Parliament buildings, Yeltsin and his supporters had built barricades and were prepared.

2) Chirac had intended to consult with his advisors before making a statement.

3) We must draw a different conclusion than the one we had expected.

4) Tyson departed from Las Vegas amidst a storm of controversy over the incident.

5) The controversy over whether or not special lanes for bicycles should be built along major thoroughfares centres on the issue of safety.

6) At the legislature today, a group of citizens protested against the federal government's proposal.

EXERCISE: Singular and Plural (149-173)

Make the changes necessary to ensure that the parts of the sentence are in agreement:

1) Either John or his brother are responsible for causing the disturbance. (164)

2) None of the excuses we were given are satisfactory. (162)

3) Each of the members feel that the application should be rejected. (162)

Choose the correct alternative:

5) The aurora borealis is still a largely unexplained _____ [phenomenon/phenomena]. (171)

6) There appear to be at least two _____ [focuses/foci] in Breugel's *Fall of Icarus*. (149)

7) There were several _____ [Attorney Generals / Attorneys General] during the Reagan administration. (149)

8) Television is generally considered to be the most influential

_____ *[media/medium]*. (168)

Correct any mistakes in the following sentences:

1) The second criteria that Locke puts forward is closely connected to the first. (159)

2) The data we were shown is not sufficient to convince us. (161)

3) At the turn of the century the press was the media that affected North Americans most profoundly. (168)

EXERCISE: Pronoun Referencing (176, 178)

Correct the pronoun problem in each of the following.

1) A shopkeeper's life is usually a very busy one. They often have to work at least twelve hours a day.

2) Frank is not as good as Henry at the high jump. He usually jumps about five feet.

3) Larson argues that the sexual stereotypes of modern Western society will not be eradicated until the economic system alters, whereas Myers feels that a degree of stereotyping is an inevitable, if regrettable, result of genetic differences. This is important to recognize.

4) Harvard must maintain the high standards that make people like Henry Rosovsky and I work twice as hard. (from an address by Harvard University president Derek Bok)

Find and correct the pronoun problems:

1) Typically, a deconstructionist searches for structures that are deeply hidden, that even the author may not have been aware of. Indeed, they are often uninterested in whatever structure the author may have declared she has attempted to impose on the text.

2) Writing business letters is an important skill to learn. Normally, of course, it should begin with a salutation.

3) Ownership rights certainly protect a sphere of liberty for the rights owners, but they may also interfere with the rights of others who are no longer at liberty to use what they previously could. If this were more widely realized we might be less likely to think of liberty as an unqualified good.

EXERCISE: *Who* and *Whom* (179)

Fill in *who* or *whom*, whichever is correct.

1) _____ will be waiting for you?

2) To _____ should I address the parcel?

3) She is a writer about _____ I know very little.

4) _____ should I say is calling?

5) Andrew Johnson was the President _____ followed Lincoln.

6) Andrew Johnson was the President _____ Lincoln preceded.

7) D'Arcy McGee was the leader _____ was assassinated while John A. Macdonald was Prime Minister of Canada.

8) It was John A. Macdonald _____ said to D'Arcy McGee, "We can't afford to have two drunkards in the Cabinet; you've got to stop."

9) It was D'Arcy McGee _____ John A. Macdonald was speaking to when he said, "We can't afford to have two drunkards in this Cabinet; you've got to stop."

EXERCISE: Part of Speech Conversions

Correct the mistake in each sentence:

1) He did not give me very good advise. (182)

2) To some extend what you say is true, but I cannot agree with you completely. (206)

3) There maybe a chance that you can still convince him to do what you want. (197)

4) She was eager to revenge what they had done to her. (206)

5) The team's four starters voted unanimous to start on four days rest. (181)

6) I loaned him the money to buy a car. (206)

7) He was careful not to loose track of the argument. (196)

8) The above quote illustrates just how short-sighted 19th-century educators could be. (204)

EXERCISE: *Like* and *as* (192)

Choose the correct alternative:

1) We should meet at ten o'clock (like/as) we agreed.

2) (Like/As) she said an hour ago when we began this discussion, we have to choose between the lesser of two evils.

3) (Like/As) Russia, Canada is dominated geographically by vast areas of frozen wasteland.

4) In many ways copper behaves (like/as) silver does.

EXERCISE: Difficulties with Meaning

Choose the correct word or expression.

1) Do you think your action will have any _____ *[effect/affect]*? (211)

2) The shopkeeper did not want to _____ *[accept/except]* a credit card. (208)

3) The tape recording _____ *[compliments/complements]* the study guide. (237)

4) The _____ *[council/counsel]* deliberated for seven hours before reaching a decision. (243)

5) One approach is to break down the questionnaire results by age and sex. _____ *[Alternately/Alternatively]*, we may study the variations among different income levels. (214)

6) He is very conservative and would never wish to _____ *[flout/flaunt]* the university administration. (273)

7) The stage can be _____ *[dissembled/disassembled]* within two hours. (254)

8) The two elements must be seen as entirely _____ *[discreet/discrete]*. (251)

9) She told me _____ *[definitely/definitively]* that she would not support the motion. (247)

10) Britain is considering whether or not to restore_____ *[capitol/capital]* punishment. (229)

11) The majority believe that theft is _____ *[amoral/immoral]* in any circumstances. (217)

12) No politician is _____ *[adverse/averse]* to publicity. (210)

13) They were eager to declare the amount as a _____ *capitol/capital* gain. (229)

14) The company always purchases _____ *[stationary / stationery]* in bulk. (331)

15) The book is laden with a preface, a _____ *[foreword / forward]* and an introduction. (276)

16) The spokesperson _____ *[inferred/implied]* that the withdrawal would be made, but he would not state it _____ *[explicitly/implicitly]*. (284, 269)

17) The judge felt that the guilt of the accused was _____ *[mitigated / militated]* by the manner in which he had been provoked; the victim was his supervisor at work, and had been _____ *[persecuting / prosecuting]* him for years. (301, 311)

EXERCISE: Mistakes of Meaning

In each of the following there is a mistake. Correct it.

1) A lot of emigrants entered Canada last year. (264)

2) Most sports stars who 'write' books do it by corroborating with a professional writer. (236)

3) The experiment would of worked if we had calculated the angles correctly. (306)

4) Anyone can park here; there are no restrictions. (228)

5) The Committee is made up of imminent people from all walks of life. (264)

6) Like all bright young women, she is liable to succeed. (295)

7) The percent of the sample that responded to question 12 was very low. (310)

8) The entire town was ravished by the violent storm. (322)

9) There were to many people there; I felt claustrophobic. (337)

10) He has little or no interest in sex, but he is otherwise a very sensual man. (326)

11) Her writing is completely eligible; I can hardly make out a word. (262)

12) Ms. Jenkins persuaded me to invest in her business, but I decided it would not be a good idea. (312)

EXERCISE: *They, There, Their* and *Were, Where* (335, 344)

Fill in the correct choice.

1) The boys told _____ mother that they would be late.

2) _____ were many people at the political rally.

3) _____ are very happy to live in such a nice house.

4) _____ are a great many machines in that factory.

5) _____ car is old, but _____ keep it in good condition.

6) _____ are many students who have not yet handed in _____ exercise books.

7) _____ you pleased that the Tigers won yesterday?

8) He could not tell me _____ the tools _____ kept.

9) My brother and I _____ walking to the store, _____ we hoped to meet several friends.

10) _____ _____ a lot of people in the audience.

EXERCISE: *Of* and *Have* (306)

Fill in either *of* or *have*:

1) I would _____ come if I had been able to.

2) I should _____ done more work at the beginning _____ the term.

3) The tragedy could not _____ been prevented.

4) It was very kind _____ you to write.

EXERCISE: Word Order

Improve the word order in the following sentences.

1) This can be the result either of natural events or human actions. (349)

2) In the end, Hitler neither conquered Britain nor the Soviet Union. (349)

3) We should first ask what are the conditions under which an electronics industry is likely to flourish. (353)

4) Passions can interfere either sporadically on particular occasions, or they can be a continual influence on one's actions. (349)

5) The conclusions we draw will be largely determined by what are the assumptions we start with. (353)

EXERCISE: Word Order

In each of the following there is a word order mistake. Correct it.

1) The Tiger supporters in the crowd were few. (346)

2) The books I lent to my friend, I need them back soon. (348)

3) The men who are responsible for installing the joists, the supervisor wanted to see them. (348)

4) He neither wants pity nor charity. (349)

5) They were given sentences of between one and three years all except those who had not committed any violent offenses. (350)

6) I and my friends usually spend holidays together. (351)

7) In this class there are three students only. (352)

8) I asked Faith how was she feeling. (353)

9) My father asked me what was I doing. (353)

10) They asked us what was wrong? (353)

11) I borrowed the young man's truck, who had bought it only the day before. (354)

12) You can order a complete computer system that will be delivered by telephone. (354)

13) Greville is now represented by the best of both his love poems and of his sonorous Calvinist laments. (347) [poet Thom Gunn, writing in the *Times Literary Supplement*, August 16, 1991]

EXERCISE: Too Many Words or Too Few Words

In each of the following there are either too many or too few words. Improve each sentence.

1) I myself I think that it is not wise to have more than three or four

children. (372)

2) In my opinion I think men are just as intelligent as women. (371)

3) It was the general consensus of opinion that no new projects of an expensive nature should be embarked upon at that point in time. (382, 386, 379)

4) The protagonist has fallen in love a girl he met at the fair the previous weekend. (385)

5) She said that she did not to work at the factory, no matter how much she was paid. (385)

6) Insects such as moths, butterflies, fruitflies, etc. can adapt very quickly to environmental changes. (367)

EXERCISE: Usage

In each sentence there is one mistake. Correct it.

1) Please do not do any changes before you have asked me about them. (404)

2) There are less people in Sweden than there are in the city of New York. (421)

3) He did a lot of mistakes on his tax form. (423)

4) Hingis does not want to go to Wimbleton nor the US Open this year. (425)

5) He could not do nothing about the problems that he faced. (426)

6) The college would like to increase the places available in residence. (414)

7) A revolution is when the government changes hands as a result of a violent uprising. (418)

8) The reason the ozone layer is being destroyed is because of the effects of aerosol sprays. (431)

9) The plaintiff now intends to try and regain custody of the child. (442)

EXERCISE: Usage

In each of the following sentences there is one mistake. Correct it.

1) According to science, it is impossible to travel faster than the speed of light. (391)

2) As he had got into the car, he turned the key in the ignition. (397)

3) The European powers wanted to colonize Africa because of the following reasons. (400)

4) There are several birds (penguins, ostriches and etc.) which cannot fly. (367)

5) He often forgets his office key at home. (410)

6) The reason she likes him is because he is a well-known personality. (431)

7) Students at this college will be substantially increased next year. (414)
8) The police did a thorough investigation, and could find no evidence of wrongdoing. (416)
9) She lied that she had not stolen any money. (422)
10) He is opposed against legalizing marijuana. (427)

EXERCISE: Putting Ideas Together — cause and effect

List as many effects as you can of any two of the following events:

1) the baby boom
2) the spread of television throughout society
3) the fall of Communism in Eastern Europe and the Soviet Union
4) an increase in the value of the American dollar

List as many causes as you can for any two of the following events:

1) the Czech Republic winning Olympic gold in men's hockey, 1998
2) the recent rise/fall in support for the federal government
3) 20th century American interventions in Central America
4) global warming

EXERCISE: Cause and Correlation

What causal relationships (if any) do you think underlie the following correlations? In each case one may be the cause of the other; it may be *one* of the causes of the other; or there may be no causal relationship. If you think there is a causal connection, state if you think it likely to be the only cause, and if not list as many other possible contributing causes as you can think of.

1) a rise in crime/a rise in unemployment
2) a rise in violent crimes (such as rape and murder)/a rise in unemployment
3) the 1990s collapse of the cod stocks off the Newfoundland coast/large catches taken by foreign trawlers outside the 200 mile limit
4) increases in government support for the performing arts/better plays being written and performed
5) Japanese children spending far more time in school than do North Americans/higher productivity in the Japanese economy
6) a large decrease in rain in Somalia/famine in Somalia

7)   record potato crops in the 1840s in Ireland/the potato famine in the 1840s in Ireland

---

EXERCISE: Putting Ideas Together (447-451; 461-62)

Fill in *but, although, however, despite, because* or *as a result*. Pay close attention to the punctuation.

1)   _____ he was sick, he could not come to work yesterday.

2)   _____ he was sick, he came to work yesterday.

3)   He was sick yesterday. _____, he still came to work.

4)   _____ his sickness, he still came to work yesterday.

5)   He was sick yesterday. _____, he did not come to work.

6)   He was sick yesterday, _____ he still came to work.

7)   She has practised for many long hours. _____, she is now a good player.

8)   She has practised for many long hours,_____ she is still not a good player.

9)   She is now a good player _____ she has practised for many long hours.

10)   _____ she has practised for many long hours, she is not yet a good player.

11)   She has practised for many long hours. _____, she is not yet a good player.

12)   _____ her long hours of practice, she is not yet a good player.

EXERCISE: *But* (449)

Exercise: Rephrase so that consecutive sentences do not include the word *but*.

1)   There is no question that the Mariners on balance have lost run-scoring potential with the replacement of Smith, Jones and Brown with Martinez, Womack, and White. But they have gained better defence and a more positive attitude. But it is not at first clear whether these will be enough to enable them to win the World Series championship that has so far eluded them.

2)   Having the right to own private property is generally considered an important liberty in this society, but for many people there will be more interference with liberty under a system of private ownership than there will be under a system such as that of the native peoples of North America (under which the land is held in common). But this does not show that a system of common use or common ownership is necessarily right for Western society today. But it should make us question our often unthinking allegiance to private property rights.

EXERCISE: Joining Words (447-450)

Fill in *but, however, though, although, despite or whereas* — whichever is correct.

1)   There is no question that the Blue Jays have on balance lost run-scoring potential with the replacement of Smith, Jones and Brown with Martinez, Womack, and White. They have gained better defence, _____, and a more positive attitude. Whether or not these will be enough to enable them to win the World Series championship that has so far eluded them is not yet clear, _____ most fans seem glad of the changes.

2)   _____ the Blue Jays have on balance lost run-scoring potential with the replacement of Smith, Jones and Brown with Martinez, Womack, and White, they have gained better defence and a more positive attitude.

3)   _____ the loss of the run-scoring potential of Smith, Jones and Brown, the Blue Jays should still produce a lot of runs from the bats of Martinez, Womack and White. Moreover, they have gained better defence and a more positive attitude.

4)   Some aspects of deconstruction proved easy to mock—none more so, perhaps, than its emphasis on the text rather than the author. 'Do deconstructionists think the text writes itself?' sceptics sneered. _____ it may well be a worthwhile endeavor to *act* as if the text has no author.

5)   Some aspects of deconstruction proved easy to mock—none more so, perhaps, than its emphasis on the text rather than the author. 'Do deconstructionists think the text writes itself?' sceptics sneered. In fact, _____, it may be an entirely worthwhile endeavor to *act as if* the text has no author.

6)   _____ their scepticism, those opposed to deconstruction were sometimes influenced by deconstructionist techniques of analysis.

EXERCISE: Joining Words

Exercise: Fill in appropriate joining words from the following list: *but, however, though, although, despite, whereas, yet, also, and, as well, indeed, in fact, further, moreover, not only...but also*

1)   Surrey has been growing enormously in recent years; _____, it now has twice the population that it had only ten years ago.

2)   The opening of the Coquihalla Highway made it much easier for cars to travel from Vancouver to Kamloops; _____, it cut almost two hours off the journey. Trucks, _____, found it almost as slow as the old route via Cache Creek, _____ the very steep grades force them to slow down considerably.

3)   _____ the opening of the Coquihalla Highway made it

much easier for cars to travel from Vancouver to Kamloops, it was not much of a help to heavy trucks. A fully-loaded transport truck can only climb the steep grades very slowly. _____, the toll charges levied make the journey more expensive than travel via the Trans-Canada Highway.

4) _____ is a fully-loaded transport truck unable to climb the steep grades at more than a snail's pace, _____ it must _____ pay for the privilege.

5) Deconstructionists followed Derrida's lead in arguing that nothing but the text is deserving of study—indeed, that there *is* nothing but the text. They argue that to refer to an author's life is to engage in idle speculation. Surely in at least some cases, _____, what the author intended to say is of more than passing interest. Surely in at least some cases, _____, information about the author's life will help to shed life on the text.

6) Deconstruction argues in favour of a separation between the text and the world when it comes to any consideration of the author as an *individual*. Deconstruction is eager to show, _____, how a text is conditioned by the *society* in which it was created—and the dominant ideology of that society. The bias is towards the collective and the unconscious. The conscious motivations and intentions of the author are deemed to be irrelevant, _____ it is the job of the critic to reveal the unconscious motivations.

EXERCISE: *Because* (461, 462)

In each of the following sentences *because* is used incorrectly. Explain why, and rephrase to correct the problem. (You may replace *because* if you wish.)

1) The compound in the red beaker is lighter than the compound in the black beaker because it weighs less.

2) Shakespeare mixes comedy with tragedy frequently because he includes comic material such as the gravediggers' scene in *Hamlet* and the Fool's banter in *King Lear*.

3) The black American family unit has broken down, because statistics show that the proportion of black American children born illegitimately has tripled over the past twenty years.

4) The fact that the proportion of black American children born illegitimately has tripled over the past twenty years does not in fact indicate any increase in the number of single parents, because two parent families are having fewer children.

EXERCISE: *Because, So, As a result* (461, 462, 466)

Fill in *because, so* or *as a result*:

1) _____ he writes carefully and checks his work, he usually

does well.

2) He writes carefully and checks his work, _____ he usually does well.

3) He writes carefully and checks his work. _____, he usually does well.

4) I think that party has done a good job in government, _____ I will vote for it.

5) I will vote for that party, _____ I think it has done a good job governing.

6) I think that party has done a good job governing. _____, I will vote for it.

EXERCISE: Punctuation And Joining Words (447, 449, 451, 466, 468)

Punctuate the following:

1) Jones was not even in the same city at the time hence he could not have committed the murder

2) The team was heavily favored to win the division three of its best pitchers however were injured for long periods hence it was unable to finish better than fourth

3) Gauthier's proviso is a general principle hence it applies both to property owners and to those whose land has been expropriated as we shall see however it is not a principle that can successfully be used as a ground on which to base private property rights

4) Mulroney was sometimes thought of as being too concerned with popularity and unwilling to lead in his actions however he frequently went against the dictates of public opinion the Free Trade Agreement and the GST for example were both opposed by a majority of Canadians should politicians in fact always follow public opinion or do they have a duty to do what they believe to be right regardless of what the majority feels if we on the left try to deny conservative governments the right to make unpopular decisions then in order to remain consistent we will also have to insist that liberal or social democratic governments only put forward legislation that is popular

---

EXERCISE: *For example* and *Such as* (470, 472)

Fill in *for example* or *such as*:

1) A number of his friends, _____ Frank Jones and Joshua Smith, have criminal records.

2) A number of his friends have criminal records. Frank Jones and Joshua Smith, _____, have each spent several years in jail.

3) At several points in the play, Antonio acts cruelly. _____, he insults Shylock even when the Jew is prepared to lend him money.

4) Christian characters _____ Antonio and Gratiano act cruelly towards Jews throughout *The Merchant of Venice.*

5) Certain forms of transportation, _____ bicycles and canoes, cause no damage whatsoever to the environment.

6) Certain forms of transportation are friendly to the environment. Bicycles and canoes, _____, cause no damage whatsoever.

7) There is a connection here between literary tendencies and political ones. Just as postmodern theorists are more alive to the collective influences at work upon the creation of a text, so too they tend to be more concerned in the political sphere with collective rights than with individual ones. The collective rights of women and of minorities, _____, tend to be given more weight than the individual rights (_____ freedom of speech) that have traditionally been the concern of the British and North American tradition. This distinction lies close to the heart of the debate over "political correctness".

EXERCISE: *So that, So...that* or *such...that* (474, 475)

Fill in *so that, so...that* or *such...that.*

1) His prose is _____ convoluted _____ it is difficult to understand what he means.

2) It is _____ a convoluted prose style _____ it is difficult to understand what he means.

3) He writes in an inaccessible way _____ the reader will sense the difficulty inherent in the ideas themselves.

EXERCISE: Comparisons (474, 475)

too	*so...that*	*so that*	*such...that*	*very*

From this list of expressions choose the one that fits into each of the sentences below.

1) After the birth of their first child they both felt _____ happy.

2) He was _____ late _____ the meeting was almost over.

3) She is now _____ a big girl _____ none of her clothes fit properly.

4) The sun is _____ bright today.

5) The sun is _____ bright today _____ you have to shield your eyes.

6) There is _____ a bright sun today _____ you have to shield your eyes.

7) I shielded my eyes _____ I could see more clearly.

8) You should do your work now _____ you will be able to enjoy yourself this evening.

9) This table is _____ big; it will not fit through the door.

10) This table is _____ big _____ it will not fit through the door.

11) This table is _____ big _____ fit through the door.

EXERCISE: *That* or *Which* (476)

Fill in *that* or *which*.

1) The essay _____ I wrote last week was eleven pages long.

2) The essay, _____ I wrote in only one night, was eleven pages long.

3) This comparison, _____ Fitzgerald first makes in the book's opening paragraph, is repeated frequently throughout the text.

4) The comparison _____ Fitzgerald makes in the book's opening paragraph is repeated frequently throughout the text.

In which of the above could *that* or *which* be omitted?

EXERCISE: Putting Ideas Together

In each of the following there is one mistake. Correct it.

1) He went away in the morning and he came home the same night and he told me that he had had a good trip. (456)

2) Although he has short legs, but he is a fast runner. (447)

3) Despite that the teacher marked hard, we all passed. (450)

4) Mark was sick because he stayed in bed all day. (461)

5) Because the players would not give up, so they achieved victory. (467)

6) Michipicoten Island on Lake Superior is very beautiful, but it is also very inaccessible. However, it is possible to reach it by private boat. (212)

EXERCISE: Putting Ideas Together (445-476)

Fill in appropriate joining words or expressions, choosing from those in the lists provided.

For (1), choose from:

as well	however
and	though
as a result	despite
; [semi-colon]	

1) The idea of building a canal from the Mediterranean Sea to the Red Sea is centuries old_____ it was considered even in the time of the Roman Empire. _____, it was not until the late nineteenth century that the project was actually begun. _____ many difficulties, the canal was finally completed early in this century, _____ for many years most ships bypassed the Cape of Good Hope. In the late 1960's and the 1970's,

_____, ships that were too large for the canal began to be built. _____, conflict between Israel and Egypt caused the canal to be closed at various times. _____, a great deal of sea traffic now once again travels right around Africa, just as it did before the Suez Canal was built.

For (2), choose from:

despite

and

although

moreover

such as

however

as a result

2) Uganda is again becoming one of Africa's more developed countries. _____ it has certain natural disadvantages, _____ having no sea port, it has a relatively good infrastructure, _____ its agricultural sector is increasingly productive. _____, it exports more products than do most of its neighbours. _____ political difficulties with rebels in the north of the country, the government remains stable. _____, many nearby nations look to Uganda for leadership. _____, Uganda is of course much less well-off than are most European countries.

EXERCISE: Run-on and Incomplete Sentences (477-478)

Correct each of the following run-on or incomplete sentences.

1) "She's miniature, her hands are about the size of my thumb," he said. (*Peterborough Examiner*)

2) How much influence the book might have, how it compares to other philosophical books, how it fits in with the current trends in philosophy, these are all very hard to determine.

3) It had taken the best part of an hour to put the plan forward, it took another five minutes before I got my answer. (F.H. Winterbotham, *Ultra Secret*)

4) The informant did not lie to us, he gave us his idea of what the people believed they were doing. (Anthropology essay)

5) Another positive element is that outside firms will bring new or substantially revitalized agricultural resources into use, they will create new employment to operate the production facilities.

6) Suppose an industry which is threatened by foreign competition is one which lies at the very heart of your National defence, where are you then? (Economist W. Hewins, quoted in the *Atlantic*)

7) Hydrochloric acid is a very dangerous substance. So always handle it very carefully.

8) The rookie sidearmer didn't merely have a fine year in the team's bullpen, his campaign ranks as one of the very best seasons in baseball history.

9) In Heriot, Scotland, a run on the bank isn't a sign of financial instability, it's just the way things always have been and still are, every Thursday from 3:30 to 4:30. The only time the bank is open. The good things in life stay that way. (Advertisement)

10) The freedom fighter spun around just in time, then he fired quickly.

11) Getting the right price for your residence is not just good luck, it's getting the right agent to help you. (Advertisement)

12) At first Bauer had no trouble with the climbing. At 7.8 km. he was second best, only Delgado was faster. (*The Toronto Star*)

13) A major breakthrough came in 1912, two BASF scientists made the world's first synthetic ammonia, which remains the key ingredient in most fertilizer. (*Financial Post*)

14) Jones argues that the world is overpopulated. This doesn't make sense because Jones says that the world has too many people but in some areas they don't have enough. (Sociology essay)

15) Television executives don't really care if a show is good or not, so long as it is popular, the larger the audience the better, TV is a mass medium. (Communications essay)

16) When Coca Cola altered its formula it forgot that the biggest ingredient in the brand's success was its traditional place in North American culture. They weren't just tampering with a recipe, they were changing a social institution. (*The Toronto Star*)

EXERCISE: Common Comma Pairings (485)

Punctuate the following:

1) she stepped gingerly over the fallen body then she screamed

2) manning's argument then is that an elected senate would be both more representative and more effective than an appointed one

3) however old you are you can still enjoy the outdoors

4) he would like to go skiing his age and infirmity however prevent him from doing so

5) the complex plot structure that byatt employs in her novel weaves together strands from many literary traditions

6) byatts novel which employs a complex plot structure weaves together strands from many literary traditions

---

EXERCISE: Colon or Semi-colon

Add either a colon or a semi-colon to each of the following sentences. (See pp. 153-154 and 159-160.)

1) Images of air and sky occur repeatedly in the first three stanzas of Heaney's poem__ "the eye concedes to / Encroaching horizon", "Between the sights of the sun", "An astounding crate full of air".

2) The company is in disarray___ it filed for bankruptcy last week.

3) This was how the Prime Minister phrased it___ "If Lindros wants to choose Oshawa over Quebec City, well then I guess he knows something about Oshawa that I don't."

4) A key feature in Locke's justification of property is the famed Lockean Proviso___ the claim that property rights can arise without consent "at least where there is enough, and as good, left in common for others."

EXERCISE: The Semi-colon

The semi-colon is one of the most useful — and one of the most underused — punctuation marks. (See pp. 153-154.) The following exercise should help to show its usefulness both as a means to more concise writing (enabling the writer to eliminate joining words or expressions) and as a way of eliminating the impression of jerkiness that short sentences create.

Rewrite each of the following, using a semi-colon in each case.

1) "Liberal" can mean many things. The Oxford English Dictionary lists thirty-seven definitions.

2) Great theatre companies often have humble beginnings. Stratford, Ontario's Shakespearean Festival was held in a tent for its first few years.

3) This policy is an unwise one for the government to follow, because it would make the poor even poorer.

4) Showing that the law has not been violated during this affair establishes at best that the Minster is not a criminal, but it fails to show that he deserves to retain a place in the Cabinet.

5) The law does not require you to compensate others for their loss if you are not at fault. It only requires you to pay compensation if you have caused the damage.

6) These theories permit people to be treated as objects because of the way in which they allow people to be used as material means for the production of morally good states of affairs.

EXERCISE: Punctuation

Correct the punctuation mistake in each of the following.

1) Mbabane which is the capital of Swaziland, is a small town encircled by hills. (485)

2) "Why did you come here," he asked me. (488)

3) We all rode in my brothers car to Ottawa. (492)
4) Both Mandela and de Klerk believed that apartheid couldn't last much longer. (492)

EXERCISE: Punctuation

Punctuate the following passages:

1) what did you think of the election he asked me i was surprised and disappointed that the republicans took so many seats i think they should bring in proportional representation soon he agreed

2) i just dont know what to do said don i cant seem to punctuate properly in english so i keep on writing incomplete sentences and run on sentences mary suggested several things that might help first of all she said you should read each word out loud and notice when you pause also she added remember that the words so and and should not begin sentences also the word because cannot begin a main clause finally the word that should not be used to join two clauses together into one sentence don thanked her for this advice then he began to write a composition

---

EXERCISE: Direct and Indirect Speech (494-498)

Rephrase so as to provide a grammatically correct introduction to the following quotations.

1) The Prime Minister asked if "Will the country accept double-digit inflation?"
2) Lentriccia argues: "Regardless of Byron's intention, the meaning of the *text* is opaque."
4) In the mid-1950s social scientists were concerned that perpetually increasing leisure time "will lead to vast social changes by the year 2000."

EXERCISE: Jargon, Abstraction, and Doublespeak (500-502)

Translate each of the following into more easily understood English:

1) The new pen has negative vulnerability to water entry.
2) The building in which the reactor is situated was apparently constructed with a view to structural rather than containment integrity.
3) The former aide to the President tries to help clients strategise whatever their objectives may be vis-à-vis Washington, D.C. or the world.

4) Since data is central to the issue of implementation guidance we believe it is advisable to examine the data that your organization is assembling, in order to maximize the actualization of projects designated for implementation, and to preclude unintended effects.

5) With regard to the staff members' requests for supplements to the level of remuneration, management is of the opinion that it would be injudicious to advocate an increment.

6) The loss of Challenger put NASA into a temporary hiatus of shuttle flights. They regarded it as certain that they would have a shortfall in the national launch capability in the near term.

7) In considering the multiplicity of factors involved, this essay will also explore possible solutions to the parameters of the problem of the bias that is particularly strongly felt in many American Caucasian communities against ethnic heterogeneity in school transportation arrangements.

EXERCISE: Bias in Language (504)

Rewrite each of the following so as to make it gender-neutral.

1) Any doctor is obliged to put his patients' concerns ahead of his own.

2) Simply increasing the number of policemen on the streets will not necessarily lead to a decrease in crime.

3) The history of mankind forms only a short chapter in the history of the planet.

4) In the 1950s most Americans worked in blue collar jobs; now the situation is reversed, with the number of white collar jobs far exceeding the number of blue collar ones.

5) In short, except for his reproductive power, a child has a fully developed capacity for love long before puberty.
      (Sigmund Freud, 'The Sexual Enlightenment of Children')

6) In most cases the genius has reached the height of his intellectual powers by his early twenties.

7) Our Stone Age ancestors are often crudely characterized as cavemen.

EXERCISE: Metaphors (505)

Unmix the following metaphors:

1) We don't want to throw the baby out with the bath water before we check to see if the coast is clear.

2) Unless every clause in the agreement is airtight the deal could come unglued and we'd be left up the creek without a paddle.

3) The government's scorched earth policy in response to the rebels has dampened hopes for an early settlement of the war.

4) We were all swamped by an avalanche of paperwork.

EXERCISE: Slang and Informal English (506-516)

Rewrite each sentence to eliminate slang words or expressions:

1) She has five kids and fifteen grandchildren.

2) The work he handed in was truly awful.

3) It is kind of difficult to understand why public perceptions of John Major changed so quickly.

4) There is a bunch of reasons why the debt became so large.

EXERCISE: Spelling (519-521)

In each sentence there are spelling errors. Correct them:

1) At the beggining of the year the commitee made its dicision. (3 errors)

2) The goverment of Malawi was long dorminated by President Banda. (2 errors)

3) A scene with over fourty charachters in it is a very unusual occurence in a Pinter play. (3 errors)

4) We have learned about garmetes, gemination, and photosinthesis. (3 errors)

5) They tried to leave serreptitiously so that the school principle would not notice their departure. (2 errors)

6) The yeild on a stock like this is likely to be non-existant; one buys it only for the capitol gain. (3 errors)

INDEX